WAKING NANABIJOU
Uncovering a Secret Past

WAKING NANABIJOU

Uncovering a Secret Past

Jim Poling Sr.

NATURAL HERITAGE BOOKS
A MEMBER OF THE DUNDURN GROUP
TORONTO

Published by Natural Heritage Books
A Member of the Dundurn Group
3 Church Street, Suite 500
Toronto, Ontario, M5E 1M2, Canada

Gazelle Book Services Limited
White Cross Mills
High Town, Lancaster, England
LA1 4XS

Dundurn Press
2250 Military Road
Tonawanda, NY
U.S.A 14150

Copyedited by Marja Appleford
Indexed by Jane Gibson
Designed by Erin Mallory

Printed and bound in Canada by Marquis
www.dundurn.com

Library and Archives Canada Cataloguing in Publication

Poling, Jim (Jim R.)
     Waking Nanabijou : uncovering a secret past / Jim Poling.

Includes index.
ISBN 978-1-55002-757-0

     1. Poling, Jim (Jim R.) 2. Mothers and sons--Canada--Biography.
3. Native peoples--Canada--Social conditions. 4. Chapleau (Ont.)--Biography.
5. Journalists--Canada--Biography. I. Title.

PN4913.P65A3 2007   070.92   C2007-903005-X

1   2   3   4   5   11   10   09   08   07

Cover photo © Dick Spooner, courtesy Tourism Thunder Bay

Conseil des Arts
du Canada

Canada Council
for the Arts

Canadä

ONTARIO ARTS COUNCIL
CONSEIL DES ARTS DE L'ONTARIO

We acknowledge the support of the **Canada Council for the Arts** and the **Ontario Arts Council** for our publishing program. We also acknowledge the financial support of the **Government of Canada** through the **Book Publishing Industry Development Program** and **The Association for the Export of Canadian Books**, and the **Government of Ontario** through the **Ontario Book Publishers Tax Credit** program and the **Ontario Media Development Corporation**.

J. Kirk Howard, President

"The time has certainly come when the innocent child should be relieved from the stigma which society has been only too ready to place upon it ... and very often block the path to its future progress and usefulness."

— 1918 Annual Report of the Superintendent of Dependent
and Delinquent Children in Alberta

To Veronica, who gave me life; and Diane, who helped me sustain it.

TABLE OF CONTENTS

ACKNOWLEDGEMENTS

THIS BOOK EVOLVED OVER MANY YEARS. IT REACHED THIS stage only because many people helped with research, manuscript criticism, and encouragement.

My niece Michelle helped confirm who my mother, her grandmother, was and where she came from.

Edmonton researcher Pat Pettitt helped track down the LaRose family line and provided invaluable assistance at the Alberta archives.

My son Jim, neighbour Jane Gow, and friend Stuart Robertson read early manuscripts and provided valuable criticism. Stuart's interest and encouragement in the project has been constant.

In Vegreville, Alberta, hospitality and valuable information was provided by Mabel Hunt, Peggy Weder, Lavonde Melnyk, and Marveline Wesley.

Erica Mansell in Innisfree set up these special Vegreville contacts and gave me much information about Innisfree and the LaRose family.

George Patzer kindly took me through the Pioneer Museum in Hanna, while Rev. Scott Gale provided me access to St. Andrew's Church records.

Thanks also to Jody Curran for sharing some of the Curran newspaper family history and to various Thunder Bay seniors who came forth in letters, phone calls, or in person to offer recollections and leads.

Special thanks to new-found cousins Linda Becker of Gold Canyon, Arizona; Kathy Munson of Iowa; Marlene Poloway of Edmonton; and Betty Matlock of Rancho Mirage, California.

INTRODUCTION

THE NORTHERN SUN, OPAQUE IN THE LAST WISPS OF morning mists, spills midday warmth directly onto Lake Superior, flattening and softening the whitecaps, and creating a deceitful tranquillity. The calm seduces even the most experienced lake traveller, smothering memories of the savagery with which this piece of water can kill.

Over the glassy horizon floats Nanabijou, the Sleeping Giant, an apparent mirage formed from the mists of great mysteries. But it is real, a rocky spine thrust out from the mainland to create the vast bay fronting Thunder Bay, Ontario, or *Nimkii Wiiwedoong*, an Ojibwe reference to the exploding thunder and lightning that rakes the bay when Nanabijou stirs. The Welcome Islands float below the Giant's feet and beyond them the mesa-like formation of Pie Island. Far beyond that, and usually lost in the immensity of the world's largest freshwater lake, is Isle Royale in the United States. The islands appear so delicate in the distance, and one wonders how the screaming tempests for which the lake is famous do not blow them off their rocky feet.

This panorama of natural beauty spreads below assorted lookouts on the hills that watch over Thunder Bay's waterfront. You can view the scene from Hillcrest Park, not far from downtown, or from Lover's Lane high above the Current River on the other side of town. The best lookout, from an emotional perspective, is just east of the downtown waterfront along the Terry Fox Courage Highway, the closest thing to a freeway in northern Ontario. Overlooking the highway and the lake is a three-metre bronze statue of the young runner frozen in mid-stride during his historic attempt to run across Canada on an artificial leg. The statue marks the spot where the twenty-one-year-old cancer patient abandoned his cross-country marathon after 5,373 punishing kilometres and 143 days after leaving St. John's, Newfoundland. He had dreamed of running ocean to ocean to raise money for cancer programs, but the cancer caught up to him and he died instead.

I know that spot well. It was part of my trap line when I was kid. Just steps into the bush from the memorial, a tragic event occurred that shattered my family's life when I was not much younger than Terry Fox.

Whenever I return to Thunder Bay, I go to the memorial and stare out over Superior's vastness and think about how each life is a circle that intersects other circles. The life circles of Terry Fox, my mother, and me intersected one day in Thunder Bay. At the intersection of those circles, Terry Fox left a legacy, my mother left a secret, and I realized I had a story to tell.

My mother always warned me that people should not disturb Nanabijou. Awakened, he becomes angry and displays his displeasure, punishing the bay and its people with wind and rain and killing lightning and ear-splitting sounds. Writing a memoir is like waking a sleeping giant. Things long ago left to rest are stirred, sometimes with unhappy consequences. We all have breathed, however, the invigorating freshness of air cleared by a storm. In ignoring my mother's warning, I hope any storms pass quickly and that tolerance and understanding spread in their wake.

Book One
WATER

1 — EVEREST FUNERAL HOME

I DID NOT CRY THE EVENING THAT SHE DIED. I STOOD IN THE doorway of the hospital room after the nurse slid her eyelids shut and stared like a deer dumbfounded by car lights penetrating the forest edge. I did not run to the bedside to touch her hand or kiss her face. There didn't seem to be any point. It was over. My mother was dead at age sixty-three, and displays of grief would be for me only, and would change nothing. So I turned and went down to the hospital parking lot, which stretches out to the edge of St. Mary's River in downtown Sault Ste. Marie.

Falling darkness turned the water a deep and dangerous black, broken here and there by the reflections of lights from Sault Ste. Marie, Michigan on the other side. The river passed swiftly below my feet, as I remembered how much she feared the water. I thought that the darkness and the lapping would bring on the tears. I wanted to cry for her, but I could not. Not because I didn't love her, not because I wasn't sad, not because hurtful events had created a gap in our closeness. The tears just would not come.

Tears never did come easy for me. I grew up in a time and family in which crying didn't count for anything. The people of my childhood lived through a terrible Depression and war. When tough things happened, you picked yourself up and moved on.

It had been a long time since I last cried. Twenty years, in fact. That dirty time in November 1960 when I leaned over my dad's coffin at Everest

Funeral Home in what is now Thunder Bay and kissed his waxen forehead, dried my tears, and became the man of the family at age seventeen.

Now in August 1980 on the St. Mary's riverbank in Sault Ste. Marie, my mother dead in the hospital behind me, I was destined to return to the Everest Funeral Home and all its agonizing memories. My mother had willed it. She had made me promise to bring her back home to Thunder Bay, Everest, and her final resting place in Dad's grave at St. Andrew's Cemetery.

So two days after her death, I fulfilled the promise and stood in the sunshine near the heart of downtown Thunder Bay, emotions exploding inside my chest, tears rimming my eyes. The viewing parlour inside Everest Funeral Home was dim and close, the air sickeningly sweet with the smell of dying flowers. When I saw her in the coffin, I bolted back outside. It wasn't so much the coffin, or the atmosphere in which it sat. I had been to Everest many times before. Poling family dead all went to Everest, then made the short trip across the street to St. Andrew's Roman Catholic Church, then up the hill to the cemetery. As a child, adolescent, and adult, I had kneeled at coffins there to touch the stiff hands of four grandparents and, most horribly, the young-looking man with a full head of black hair. My father died on us when he was forty-four, and when he did, I knew that nothing else in life could ever hurt as much.

Everest itself did not scare me. I was there as promised. I brought my mother home from the place where she had fled when my father died. She had made me promise to ignore the feelings of her second husband and to take her body out of Sault Ste. Marie, the Soo or Sault for short, and bring her to Thunder Bay to be buried beside Dad. She knew this request would hurt Bill Brooks, the Algoma Steel foreman she married after moving to the Soo to escape the misfortunes that had fallen on us. She had been adamant, on her deathbed and in her will written at Christmas 1978, soon after she discovered her bladder cancer: "In the event of my death I am to be brought home to Thunder Bay and buried with my beloved husband Ray Poling. No ifs, ands or buts. That's the way I want it."

The will indicated that she knew she was relegating Bill Brooks to be a bystander mourner at her funeral, with the added hurt of knowing she had married him out of necessity.

She wrote, "Sometimes circumstances force one to do things that we do not care to do. I know, Jim, you did not approve but in my case it was a necessity so my kids could live and eat the way they were accustomed. I love you all dearly and just feel badly I was unable to share my home and feelings openly. But then I'm sure you understand."

I was not sure that I did understand. I never took to Bill Brooks, but then how many young men accept the new husbands of their widowed mothers? Bill would arrive at Everest soon for the wake, and I felt sorry that he had to come to this strange place in a strange city to see his wife buried with her first husband.

The body of my mother, Veronica, had arrived earlier in the day in a hearse, another bizarre twist she had thrown into her funeral arrangements. She had insisted that I promise to have her driven from the Soo to Thunder Bay, called Port Arthur and Fort William when she moved to the Soo. She feared flying as much as she feared the water and could not tolerate the thought of being on an airplane, even as a corpse. So I hired a hearse to drive her body seven hundred kilometres on a two-lane highway around the rocky shore of Lake Superior. The ride must have been rough because when they opened the coffin for the viewing, there was a dark red bruise at the corner of her mouth.

Seeing her bruised face was the final drop of water falling into a glass filled to the rim. My sorrow overflowed and I turned on my heels and hurried outside. Emotions washed over me like the waves beating against the stone breakwater in Thunder Bay harbour. To hold them back, I lifted my head and stared at the cars whizzing by on the street where maroon and yellow streetcars once clattered and clanged their way to and from downtown. In the old days, people hopped on and off the cars as they pleased. Those not in a hurry, or not too tired, walked the sidewalks, pausing occasionally to exchange greetings and news with a friend or neighbour.

The only person on foot on this day was an older lady carefully navigating the broad steps of St. Andrew's Church, a centre of our family life a lifetime ago. Soon I would cross the street and climb those same steps, following slowly and sadly behind a coffin in a family ritual repeated many times in the past.

The distraction of the cars and the lady climbing the church steps were not enough to stop the dam that was about to burst inside me. As the final stress fractures started to let loose the sobbing, pinpoints of red light blipped weakly along Algoma Street, becoming stronger and more urgent as they came closer. They stopped down the street from the rear of St. Andrew's and I knew they were at St. Joseph's Hospital. More flashing lights gathered and stopped, congesting the street outside the hospital entrance.

St. Joseph's had never seen such a traffic jam of emergency lights before. This was no delivery of bumped and bruised victims of a two-car fender-bender. Something big was happening and my reporter instincts yanked me off the edge of an emotional breakdown and told me to find out what it was. I loped across the street and almost ran down a passerby hurrying from the hospital scene. I couldn't wait to get the details, so I stopped him to ask what the commotion was about.

The man explained breathlessly that an ambulance had brought Terry Fox into the hospital. The news jolted me. What were the chances of me running across Terry Fox, someone who had become an important part of my work as a journalist? I asked what happened. Was he hit by a transport?

Reporters always conjure up the worst scenarios. Terry Fox smacked down by a runaway transport while he ran his Marathon of Hope for cancer was a story too huge to even imagine. The passerby said he didn't know, but one of the cops thought he was sick again.

I stopped to consider the information. Terry Fox was a skinny kid with ruddy-faced determination and a head of curly hair that looked like steel-wool pot scrubber. He lost a leg to cancer and dreamed of running across Canada from sea to sea to raise money for cancer research. He travelled from his West Coast home to St. John's, Newfoundland in April and on the twelfth of that month in 1980 dipped his artificial leg into the Atlantic Ocean and started running the roughly 7,500 kilometres back home to the Pacific.

His Marathon of Hope began as the usual oddity in the news. People often biked, marched, or rolled hula hoops along the highways to raise money and attention for one cause or other. The reporters in the towns they passed through paid small attention to them.

Sometime during the spring, the Terry Fox run had grown beyond just another highway sideshow. It appeared organized and determined.

By June he had ran all the way into Ontario, and the people of the country's most populous province began to pay attention. The white T-shirt, running shorts, and artificial leg that he threw forward in a trademark gait, began making the daily news. He became a star in southern Ontario, and as he rounded the top of Lake Superior, people realized that this crazy kid might run all the way across the country on one leg. People gathered at the roadside to cheer him on. Donations piled up like a blizzard pushing snow against a fence. National reporters elbowed aside the locals to get at the story.

I owned part of this story. I was the bureau chief for the Canadian Press (CP) — the national news service — in Vancouver and Terry Fox lived in the Vancouver suburb of Port Coquitlam. I had already began sketching some plans for when he crossed the Prairies, ran through the mountains, and down the slope to the Pacific where he would dip his plastic leg in triumph. This would be a dream news event: a starry-eyed cancer kid completing an incredible journey of hope, courage, and sheer guts.

The only reason I wasn't back in Vancouver making coverage arrangements for his triumphant return was Veronica's illness and now her death.

Being in Thunder Bay with Terry Fox in some kind of trouble could be considered, in other circumstances, a stroke of journalistic good fortune. I needed to get into that crowd, gather up the details, and telephone them fast to CP in Toronto. They would be stunned to hear their British Columbia bureau chief dictating this international scoop from Thunder Bay. I composed pieces of the story as I ran down the street, even though I didn't know what it was yet, and I thought how important it was to be in the right place at the right time. I had a knack for stumbling into stories, and this was just another example.

My mind roared ahead, then my feet slammed to a stop. I turned and looked back. There was the Everest Funeral Home, still sitting on the corner. The coffin still occupied the viewing room. My mother still occupied the coffin. Bill Brooks and others soon would arrive for the family gathering, followed by the wake. The deceased's eldest child, the guy in charge of all the arrangements, was running down the street to cover a story.

I turned and sauntered back toward Everest. Even I couldn't do this, leave my mother's funeral to cover a story. I had skipped many family events to cover good assignments. Off somewhere taking notes when the kids were out trick-or-treating for Halloween. Parts of two Christmas seasons away reporting in Cuba. Numerous birthdays and anniversaries, hockey games, and concerts missed. Gone for eight weeks wandering Saskatchewan for stories just days after our twins were born. My wife, Diane, at home alone with two newborns and two toddlers in a strange place while I interviewed disgruntled wheat farmers, worried business people in dying prairie towns, and pilots rescued from crash sites in the far north. Even I couldn't be so shameful as to walk away from my mother's funeral for a story.

I was a reporter because of Veronica. Not only had she tricked me into that trade, she had led me in that direction since I was a child. She was a storyteller, a great storyteller, and it is no surprise that I grew up wanting to tell stories.

Thunder Bay was a perfect nurturing place for storytellers because it wallowed in Ojibwe legends. The city lived in the shadow of Nanabijou, the Sleeping Giant that dominates the eastern horizon. Storytellers say that Nanabijou is the sleeping body of a great chief who protects the rich silver deposits at Silver Islet near his feet. When anyone tries to get near the silver, he awakens and terrorizes the people with flying bolts of lightning and awesome thunder that shakes the hills and whips the lake into a fury.

That was legend. Terry Fox down the street was fact. Not knowing what was happening to him at St. Joseph's and what would happen to the Marathon of Hope, gnawed at my reportorial instincts and pride. It hurt that this was one big story that I would read about and not write myself.

I went back to Everest and Veronica and the folks filing in for the viewing. I tingled with the voltage of being close to a big story. There is no bigger charge than reporting fast-breaking news. Being fast, being first, and being accurate. It seemed incredible that I had to turn my back on this one. Little did I know, however, that while Veronica's death denied me one big story, it would lead me into the greatest reporting assignment of my life. An assignment in which I would discover who my mother really was and where she came from.

2 — LaFRANCE

ALL I KNEW ABOUT MY MOTHER WAS WHAT I HAD OBSERVED growing up as her son and what she had told me. What she told people did not always match reality. Her storytelling often mixed fact and fiction. Who she said she was and where she came from turned out to be "faction," a blend of fact and fiction.

Veronica enhanced real-life situations with dramatic imagery. One day she hauled me to an upstairs bedroom of the home we shared with her parents and balanced me on the windowsill. An inmate at the Port Arthur jail was to hang that morning. When they hanged someone back then, they lowered the flag atop the jail building as a signal that the deed was done. We had no hope of seeing anything — the jail was a good two miles away — but Veronica was a storyteller and by placing me in the window, she could tell a story of crime and punishment with more impact by urging me to look hard to see the flag being lowered. The hanging was real, but seeing the jailhouse flag was fantasy.

She had a flair for drama. Many years after the hanging, she presented me with a wrapped gift. I undid the wrapping to reveal a plastic Indian doll, a chief with removable headdress. She told me that this was the last toy she would ever give me because I was a man now and it was time to put away the toys of childhood.

Another time she took me by the hand and led me into the basement to her cherished cedar hope chest. She sat me down on it and said she was going to tell me the story of her family. The story stayed with me the rest of my life and became an important clue in my search to discover who she really was. She told it slowly and with the flair and expressions of a great actress.

Not long after Europeans first occupied Canada, a dashing young man in Normandy shot another man in a duel over a woman. He fled to the New World. The ship carrying him to Quebec City foundered in a storm and crashed onto the rocks. The young man was tossed overboard and washed onto a riverbank. He opened his eyes to see a beautiful Indian princess nursing him. She healed his injuries and restored his health and they married. So began the LaFrance family in Canada.

As with most of her stories, parts resembled the genuine history of the LaFrance family. Other parts were sheer fantasy. She took some facts and blended them with her fantasy, and the reason she did so became evident only long after her death, when I discovered who she was.

Her parents were the LaFrances, Joseph Isidore and Louise LaFrance, both railway people. Both grew up beside railway tracks, where the shrieks of steam locomotives and thumps of shunted cars were the sounds of life itself. Most people they knew had lived and died within earshot of the tracks, spending their lives devoted to ensuring that the trains ran on time. Their days were tied to arrivals and departures, frequent separations, and worry about accidents. Despite that, railway life was a good life that brought special privileges, respect, and good pay for a locomotive engineer.

Railway life brought Louise and Isidore together when the new century turned. Both their families had migrated to Chapleau, a frontier town carved out of the northern Ontario bush in 1885 as the Canadian Pacific Railway moved west to fulfil the national dream of a rail line from Atlantic to Pacific. Louise grew up in the rail camps along the Ottawa Valley and beyond — as construction crews pushed the rails relentlessly west. She and her sisters and brothers lived wherever their father Oliver Aquin, an immigrant from France, could find work building the railway as it moved along through places such as Black Donald Creek, Chalk River, Mattawa, and Nosbonsing. When the rails stretched west beyond Chapleau, Oliver stayed behind in the North Bay-Sudbury-Chapleau region with crews tending the track beds and switches and watering and fuelling stations.

Marie Aquin, Oliver's wife, bore all her children in the rail country bush, and they grew up playing beside the tracks, sometimes finding their home was a converted rail car. There were nine of them, seven girls and two boys, and they built good lives by sticking together and helping each other. Their lives developed some permanency as Oliver advanced in the track gangs and became a section foreman. The family settled in Chapleau about 1902 and stayed there, Oliver dedicating his life to railway work until one evening one of the kids went to fetch him for supper and found him keeled over dead at sixty in his foreman's shed.

Lambert LaFrance was a different piece of history. His ancestors were among the first to settle in New France. They had left France more than two centuries earlier, eventually settling at Bic, Quebec on the south shore of the St. Lawrence River where it begins to join the Atlantic Ocean. Life was good there, after the initial horrors of cold, starvation, and Native attacks. The land had been broken and settled to provide all the pastoral comforts of farm country plus the attractions of seaside living. Why Lambert would uproot himself is a mystery, considering the pain his ancestors suffered to create a little paradise there.

His Canadian family history did not begin with an Indian princess, as my mother told me, although Natives played large roles in the lives of the LaFrances. It began when Nicholas Pinel signed a contract on April 5, 1645, to help colonize France's settlement at Port Royal in Acadia, now part of Nova Scotia. He agreed to live in the new country for three years, working as a village carpenter. When the contract expired, he found himself still alive, unlike many others who succumbed to the weather, disease, or Native attacks. He decided to stay on in the New World and sent for his family.

A diffident French bureaucracy and wars with the British and Natives stunted Port Royal's growth. The French spent little effort learning about their new territory. They were too busy basking in their own glory to develop a good understanding of North America. The Port Royal mission languished and Pinel moved to the Cap-Rouge River area near what later became Quebec City, but settlement also was difficult because of regular attacks by the Iroquois. He moved to Sillery, where more people offered more protection from the Native attacks and where the Jesuits established their first North American mission.

The Iroquois hated the French for siding with traditional Iroquois enemies, and their travelling war parties continued to make life difficult for the settlers even at Sillery. Nicholas Pinel joined a group organized to fight off their attacks, but his ten-year lucky run in the New World ran out in September 1655 when he was killed in a fight with a war party. His family carried on, later adopting the name Pinel dit LaFrance in the French custom, common in New France, of refining the identification of families. A Pinel dit LaFrance was one of the family of Pinels who originally came from France. Eventually the name became LaFrance, or Lafrance, meaning "of France" or "from France". That history of the LaFrance family founding in North America is a mile off from Veronica's rescued-by-an-Indian-princess tale. However, I discovered later there was a reason for introducing an Indian princess into the family.

The promise of opportunity tugged Lambert LaFrance west from the comforts of the south shore to the bug-infested forests along the Chapleau River. The CPR became the doorway to thousands of miles of unsettled territory in a massive effort at nation building and would lead to jobs and business prospects. Lambert and his wife of four years, Adele Roy, arrived when the town was a muddy slash line with seven or eight log cabins, some tents, and a boxcar converted to a telegraph office. The trains stopped seven miles to the east because that's as far as rail construction had gone, so they made their grand entry into Chapleau on a rail handcart. They opened a boarding house for railroaders near the Chapleau tracks, and it became known as the best place to get an excellent meal in Chapleau.

The LaFrances had ten children, three of whom died young in the wild Chapleau bush country. For those who survived to adulthood, it was inevitable that they would become railroaders or marry railroaders. Isidore was mesmerised by the comings and goings of the black locomotive giants and was riding them as a CPR employee before his sixteenth birthday. His brother Adélard had more interest in the bush and the Ojibwe communities at Missanabie and Biscotasing, home for several years of the Englishman Archie Belaney, also known as Grey Owl. The railway settlements attracted the Natives looking for trade and Adélard, two years younger than Isidore, discovered trading could be profitable. He opened a trading post at Missanabie in 1908 and began buying furs from the Natives. He later moved the operation to Chapleau, then Sudbury, where it continues to operate today as the furrier Lafrance Richmond Furs.

By the turn of the twentieth century, Chapleau was a human anthill, a brushed-out busy speck in hundreds of square miles of threatening northern forest. It offered little in terms of natural beauty, plopped down on the lowlands beside the slow-moving Chapleau River, surrounded by swamps and tracts of funereal black spruce and emaciated jack pine. There were few of the granite outcroppings, hardwood hills, or patches of majestic white pine that made the bush country west, south, and east of Chapleau so richly picturesque. It was about as isolated as you could be in the lower half of Ontario. The closest towns of any consequence were Sault Ste. Marie, 180 kilometres south-southwest the way the crow flies, and Sudbury, 250 kilometres south-southeast in a straight line. There was no highway connecting the town to the outside until after the First World War.

The town went up in too much of a hurry to allow for any thoughtful planning or significant architecture. Most of the houses were wood-frame, two-storey boxes the shape of the hotels in a Monopoly game. Buildings usually were clad in clapboard because sawn lumber from the bush was more readily available than manufactured brick. Houses and businesses spilled along either side of the tracks, which were numerous because Chapleau was a divisional point where crews and equipment were changed. This required sidings for maintenance and repair facilities, supply depots, and auxiliary equipment. Aside from the bustle of railroading, it was a bleak place, especially during the long winters of snowdrifts, icy winds, and freezing temperatures that could kill anyone without heated shelter.

Time out from railroading focussed on home and church. Many Chapleau townsfolk were Roman Catholic, French and English alike, and built themselves what probably was the finest building in the town — Sacred Heart of Jesus Church, or Sacre-Coeur. They built it in 1885 the same year the CPR established Chapleau, but the church rapidly became too small for the growing population and a new one went up in 1891. It burned in 1918 and the brick structure with two bell towers, still active on Lansdowne Street, replaced it.

Church gatherings were a main entertainment outside the home, bringing together families such as the LaFrances, the Aquins, the Tremblays, and the Burnses. Sacred Heart Church developed a unique experiment in Canadian culture in Chapleau's early days. The town was so small and so isolated that it was difficult for different ethnic groups to remain apart. Sacred Heart became a truly bilingual and bicultural parish out of necessity and still is, right down to the stained glass sacristy windows — St. Patrick on one side, St. Jean-Baptiste on the other. The church became even more a centre of town life in the years following 1911 when a young, energetic, and personable priest named Father Romeo Gasçon arrived. A born organizer, he threw himself into the community's affairs and became friends with many of the townspeople, including the LaFrances. Their lives became part of his life.

The LaFrances met the Aquins when the latter moved into town in 1902. The meeting was inevitable — two large families in one village could not avoid each other. Besides, no one could miss Isidore LaFrance on the street. He seemed as tall as the trees, a kind-looking giant with a perpetual half grin and large and dark friendly eyes. He dressed sharply and always was well-groomed even when crossing the tracks in grease-smeared striped overalls and a big lunch pail under his arm.

Louise Aquin turned heads as well. She was tall, unusually so for a woman of her times, not far from six feet in her shoes. She had piercing eyes. They were clear, knowing, and persistent, and certainly in later life could quickly search out fibs that might float from the lips of a grandchild. She was talented in music and remarkably articulate for a young woman with little formal schooling. She was bilingual, speaking French and English equally well. She often sang solo at Sacred Heart, her soprano voice soaring to the ceiling and beyond. Anyone who ever heard her hit the high soprano notes of "O Holy Night" on Christmas Eve would never forget it.

They dated, mainly attending family and church and sporting events. Before long, Isidore and Louise were married in the old church in 1904. Sacred Heart was the scene of many such family weddings. The Burnses, Francophones despite the Scottish name, also met the Aquins, but the Burns boys found the LaFrance girls

Courtesy of Jim Poling Sr.

Louise and Isidore LaFrance in their thirties and childless after a dozen or so years of marriage. Both were tall for people of the times, Isidore well over six feet and Louise close to it.

more interesting. Three Burns brothers ended up marrying three LaFrances, all sisters of Isidore. These were remarkable times of large family gatherings celebrating engagements, marriages, and births. Talk and food were the centres of the celebrations. If a piano was handy, there was singing and often the main voice was Louise Aquin LaFrance, principal soloist at Sacred Heart.

Booze, not often openly used in conservative families, made an occasional appearance. One memorable appearance was during Christmas holidays when family celebrations were breaking out all over town. These people, their lives tied to the railway, knew all train schedules down to the minute and the contents of every rail car. One night, one of the Tremblay boys, who had married into the LaFrance family, led a party to the tracks with a brace and bit and several buckets. It was a bitter night with the white of one's breath barely visible in the fog of blowing snow. One of the boxcars contained a shipment of fine Scotch whiskey that was headed west. They drilled through the boxcar's wooden floor and into an oak keg and caught the whisky in pails as it drained through the hole.

Isidore had started work at the Chapleau rail yards in 1899 at age fifteen. He quickly worked his way into a locomotive cab as a fireman and in 1902 advanced to locomotive engineer. At nineteen years old, he was in command of a roaring locomotive beast thirty metres long and weighing close to three hundred tons. Being a locomotive engineer had its benefits: good pay, status, and the joys of exercising command and control in an important job. But it also brought sacrifice. There were long stretches away from home and family.

Railroading was dangerous work. Construction accidents were common, as were collisions resulting from inaccurate timing and crashes set up by Mother Nature. The LaFrances were not immune to the tragic consequences of railway life. In 1906, Lambert received word that his brother Napoleon had been hurt while working on a construction train carrying gravel west of Chapleau. The train pulled in to Chapleau with Napoleon, his leg severed when he had slipped between two cars. Lambert held him in his arms as the train travelled to Biscotasing where medical help was available. When the train reached Biscotasing, Napoleon was dead, having bled to death in his brother's arms. His name is engraved on a workers' memorial plaque near the Chapleau station.

Five years later, Isidore braked a locomotive as it rolled into Chapleau station when a small engine wheel broke off. The engine stayed on the tracks and no one was hurt. CPR bosses tried to blame the incident on Isidore, so he told them to shove the job and applied to the Canadian Northern Railway (CNoR), which was rapidly expanding out West.

He and Louise found themselves far from the warmth of family life in Chapleau. They were stationed in Port Arthur, the main eastern terminus for the new railway, and Isidore began running the big engines in every division between Hornepayne on the east and Edmonton on the west.

The LaFrance-Aquin-Burns family circle mourned the move of the eldest LaFrance son and the eldest Aquin daughter. Louise and Isidore were key family players — sociable, friendly, and just nice people to have around. Free rail passes were plentiful in the family, however, and there was enough back and forth between Chapleau and Port Arthur to hold family ties intact. Then, in early 1918, the Chapleau families learned that Isidore and Louise had left Port Arthur. Inexplicably they moved west and were living in the unheard-of village of Hanna, somewhere out on the plains of east-central Alberta.

Then came news from the West of the arrival of a long sought after baby. Isidore and Louise, who'd been having trouble conceiving and were now into their thirties, finally had a child. Father Gascon, who had a habit of appearing at important times in people's lives, carried details of this miraculous child back to Chapleau. It had seemed somewhat odd, but this impoverished and busy priest had travelled west just to visit Isidore and Louise and reported them well settled into family life with their new daughter, Veronica Cecile LaFrance.

As quickly as they had disappeared out West, the LaFrances reappeared in Ontario, at Port Arthur. That, too, seemed odd. A year out West, then back to Ontario. But it was no secret that Isidore loved Port Arthur and people just assumed the LaFrances had not taken to the Prairies.

Port Arthur felt more like home to the LaFrances. Isidore relished running his locomotives along the Lake Superior shoreline. He was fascinated with the spectacular views. The Great Inland Sea dominated all views to the east for at least 180 points on the compass. From almost any hill along the waterfront, the horizon was filled with water. Water moving relentlessly eastward on an incredible journey to the Atlantic Ocean. Only a few island dots, and of course massive Nanabijou, interrupted an otherwise unbroken view of water that stretched from the Port Arthur waterfront to Sault Ste. Marie, 450 kilometres east.

Nanabijou is the Sibley Peninsula, a rocky spine roughly thirty kilometres long and ten kilometres wide that juts into Lake Superior from the north to form the vastness of Thunder Bay. Seen from the cities of Port Arthur and Fort William, amalgamated as Thunder Bay in 1970, it does indeed look like an Indian giant wearing full headdress, sleeping on his back with his arms folded across his chest. It is an amazing piece of nature that Canadians, in a 2007 Canadian Broadcasting Corporation(CBC) poll, voted one of the seven wonders of Canada.

The legend of the Sleeping Giant is myth, but the silver treasure is real. There have been attempts to mine it, the most successful in the 1870s and 1880s. Miners extracted tons of silver and Silver Islet became known as the world's richest silver deposit, but Nanabijou constantly fought back, raking Lake Superior with vicious storms that made mining operations miserable. In 1884, a shipment of coal needed to fuel the pumps that kept water out of the mine did not arrive on time. The pumps fell silent, the mine flooded, operations ceased, and the mining families moved away. Nanabijou had succeeded in protecting at least some of his treasure.

Long before the silver seekers came, the mainland shore opposite the rocky peninsula was Native territory. The Ojibwe Natives lived along the

Courtesy of Thunder Bay Historical Museum Society.

Nanabijou, the Sleeping Giant, as seen from Hillcrest Park overlooking the part of Thunder Bay known as Port Arthur until the early 1970s.

shoreline where the Kaministiqua River joins Lake Superior, or the Big Lake, in what used to be Fort William. The North West Company built a fur trading fort there just after the turn of the 1800s, and it became a major rendezvous point for fur traders heading west or returning to Montreal. In 1868, Simon Dawson began building a road from the Lakehead waterfront to the Red River colonies out West. It ran straight up the hill from the lake, later becoming the forked road where Everest Funeral Home and St. Andrew's Church faced each other.

Until the railway came, the road leading away from the water was the path used by settlers, surveyors, traders, and soldiers sent to put down the western Métis rebellion. Many a traveller leaving the waterfront from the Port Arthur side must have stopped along the road where it tops the hills to look back and absorb the spectacular views of the lake, the islands, and Nanabijou.

Isidore rented a house up that hill when he returned from the West with Louise and their new baby. It was near Hillcrest Park, a flat spot from which you could drink in the entire panorama of the Thunder Bay region. You could stand on the rock wall and look down at the brick-chimneyed rooftops of the houses that spill into downtown. These were the homes of the working class, the immigrants who melted into a Lakehead society that seemed less hyphenated than other parts of Canada. They were mainly Finns, Swedes, and Italians and the rooftops of their edifices poked up from below the hilltop — St. Anthony's Catholic Church and the Scandinavian Boarding House. Everything looked so much smaller from up there. There was a sense of being airborne. The rectangles and squares of the commercial buildings of downtown were tiny. Even the gargantuan concrete tubes of the grain elevators that blocked access to the water's edge appeared less significant. Only the Giant itself, despite being twenty-five kilometres straight out from the park, gave any sense of bigness.

The LaFrances' house was a two-storey wooden place at 385 Cornwall Avenue on the hillside overlooking the lake. It was anchored to the rocks just below where High Street ran past Hillcrest Park, and if you craned your neck from an upstairs window, you could view the lake. It was a short walk over the brow of the hill to Hillcrest Park, with its flower gardens and a long rock wall with imbedded cannons pointed out over the harbour. On cool, spring days, kids climbed onto the cannons to feel the warmth that the black iron had absorbed from the sun. Opposite the park are some of the city's finest old homes, built there long ago for the splendid view.

Hillcrest Park was a popular place to stroll. It was almost like a park in the LaFrances' backyard where they could let Veronica loose to run and laugh and point at the flowers. For longer outings, they would drive her to Boulevard Lake on the east side of town where people strolled the lakeside or sat and had picnics while looking out over the water.

Isidore walked down the hill from his house to the CNR roundhouse where his locomotives were kept. He could see the rising sun turn the skies above the Giant to the pink of the amethyst so abundant in the area's rock. Then to a deeper pink purple and finally blood red as the sun lifted above the Giant's feet. In the evenings, the setting sun sun made it iridescent, then sharpened its features until its cliffs and crevices became visible.

The joy the LaFrances felt at watching Veronica frolic at Hillcrest Park or beside Boulevard Lake evaporated unexpectedly one morning when she was four years old. Veronica's get-up-and-go personality usually woke the household, but on this morning the house was quiet and there was no sound of activity in her room. Louise and Isidore found her in bed, unusually subdued and chilled and tired. When Louise helped her up, her legs didn't want to hold her, and as the hours passed, they became more wooden. Within days her legs were paralysed. The doctor whispered the news: infantile paralysis — the dreaded poliovirus — crippler and sometimes killer of children and young adults.

The LaFrances were shattered. Their little family was a dream come true, a dream that had survived the greatest threat to human life of their time — the Spanish flu that in 1918–19 killed 50 million people worldwide. Isidore fell ill with that deadly scourge while on a road trip but recovered. His younger sister in Chapleau caught it and died. Now having narrowly escaped that outbreak, the LaFrances were visited by a new scourge that had appeared as a serious threat to children in 1916. Each summer after that brought new outbreaks that peaked in the late 1940s and early 1950s.

Veronica lay in bed for more than two months, unable to move her legs. The only good news was that her breathing remained unaffected, and she was not trapped in one of the iron lungs that lined hospital wards, filling them with the eerie rhythm of velvet wheezing. The poliovirus attacks and destroys motor neurones, sometimes concentrating on the limbs, other times favouring the respiratory neurones. Veronica was fortunate; the virus hit only her legs.

The disease struck Veronica in 1921, the same year it caught Franklin D. Roosevelt, leaving him without the use of his legs. His case showed the world that the disease could strike anyone, and his struggle to regain the use of his legs set a courageous example for others. His legs never did return to normal, but Roosevelt pushed on and became U.S. president, leading the nation through some of its most difficult times.

Veronica recovered. Slowly her legs grew stronger. She began to walk again with the help of crutches and then a brace on her left leg. She learned to pitch the braced leg forward in an attempt to run with the other kids who lived in the Cornwall Avenue area. The leg brace and her drag-kick-and-hop walk were playground novelties when she entered St. Andrew's Catholic schoolyard just days before her seventh birthday. Few kids had seen leg braces before, although they would appear more and more over the years.

St. Andrew's was downtown, part of the Catholic institutional complex that covered most of the area bounded by Arthur, Court, Algoma, and Camelot streets. The school fronted Arthur Street, Port Arthur's main drag at the time, along with the church hall, rectory, and church. Behind them facing Algoma Street were St. Joseph's Hospital and the convent of the Sisters of St. Joseph. The extended block was a one-stop destination — schooling, health care, spiritual life, and social activities for the many Catholics who occupied the houses on the neighbourhood just above downtown.

The school was a two-storey, free-standing, red-brick block with a bell tower on the four-slope roof. It was a centre hall plan with front and rear double doorways where the kids lined up when one of the nuns in black-and-white habits appeared and clanged a heavy brass hand bell. The junior grades spilled into the lower classrooms while the older kids climbed the stairs. The classrooms occupied corners, each side of which had large rectangle windows through which outside light could spill.

The LaFrances moved to 28 Peter Street, which was only three long blocks up the hill from St. Andrew's. It was walking distance for a kid with a leg brace and, although the LaFrances would change houses over the years, they stayed within the hillside neighbourhood bounded by Algoma, College, Arthur, and Dawson streets.

The disability did little to hold Veronica back. She was naturally gregarious, an expressive child. She wore her emotions on her face, with the expression of her big eyes, the shapes of her mouth, even the wrinkles of her nose transmitting her feelings. She loved to tell stories to the other kids and did so with the flourishes of a child actor. Other kids liked her because she was fun-loving and liked to laugh. Asked to describe her most memorable trait, most of her playmates would say her infectious laugh. Outgoing as she was, she liked to keep secrets. She teased friends about knowing something they didn't know while they pestered her to tell them.

Other kids loved playing at the LaFrance houses — the McCuaig Block at College and Tupper streets, then 63 Peter Street, a couple doors north of Van Norman Street. As an only child, Veronica got the best of everything, including attention. Most of her friends were from large families and had to share everything with their siblings. Her best friend Doris Shaw often came to the house for sleepovers, and they would stay up late giggling and laughing and playing with Veronica's little white Pomeranian.

After she recovered from polio, her childhood years took flight and soared to heights that every child should be so lucky to enjoy. Friends were numerous, money was not a problem even in the Depression years because locomotive engineers continued to work. Life at the LaFrance house was secure, warm, and comfortable.

Isidore made his regular runs east to Capreol and as far west as Edmonton, suffering the stress of delays, bad weather, and accidents. When he would return from a run depressed, Louise would know immediately what was wrong — his engine had hit a moose on the tracks. He always felt sorry for the animals, and he fretted that they would stand staring at his headlight while he wrangled to stop tons of locomotive pulling tons of cars.

Louise devoted her time to the church and politics. She became diocesan president of the Catholic Women's League, an executive member of the women's Liberal association, and an active member of the St. Joseph's Hospital auxiliary. Church was a central part of her life, as it had been at Sacred Heart in Chapleau and briefly at St. George's in Hanna. She could often be found changing altar cloths on the ornate altar at St. Andrew's. Sometimes when an altar boy didn't show for an early weekday Mass, she filled in even though it was not a woman's place to be on the altar during Mass. Girls were not allowed to serve on the altar then, but either Louise LaFrance's strong will or a progressive priest broke the rule on occasion. On Sundays, Veronica would stand beside her father in their favourite pew and stare up at her mother, framed by the impressive St. Andrew's Church pipe organ, filling the small cathedral with the soaring notes of a soprano soloist.

Isidore's rail pass allowed the family to travel to Sudbury and Chapleau to visit family. The LaFrances and the Aquins were large growing families in the 1920s and reunions were happy and hectic. Veronica grew to love visiting her cousins' homes in Chapleau and Sudbury. Uncle Adélard, whose fur trading business flourished and expanded into actual manufacturing of fur garments, built a cottage on Lake Panache west of Sudbury, and it became the site of many family reunions. The Port Arthur LaFrances visited frequently and Veronica once confessed to a younger cousin that she loved the cottage during the day, but it frightened her at night.

Because she was an only child, Veronica loved these visits among her cousins. Her cousins also enjoyed her visits because she was lively and told outrageous stories and was quick to lead the others in singing. Her cousin Simone, Adélard's youngest daughter, recalled watching her older cousin with wonderment, admiring how good looking she was. Decades later, she still remembers Veronica's fine dark features and terrific smile.

Veronica's lame leg strengthened, and soon she was almost indistinguishable among the other kids in the schoolyard. The brace was gone and the drag-and-kick step faded into a limp that one had to watch for to notice. When the leg brace disappeared so did the long black ringlets, replaced by a shorter, big girl cut. She grew it back during her teens, letting it hang just above her shoulders or folding and tying it into a bun.

By the time she finished Grade 8 at St. Andrew's and began to hike the Van Norman Street hill to the Port Arthur Technical School, the dark hair was longer and pushed back behind her ears. She was a beautiful young woman, petite and slim with a finely sculpted nose and mouth, high cheekbones, and dark, expressive eyes. She favoured pants because anyone who looked closely below her skirt or dress could notice the thinness of her left calf and ankle — the only visible trace of the polio.

Her teen years were not exciting times in the early 1930s. Young women went to school and returned home promptly. Dating was not allowed during the early teen years. Entertainment was going to a movie in a group on a Friday night or attending the young people's club at St. Andrew's Hall on Sunday evenings.

Veronica reunited with friends from the Cornwall Street neighbourhood when the Chester family moved onto Van Norman Street below Peter Street and just around the corner from the LaFrances. Audrey Chester and Veronica walked up to Tech School every day. After the high school years, they both went to work for the Port Arthur Public Utilities

Courtesy of Jim Poling Sr.

Veronica at 19 looks pensive and reserved. In fact, she usually was the centre of attention with her hearty laugh and impish sense of humour.

Company, which ran the city's telephone service. They became operators, a job that perfectly suited Veronica's happy disposition and voice.

You needed a sunny disposition to work as a Port Arthur telephone operator in the late 1930s. The work week was forty-five and a half hours and each of the thirty-nine operators handled 136 calls an hour during the busiest times. Port Arthur had roughly thirty-five hundred subscribers at the time, a drop from pre-Depression years when people had more money to spend. The girls sat at a long switchboard panel plugging and unplugging cords and asking: "Number, please."

It was not simple work. They had to deal with all sorts of people and had serious responsibilities. Telephone operators took fire calls and reported them to the fire department. After alerting the firemen, the operator then called the pumping station nearest the fire to alert them to increase water pressure to the hydrant. They had to be cool-headed and precise. For all of this, they received roughly five hundred dollars a year wages for starting operators and eight hundred dollars a year after three years.

Despite the responsibilities, long hours, irritations, and low pay, they were not easy jobs to get. The telephone company had strict requirements, physical and moral. Candidate operators had to be eighteen to twenty-four years old, stand at least five foot five inches, and have a reach of three feet six inches. Veronica, at five foot two inches, seemed to have slipped past the height requirement. PUC operators required a high school diploma, good eyesight and hearing, normal speech, and clear enunciation. They had to be unmarried, preferably living at home with their parents, and had to remain unmarried to keep their job. They had to produce a medical fitness certificate once a year and could not use tobacco in excess.

It was a job suited to the times, a period of transition in Canada. Transition from a slower and simpler life to the fast pace that eventually led to the frenetic madness of today when people barely have time to think, and many of them don't. The era of the telephone operator lasted longer in Port Arthur than many other places. Voters refused to approve autodial systems in the late 1930s and autodialling did not come into being there until 1949. No doubt it was coincidental, but much about life began to change at the same time.

When they started as operators, Veronica and Audrey could walk to their jobs downtown. It was only a few blocks downhill through leafy streets where houses were not quite worthy of *Better Homes and Gardens* but certainly were neat and practical. Fewer people owned cars and walking to work could be a social occasion. It was almost impossible to walk down Arthur Street without meeting a friend or a relative. There was a malt shop just down from St. Andrew's, and you could stop there for a soda or a milkshake and talk with others who strolled in coming or going from their business. Not only was there time to talk to people, stopping and chatting was expected.

If you tired walking up the Arthur Street slope, you could ride one of the streetcars that rattled and screeched along the iron rails imbedded in the Arthur Street pavement. You could hop on pretty much anywhere if you were swift and nimble enough to grab the handrail and swing onto the platform.

Audrey often invited her teenage girlfriends to her house on Van Norman Street. Mrs. Chester would play the piano and they all would sing along. Veronica was front and centre, singing and clowning and at the centre of attention. At one session, Veronica passed by the living room window and noticed a young man coming out of a house down the street. He was tall and skinny and wore a fedora cocked to one side of his head.

The girls began to take a special interest in 331 Van Norman Street, a two-and-a-half-storey brick house with a veranda off the second-storey main bedroom. The house was whistling distance from the religious property that held St. Andrew's Church and School and St. Joseph's Hospital. A young man came and went with another man roughly the same age. Sometimes a couple of girls close to their own age were seen coming and going from the house.

One day after watching the young man from behind the Chester's curtains, Veronica announced to the group of giggling girls that that was the guy she was going to get. The girls believed her. They knew that when Veronica LaFrance made up her mind to get something, there was no questioning her.

3 — THE LOON PEOPLE

THE POLINGS ARRIVED IN PORT ARTHUR IN 1937 LOOKING like the Joads on their move west from Oklahoma to California in Steinbeck's *Grapes of Wrath*. The older boys were lean and wiry from the hungry days of the Depression just ended. They pushed up the front brims of their fedoras with their thumbs just like Henry Fonda in the movies. They arrived in a jalopy of the day, Eva Poling and all the kids and whatever they could carry jammed into the seats and the trunk. Bob, the eldest and Ray, two years younger, did the driving. Robert Sr. already had gone ahead to take up his job at the new paper mill built on the shoreline in Port Arthur's extreme east end.

They had loaded up close to twenty years of living in Sault Ste. Marie at the east end of the lake and headed west through Michigan, Wisconsin, and Minnesota. There was no road between the Soo and Port Arthur, just a lot of spectacular bush scenery along Superior's north shore. Travelling west meant going through the States, the first leg being the short ferry ride across the St. Mary's River dividing the Canadian Soo and the American Soo.

The border didn't mean anything to them. They had come to the Soo originally from Minnesota where the three oldest children had been born. The trip was an opportunity to visit relatives, including the Desilets, Eva's parents, in Superior, Wisconsin. They also would visit the Cloquet, Minnesota area where they had lived before the Great Fire of 1918.

Robert Sr. had worked in mills in Cloquet and International Falls before crossing the border to Sault Ste. Marie, Ontario, the site of a new paper mill. No one could ever recall how Robert got into paper mill work. It certainly wasn't because of his size. Mill work involved much hard labour in the early days, from wrestling logs in the mill ponds or yards to stirring pulp and pushing about rolls of finished product. Robert was tiny, under five foot nine inches, and boasted he was 110 pounds soaking wet. His wife and friends called him Tom, a nickname someone gave him after observing that he looked like Tom Thumb.

Nor could anyone recall how he got to Minnesota. He was born in Atlanta, Georgia, where his maternal grandfather Hiram Walker kept slaves long after the Civil War and Emancipation. The story was that most of them preferred plantation life to going out on their own. His dad, Isaac Elmer Ellsworth Poling, was a carpetbagger who wooed Hiram's southern belle daughter Mattie. The marriage went bad almost immediately because Isaac turned out to be a shifty gambler, but not before there was a pile of kids who were shuffled back regularly between Ohio, Isaac's home, and Atlanta. Ernie, a couple years younger than Robert, often recalled standing with one of his brothers on a railway station platform with tags on their coats, so they would not be lost on a trip to their grandparents' plantation.

Robert claimed that the unsettled family life left him out on his own at age ten. Who knows if that was a bit of an exaggeration, but we do know that he was out wandering when he was quite young, loading bricks for ten cents a day. As a young man, he found himself in the northern Minnesota woodlands, where the forests provided much work for those with a strong back and an appreciation of solitude.

Isaac's life of drinking, gambling, and shattered family life was an aberration in the Poling clan. The Polings were known as religious people from Manhattan through to New Jersey, Virginia, West Virginia, and Ohio as they had expanded and spread out. Isaac's father, George Washington Poling, was a Salvation Army preacher in Ohio and part of a family branch that produced seven consecutive generations of ministers.

The first Poling to reach America's shores was Thomas who arrived on the ship *Scorpion* at Lynn, Massachusetts in 1642. He had sailed out of Gravesend, England, leaving his home in Sussex. One of his sons, John, became associated with Lady Deborah Moodie, an eccentric aristocrat who fled England to escape religious turmoil. She was an Anabaptist, someone who believed that baptism is for adult believers only, not infants.

Lady Moodie found the religious climate in America even more severe under the Pilgrim society. Her Anabaptist views were heretical, and she moved again, this time to New Amsterdam, now New York City. The Dutch, who controlled Manhattan and the surrounding area before losing it to England, granted her and twenty followers, including John Poling, religious freedom and some land on Long Island.

The Polings thrived in what later became Brooklyn and then branched out to New Jersey and beyond. John's great-grandson Jonathon was a Methodist circuit rider known to have galloped the Appalachians with a Bible in one saddlebag and a revolver in the other. He became the patriarch of a family branch that produced a remarkable string of seven consecutive generations of Protestant ministers. Three of his grandsons were Daniel Shobe Poling, an Evangelical Association circuit rider; William, an English Methodist preacher in Pennsylvania and later Wisconsin; and George Washington Poling, who joined the Salvation Army when it came to North America. Daniel carried on the family tradition of producing preacher heirs: a son, Rev. Charles Cupp Poling; a grandson, Rev. Daniel A. Poling; and a great-grandson, Rev. Clark V. Poling, who ended the string when he died a hero in the Second World War.

George Washington Poling had no such luck in raising priestly boys. In Isaac, George produced a son who in one short lifetime used up all the good works and prayers of those many generations of preaching Polings. One of Isaac's many sins was to name his son Robert Lee after the great Confederate general. This had George spouting some distinctly unreligious words, which is forgivable considering he had fought valiantly for the Blue — even against his half-brother Wilson — and had named Isaac's brother, Ulysses Grant Poling.

Robert met Olivia Desilets in Minnesota. She was the daughter of a French-Canadian family who lived near Rat Portage outside Kenora, Ontario. Robert and Olivia, called Eva, courted, then married, and had the first of three of their eight children before moving to Canada when Robert got a job at the paper mill in Sault Ste. Marie, leaving America and the American Polings behind. It was just as well. Leaving one's native land and extended family is a terrible wrench, but these were tough times to be a non-religious Poling. U.S. Prohibition was in place and the Poling clan was at the front of the battle against demon alcohol. Rev. Daniel A. Poling had documented in detail the evils of drink in his satirical book, *John Barleycorn: His Life and Letters.* He also campaigned against smoking and numerous other bad habits and sins.

Courtesy of Jim Poling Sr.

Eva Desilets and Robert Poling in their 1913 wedding photo. They married in the pulp and paper town of Cloquet, Minnesota, eventually moving on to the Ontario mill towns of Sault Ste. Marie and Port Arthur after the Great Fire of 1918 destroyed much of Cloquet.

Robert Lee wanted nothing to do with religion or Prohibition or people who called smoking a disease of the devil. John Barleycorn was a frequent and welcome guest in his house and later the houses of his sons and grandsons. Any preaching done under this branch of the family tree would be over a few cold beers or a couple of glasses of Seagram's, or maybe both. His good wife later helped Robert find religion, but it was

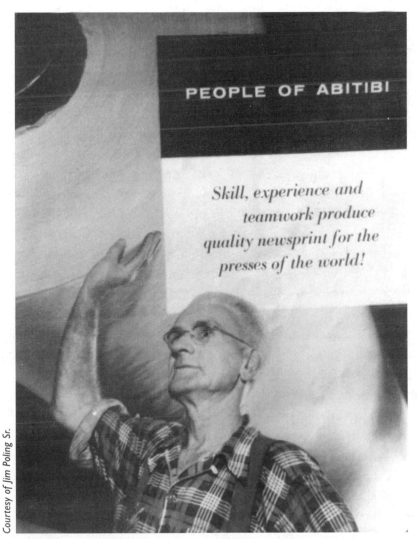

PEOPLE OF ABITIBI

Skill, experience and teamwork produce quality newsprint for the presses of the world!

Robert Lee Poling was born in Georgia but moved to Canada to work in paper mills in Sault Ste. Marie and Port Arthur. He was mill boss at Abitibi in Port Arthur when he retired in the 1950s.

religion backed by a strong shot and a good smoke, and it took a back pew to his greatest love, the outdoors. Like his West Virginia ancestors, Robert Lee Poling was a man wild for the bush and he taught his kids the joys of packing canoes, landing trout, and knocking down autumn-fat deer with an old .38-55, a rifle he said was so powerful it killed them, cleaned them, and packed them out of the bush.

In the Soo, he supplemented his mill income by operating a souvenir shop out of the Windsor Hotel and used it as a base for a guiding business. Americans flocked off the ferries near the hotel's back entrance, and a lot of them were looking to experience the joys of the great pastimes of the day, fishing and hunting. Robert Poling guided them into the bush country north of the Soo and established himself as someone as at home on the northern lakes as a loon. The two older boys followed the old man much like two loon chicks paddling beside their mother.

When the family spilled into Port Arthur, Robert Poling already had arranged the house at 331 Van Norman Street. It was on the south side of the first Van Norman Street hill, and backed on the large houses on Arthur Street, later named Red River Road. From the backyard you could see between the Arthur Street houses to the Cenotaph in the park, below the grey stone façade of Port Arthur Collegiate Institute. At the tip of the park were Central School and the start of downtown.

The four bedrooms on the second storey of 331 Van Norman Street and the small apartment on the third made it a good fit for a large family. Especially a family with such a wide age spread. Bob was twenty-three, Ray twenty-one and the others — Eileen, Jack, Theresa, Zita, and Len — were all a couple of years or so apart. There also was a baby, Gerry.

The family settled quickly into the community, installing the younger kids at St. Andrew's School and joining St. Andrew's Parish. Bob and Ray found work, the former as a welder and latter as a chauffeur for the Greer family who owned the turreted mansion on Court Street overlooking McVicar Creek. They also got extra work fighting forest fires, a hazardous job that almost cost Ray his life. They were hiking out of one fire area, Ray bringing up the rear, when the crew stopped for a break. Someone noticed Ray was missing. They backtracked twenty minutes before finding him passed out in bush. He suffered an appendix attack and by the time they got him out of the bush and to a hospital, the appendix had ruptured.

Veronica passed the house at 331 Van Norman Street daily, no doubt craning her neck to catch a glimpse of the fellow she had seen from the Chester's living room window. It was inevitable that they should meet and they did — down the hill at the St. Andrew's youth group. The church hall had pool tables, a snack bar, and bowling alleys and was the meeting place for an active group of young people.

It didn't take long for Veronica to fulfil her prophecy. She got the guy who she had seen coming out of the house at 331 Van Norman Street. They joined the Port Arthur Catholic Young People's Society, a social club based at St. Andrew's, offering wholesome fun for men and women eighteen and over. For a $2 annual membership, they could join outings, spaghetti suppers, and twenty-five-cent dances such as masquerade balls. Ray and Veronica and friends from the club often went on hikes to Mount McKay and spent Sundays where so many other Port Arthurites did — picnicking at Boulevard Lake, the recreation area created within walking distance from downtown by the damming of the Current River. When a car was available, they

Courtesy of Jim Poling Sr.

Veronica and Ray did much of their dating in the outdoors. They took fishing trips to MacKenzie Falls just east of Port Arthur, plus hikes to Mount McKay, overlooking Fort William. Here they are pictured at Kakabeka Falls, a popular Sunday drive destination from Port Arthur, now called Thunder Bay.

also motored down the east highway to MacKenzie River to fish a foam-flecked trout pool below rapids created by the river's fall toward the Big Lake. They double dated, often with Ray's brother Bob and Veronica's childhood friend Doris Shaw.

While life was quiet at the LaFrances, it was bedlam at the Polings. With eight kids ranging from a preschooler to grown men, every room at 331 Van Norman Street bulged with constant action. Eva was always in the kitchen, which was impossibly small for feeding such a large family had it not been for the huge summer kitchen off the back. There, kitchen supplies could be stored among the gun racks, fishing rods, and camping gear. When the action went beyond control, little Robert Lee waded in and restored order. One day, he was repairing the kitchen ceiling when Bob and Ray began to fight. Both were big boys, each over six feet tall and lean and stringy. Robert Lee was standing on a cupboard counter when the battle began. He leapt from his perch, landing with a hand on the back of each combatant's neck. He banged their heads together and knocked them both cold onto the kitchen floor.

Neither Bob nor Ray was one to fight, but most brothers do have occasional differences. Both were quiet to the point of being shy, the tall quiet types for whom minding your business was a virtue. Both were open books. What you saw was exactly what was there. Ray was one of those rare individuals whose smile would broadcast ten thousand watts of trust and confidence. He was what was known back then as a genuinely true guy. He had that lanky Jimmy Stewart look with the dark wavy hair that was a Poling trademark. He dressed immaculately and to see him walking downtown in a three-piece suit and polished white bucks you would never imagine he could break trail with the best of bushmen.

He and Veronica made an attractive couple, though mismatched in size. Veronica was petite with a distinct French-Canadian beauty. Her facial features were delicate except for prominent cheekbones that rode high below brown eyes often filled with amusement or mischief. Dark hair swept back behind her ears accented the playful look. Her mother had written in her baby book that Veronica was a happy child. She carried that happiness into adulthood. If there was a party, you knew she was in the centre of it. Everything in her disposition gave the appearance of a woman who was an open book, but she wasn't. At times she exhibited a quietness that gave her an aura of mystery.

There was no question about love at first sight. In 1938, not more than a year after Ray moved to Port Arthur, they were engaged. On November 30, 1940, a bitterly cold day even by northern Ontario standards, the LaFrances and Aquins from Chapleau and Sudbury and North Bay gathered with the Polings and Desilets from Port Arthur and Minnesota under the high arches of St. Andrew's as Isidore made the long walk down the aisle with Veronica on his arm. Waiting in front of the gilded white Gothic altar among the groom and groomsmen and dressed in celebratory robes was a familiar figure. Father Romeo Gasçon of Sacred Heart Church in Chapleau opened his book and began the wedding service. Father Gasçon still had a habit of showing up at important times, so no one would have been shocked to see him there as the presiding priest. The shock arrived decades later when I sat in St. Andrew's storage vault with the musty 1940 marriage register cracked open and saw what Father Gasçon had added to the record that day.

The marriage had a rough financial start. Ray found full-time work at the Provincial Paper mill and it looked like he would follow his dad in the

Courtesy of Jim Poling Sr.

It is not known if Ray Poling knew Veronica's secret when they married on November 30, 1940. Ray's eldest brother Bob said no one in the family knew, and his brother never mentioned it to him. The priest who married them did know because he had an important role in the secret.

papermaking trade. A runaway lift truck ended that plan. It pinned Ray against a wall, mangling his left arm. The doctors put it back together the best they could but said the nerves were dead forever and suggested amputation because that would allow him to apply for a disability pension. He refused to give up the arm for a pension and began working with it, exercising and lifting weights. It recovered. He always carried a rubber ball in his left hand, which he squeezed to build strength in his fingers. Later he got seriously into fly-fishing, using the rod left-handed to work the injured arm.

There was little money coming in while he struggled to gain full use of the arm. Both the Polings and the LaFrances helped out, and many of the groceries were put on credit at Wilmott and Siddall, the neighbourhood grocery store across the street from Port Arthur Tech. Never once did Ron Wilmott or anyone else at the store push for payment. For years after, the Poling families refused to consider buying groceries anywhere else. Eaton's downtown location had a grocery section and prices were cheaper, but Ray ordered that all groceries be bought from Wilmott no matter how much the bigger stores cut prices.

Ray got work as a pitman doing minor maintenance for the city transit system. He worked on the street railway cars, then the electric buses. He later got a job selling life insurance, which suited him perfectly. He was personable, an impeccable dresser, and had an interest in people, and did well at it.

The early years of marriage also brought another misfortune. A boy, named Richard, died at birth, and there was some concern that other children would not be possible. A couple years later, in February 1943, Ray, still an American citizen, walked beaming into St. Joseph's Hospital and planted a Stars and Stripes at the bedside where Veronica was showing off their first child — me. The flag fulfilled his belief that a child born under the U.S. flag could claim American citizenship. That was nice, but he forgot to register me the with the U.S. government, an omission that no doubt saved me from having to dress in combat gear and wade through the rice paddies of Vietnam some twenty years later.

Isidore and Louise LaFrance, originally denied children by fate, gave thanks for a grandchild who was joined by Barbara Ann in 1947 and Mary Jane in 1953.

4 — McVICAR CREEK

WATER WAS LIFE IN PORT ARTHUR. IT FLOATED THE LONG ships that carried off western grain; it made the shipyards ring with activity and supplied liquid for the chemistry that turned logs to pulp and then paper at the mills crouched along the waterfront in spaces where the grain elevators did not sit. It nourished life with the jobs it provided and soothed the spirit with its beauty. Every path led to water. Every piece of water led to a larger piece of water that eventually found its way to the biggest piece of freshwater of them all, Lake Superior, the Big Lake. The Current and McIntyre Rivers, McVicar Creek. In the lowlands of Port Arthur's flat-chested and homely twin, Fort William, the Neebing River and the Kaministiquia, which divided into the McKellar and Mission Rivers, all paid homage by ending their journey at the Big Lake.

Water was central in many local legends. The Three Sisters, or Welcome Islands, off the Port Arthur waterfront, are said to be three Ojibwe sisters turned to stone and cast into the water after they killed their younger sister out of jealousy.

West of the Big Lake at Kakabeka Falls, some say that on certain days you can see the figure of Green Mantle, an Ojibwe maiden, in the mists of the falls of the Kaministiquia. Legend tells of the young maiden misleading a war party of Sioux enemies to their deaths over the stupendous falls, sacrificing herself but saving her village.

Water also was central to the life of the Polings, much to Veronica's chagrin. She hated the water and I learned this early. My first memory of her is from Loon Lake, the popular cottage lake just east of Thunder Bay. I was an infant on my very first excursion into the northern Ontario wilds. I remember the water gurgling a mild protest against the push of the paddle. The canoe whispered a calming lullaby to the lake, a fair-weather friend that could turn as tempestuous as it was now tranquil.

Far in the distance, a magnificent black steam locomotive boasted its size and superiority over everything along its moving landscape. Not the boldest of birds, not even the cocky jays, dared to call while the pounding engine issued shrill screams that pierced the chilly air then floated into the distance like wide wet vowels. These were the urgent calls of a passenger train at full throttle, rocking and clicking and clacking, hell-bent to keep time with the fine Hamilton railwayman's watch held in the flat of the engineer's broad hand. The whistle calls intensified as the train thundered past Loon Lake, only to be swallowed by the advancing dusk as it roared west toward Port Arthur at the head of the Big Lake. There would be no stop at the brick-red Loon Lake station today because it was too late in the year. Summer was almost a memory and three seasons must change before the shrieking steam engine decelerated to chuffs and puffed and panted to a stop beside the lake, disgorging cottagers and their kids and men wearing wide-brimmed fedoras and carrying tubular fly-fishing rod cases. The lake returned to the bush for another year, except perhaps for the solitary trapper or rock hound and two adults and a baby making for the far shore in a nasty little thirteen-foot cedar strip and canvas canoe known as the *Undertaker*.

The passing of the train was momentous, though not because of its failure to stop or because its fading whistle accentuated the isolation. It was because Veronica, in spite of her terror of water, removed one hand from its death grip on the gunwale for a second or maybe two, to perform a perfunctory half-wave before regripping the varnished wood. The wave was more from habit than bravery because Veronica grew up in a railroader's home and railroad folks wave at every passing train. Not waving on this night would be a special breach of railway etiquette because the tall man in the pinstripe overalls pushing the locomotive throttle with one hand and checking the precise Hamilton watch in the other was Isidore LaFrance, running flat out on the home run into the Port Arthur roundhouse. A lifetime of waving at trains, especially one commanded by your dad, could not be overcome by the numbing fear of riding in a deathtrap canoe carrying the man you love in the stern and your first-born on the cedar strip floor beside the box of groceries.

Veronica loathed the water and all forms of water transport, unreasonably so in those early days. The rationale for her fear and loathing would come later, after years of living in a family obsessed with crossing water in things that would float, or often only half float.

Why we were in that canoe on that lake in the autumn of 1944, I cannot say. Nor should I be expected to say considering I had entered the world only eighteen months previous and was just then experiencing the first sights and sounds to be committed to memory. Perhaps my father was without work, or perhaps it was one of those last precious holidays given to people before they shipped out to the killing grounds in Europe and the Pacific. Others had gone already. Ray's younger brother Jack was in a British hospital after riding the tail of a flaming bomber into a field somewhere in Wales. Terri, one of Ray's three sisters, was destined for the WACs and two future brothers-in-law, Gus Hungle and Sandy Brown, were at sea or about to be.

Already the Polings had one posthumous war hero, whose life was snuffed out by a Nazi U-boat ten days before my birth. Capt. Clark Poling, a thirty-year-old U.S. Army chaplain and a distant cousin, was one of the famous Four Chaplains aboard the troop ship USAT *Dorchester* sunk en route to Europe. The *Dorchester* was a down-at-the-keels coastal liner that had sailed in luxury before being pressed into war service to ferry troops across the Atlantic. It carried 902 persons as it steamed through the icy blackness of the patch of Atlantic known as Torpedo Junction, 250 kilometres off Greenland just after midnight on February 3, 1943. Most of the troops were sleeping when the torpedoes hit, killing many instantly and leaving the others scrambling to reach the decks for life jackets. There were not enough for everyone, so Clark Poling and three fellow chaplains removed theirs and gave them to soldiers beside them. As the *Dorchester* tilted and prepared for its horrible slide to the bottom, the four chaplains linked arms at the deck rail and prayed, sang, and offered hope to the soldiers in the water.

"It was one of the finest things I have ever seen this side of Heaven," one of the 250 survivors said later. The other 672 soldiers and sailors on board died.

The story of the *Dorchester* torpedoing and the uncommon valour of the four chaplains is immortalized in the Chapel of the Four Chaplains at Temple University in Philadelphia. It opened in the early 1950s, dedicated by Clark's dad, Rev. Daniel Poling, and his friend President Harry Truman.

Whether they were preachers or papermakers, the Polings loved the outdoors. And that love was the reason that Robert Lee Poling's second eldest child, Raymond Marcel, was paddling the *Undertaker* across Loon Lake with his wife, Veronica, and me. Why a supposedly sane man like Robert would allow his son and family to borrow and actually use that canoe remains a puzzle many decades later. My grandfather's canoe was the most homely, most ungovernable, and crankiest little beast ever to kiss the water. It lived long and dumped many, but never my grandfather, and he loved it.

War raged, but Loon Lake was another world. After the passing of the train, the lake regained its solitude. A raven returning to nest croaked. A trout splashed off the starboard stern, causing my father to bend forward and reach for his fly rod, an action immediately halted by a scream of terror:

"Ray, I told you before, you're going to tip this damn canoe and drown us all!"

My father stared down at me curiously, then wistfully out at the widening ring of the speckled trout rise. I am certain that it was only my presence that caused him to set the rod down. A frightened wife, yes, even a wet wife clinging to an overturned canoe, was not reason enough to pass on a trout like that. A baby was.

For my part, speckled trout belly flopping for flies held no interest. The outside world was just too big and too amazing to try to bring into focus, let alone try to comprehend. My world was in front of me in the form of that grocery box with intriguing bags, cans, and bottles sticking out the top, so tantalizingly close to my stretching little fingertips.

"Oooh, nooo!"

This sudden sound startled me, and of course my mother, who immediately concluded that it announced the inevitable end of us all. It was a sound I was to hear many times in the future in many variations. Sometimes it was multisyllabic, with the *oooh* and *nooo* stretched out like *oooh-ah nooo-ah* to emphasize disbelief so complete that it contained anguish. Sometimes the last sound was repeated, as in *oooh, no, no, no, no,* which was accented by a violent sideways shaking of the head from which the sound was emanating. This day the sound was just mournful, so rounded that it floated across the lake and into the trees, skipping lightly off rock faces, never bouncing back as a sharp echo, but simply floating on a course into the next valley and beyond.

For me growing up, *oooh nooo* became a bush sound as familiar as the crack of a long fallen branch crushed by something dark and unseen. Or the syrupy and insistent trill of the vireo or the thump of a bear paw dismantling a stump alive with breakfast grubs. A bush sound that always announced that my father was near and in some momentary distress.

After my initial fright, the sound made me laugh with delight and I rocked forward and backwards clapping my hands, hoping to hear it again. "Oooh, nooo, no, no, no!" The sound flew from my father's mouth as he flailed away with a paddle, trying to put the canoe into a 180-degree turn and full reverse at the same time.

"Oh, Ray, what happened now? We're sinking, aren't we?" my mother, her voice tight with fear, asked from the bow. Her question would have been answered if she had simply turned her upper body and looked into the canoe wake. Such movement is not possible when one's fingers are squeezing the grain out of the cedar gunwales and one's elbows are tightly locked as if stricken with rigor mortis. Whatever the problem, my mother was not going to view the wake because she was convinced that even a wrinkle of the nose would spin the *Undertaker* like a top and drown us all. Nothing could loosen her death grip on the canoe until its nose touched the sandy shore on the other side of the lake and my father pried her fingers loose.

Why she so feared the water I do not know, probably because I didn't ask her, just as I didn't ask her other things that I should have. I had no fear of the water and proceeded to stand in the canoe to get a better view of the problem. I already knew what the problem was, of course, because

I created it but wanted a full view of the action, and my effort to hoist myself by the gunwale set the *Undertaker* rocking and elicited another scream from the bow.

"Ray, for God's sake, we're tipping! Hail holy Queen, mother of Mercy and Light ..."

My father's hand let go of the paddle that was executing a fast right turn to push me to the canoe floor. Before it did, I got a pretty good look into the wake where a little brown paper bag made its final bob before its bottom gave way, creating a starburst of dazzling white crystals dissolving as they sank into the dark waters of Loon Lake. Our family cache of sugar, not replaceable under war rationing, was gone.

The remainder of the ride across the lake was jerky as my father interrupted his normally rhythmic paddling to tap my fingers while they tried to extricate another bag from the grocery box and continue this delightful new game. Far too soon, however, the bow of the canoe scrunched into the beach sand, my mother leaped to safety and pulled me from the clutches of the demon craft.

I have no recollection of what happened after that. I learned later that we had two or three days of golden autumn filled with walks across the forest floor newly matted with yellow brown birch and poplar leaves. At night there were quiet talks at campfires that flickered orange yellow and listened for a train whistle meant just for us. My parents talked and crooned the old songs like "By the Light of the Silvery Moon" and "Shine on Harvest Moon" and drank strong tea without sugar. They cut it with thick and sickly sweet Carnation evaporated milk, cans of which sat on the oilcloth tabletops of every cabin in the Canadian bush, wooden matchsticks sticking in their tops to keep the pouring holes from crusting over. No doubt John Barleycorn stopped by the fire to help shake off the chill.

I don't remember the quiet talks by the campfire or the autumn walks, but I do remember dozens of later Loon Lake visits. We didn't own a camp as they are called in the North (as opposed to "cottage" in the south), but there was always one to rent or borrow or visit. I learned to dog-paddle there because I couldn't stand the oozing bottom of the lake between my toes. I got my first dog bite there, a full canine slash to the right thigh, and set off a hell of a commotion when someone who had obviously failed animal identification put up the alarm that a wolf had attacked me.

I came close to drowning there twice, nearly fulfilling my mother's prophecy that water eventually would take all of us. Once I got in over my head and was pulled to safety by a friend. Another time I was riding in the bottom of the *Undertaker*, paddled by my dad, when his little brother Gerry stood in the bow and dumped us all into the lake. I remember floating near the bottom, my hand touching the light brown sand ribbed like snake's tracks by the creek's current and seeing little fishes darting into a patch of thin green reeds. It was quiet down there. Everything moved in slow motion, and I was sleepy and ready to dream until I saw my father's contorted face appear, the wavy dark brown hair flattened back against his head, his open fingers stretching out to grab my long blond hair that had yet to see its first cut.

When I awoke onshore after my dad's artificial respiration had produced a thankful gurgling, I heard another of his expressions, the one reserved for times of great anger when immediate danger had passed: "Jesus Mexican Murphy!"

Veronica was not present so was spared the agony of seeing the near drowning of her first born. However, when she learned about it, she shook her head and uttered a line reserved for the Polings and their wild bush ways: "You're all crazy. Crazy as loons!"

After the sugarless outing in the autumn of 1944, I never again saw Veronica in a canoe or boat of any kind. She could not avoid the water, however. It was everywhere and in particular it was near our house, in the form of McVicar Creek.

McVicar Creek was no turgid urban trickle in those days. To the neighbourhood kids, it was an artery in the heart of Borneo. It entered the city from somewhere far off the northern edge of the city map and plunged through pieces of heavy bush, revealing itself to the backsides of a couple of middle-class neighbourhoods before crossing under River Street. There it made a sharp left turn in a grass and rock meadow before beginning the plunge down the steep hill to the Port Arthur waterfront, passing under Algoma, Court, and Cumberland Streets to achieve its true purpose: delivering itself to the vast inland sea of Lake Superior. It wasn't so narrow a creek that you could jump it, but it slowed its pace in spots where you could ford it in times of low water. In the spring and times of heavy rain, it roared and threatened to be as big and bold as its nearby river cousins.

McVicar Creek was the jungle of our young lives. Above the River Street Bridge, there were pools for swimming and meeting places to discuss secret plans. Below the River Street bridge, we dangled worms to entice the last of the little speckled trout struggling against urbanization and trekked and hunted the strip of woods that clothed the creek's path to downtown's edge. This little forest was perfect for conducting war games and for hiding and spying on the people who walked the McVicar Creek path to Algoma or Court Street before veering right into downtown.

We lived in make-believe kiddie pueblos among the rocky outcroppings overlooking the creek behind the intersection of Dawson and Jean Streets. Smooth flat tabletop rocks provided our beds where we lay and stared into the summer skies and let the clouds stimulate our imaginations. The fluffy cloud shaped like a contorted cross definitely was an angel carrying a candle. Others were elephants and airplanes and other objects that sparked eye-of-the-beholder arguments. The smaller rocks were our tables and chairs where we feasted on the snacks our mothers gave us before letting us loose for days that started immediately after early breakfast and ended at the 9 p.m. city curfew with only meal breaks at home as interruptions. Sometimes we shared candies bought at the corner store with the pennies we got from the pop bottles our grandmothers gave us to return. Throughout the day, our playtime business took us down to the creek for exploration, swimming, war games, or searches for adventure.

We roamed as we wished, spending hours at a time out of parental sight. Surely there was evil about in those days, but it didn't seem to manifest itself often. We knew from our parents' warnings not to play south of the Cumberland Street bridge because bad men gathered there to drink cheap cologne and shoe polish mixed with pop, anything from which they could get a bit of alcohol. We also knew from our own experience not to play in the trash left on the north side of the creek at Algoma Street by the Port Arthur Brewery, which made beer with a picture of the Indian princess Green Mantle on the label. Rats — black, vicious rats with red eyes and sharp teeth — lived there and more than one kid had felt their bite.

Veronica spent much of her time as a young mother planning how to keep me away from the creek. Her strongest weapon was exaggeration. She laid on me tales of the evil men at the mouth of the creek and the dangers facing little boys who played by the creek. *Who knows what lurks in the bushes? Any little boy who falls into the creek is swept away out into the lake and into the clutches of Nanabijou. You've heard him roaring, haven't you, on those stormy days?* Interesting, but I preferred the story of the ancestor shipwrecked and found by the Natives. I imagined myself being pulled from the water, nursed back to health, and becoming a member of the tribe, hunting and warring throughout the river forest.

Mothers worry too much and Veronica's cajoling and stories of danger could not keep me away. There was too much water, too much lure of water, for any mother to keep her children away from it. What she didn't know wouldn't hurt her, and there was much she didn't see. Like the day our terrier, Trixie, and I were carried away by the spring-swollen creek. An ice jam saved us from being swept into the arms of Nanabijou, but when we returned home soaking wet and shivering, Veronica made me promise I would never go near the creek again. It was a promise that would be broken many times.

Our home then was the LaFrances' two-storey red-brick house at 402 Dawson Street at the northeast corner of College Street. They had moved to the new place, three blocks over from 63 Peter Street, the year before Veronica and Ray married.

We originally had lived in the top storey of 331 Van Norman Street, then on Rockwood Avenue in our own tiny bungalow. Veronica used to tie me to the fence there so I could watch all the comings and goings in safety, but we didn't stay in the little wartime house very long. Things had not been going well over at 402 Dawson Street where Louise and Isidore had become empty nesters. Louise was stricken with arthritis. The pain in her joints worsened, then began to twist her fingers and legs. Walking became difficult and it was soon obvious that she was a victim of the most crippling type of arthritis. Within a year of so of my birth, she rose from her bed only with great difficulty and we moved into 402 Dawson Street, so my mother could help her father care for her.

This marked the end of Veronica's sheltered and somewhat pampered life. What had once been a life of a majority of joy would be transformed into a string of heartbreaks. Caring for her bedridden mother made for long, hard days and sleepless nights when the pain had Louise crying in the night. Worse was watching the searing pain suck the power out of such a strong, independent woman.

Still, life at 402 Dawson Street was close to as good as it got in the 1940s. For us kids, the neighbourhood was a quiet pool at which to rest before starting the serious part of life's journey. Dawson Street, once a dirt trail but now an asphalt stream lined with stone curbs and sidewalks that held the roadway back from double-storey houses, tumbled over the Port Arthur hillsides toward the Big Lake. Middle-class working people lived along Dawson Street. My grandparent's house was not large, but it sat prominently on the northwest corner as one of the nicer places on the street. It was two storeys but tightly designed and looked larger than it was because of the semi-mansard roof that eliminated the typical "A" peak at the front. Its red brick and red mortar gave it a solid protective look.

The neighbourhood was typical of less busy times. Most of the houses were two or two and a half storeys, with the lower levels made of brick and the upper levels cedar or clapboard. All had porches — some open, some closed — for sitting out and watching weather or the kids at play. Grass medians separated the concrete sidewalks from the asphalt road, curbed with black granite rocks. There were no driveways and anyone who owned a car parked it at the rear of their house accessed by the back alley.

There was a telephone pole at the corner in the front of our house and every kid in the neighbourhood had put his or her face to it and covered their eyes while counting down the time to hide in a game of hide-and-seek. I can still feel my face pressed against that pole, nostrils inhaling the bittersweet scent of cedar and creosote, fingers tracing the bite marks of linemen's spikes in the dry roughness of the wood.

Along the College Street side of the house, there was a white and green fence with a side gate. The fence had a sculpted look because its boards were deliberately cut uneven at the top. At the rear of the property, the fence connected with a white and green clapboard garage with double barn-style doors. Inside was the black early 1940s Chevrolet that Isidore kept spotless for family Sunday drives.

The most interesting feature of 402 Dawson Street was a side portico, an enclosed bricked porch area with country church–style windows along the side and front. It served as an entranceway to the house and a place to sit and look out at the street out of the weather. It was a great place for Trixie and me to hide when we were in trouble, like after our near drowning at the creek.

The McVicar Creek incident was the last great adventure for Trixie. Not long after, she was strolling across the street in front of 402 Dawson Street when a speeding car smacked her. My dad and I bundled her into a blanket and took her down to a vet who operated out of a rough board shack on the Port Arthur waterfront. It was a dark, foul place that smelled of dogs and whisky and mange medicine. The old vet laid Trixie on a kitchen table and put her back together with some rough stitches, but she was blind after that. I remember the mixture of pride and sadness I felt watching her stumble around my grandfather's house, walking into walls and falling down stairs. I was proud of her courage but saddened by the pathetic images of her trying to exist without sight. None of us, Veronica especially, could stand to watch her and soon we returned her to the old vet, and she didn't come back home ever again. It was a heartbreaking time, but it taught me a lot about life and my mother — someone with an uncanny understanding of animals.

Not long after the McVicar Creek incident, there was another dangerous meeting with water. A bunch of us kids were sliding on the rapidly shrinking snow on Prospect Hill. God made this hill for kids. Bald as a bowling ball, the hill and surrounding field covered a huge area bordered by Dawson Street on the north, Prospect Avenue on the east, High Street on the west, and Prospect Public School on the south. It was a sliding hill extraordinaire in the winter. We learned to ski and toboggan there and in summer ranged through it with our bikes, pretending we were army patrols going through the mountains. It was the site of plenty of broken bones, black eyes, and bleeding noses. If you got a good slide from the top, your toboggan would zoom across Prospect Avenue into someone's hedge. Biking down the hill was sheer madness.

The hill's greatest danger appeared only in spring. Beside Dawson Street was a deep depression in the side of the hill and it filled with runoff water, occasionally to a depth of six feet or more. It froze and thawed and refroze in spring. Older kids, like us eight-year-olds, knew instinctively to stay away from that hole. Nobody told us about it. It was just something you knew from being out in the neighbourhood. My sister Barbara, then five years old and three years my junior, had not been blessed with the instinct. She decided to walk on it and plunged through. The rest of us kids were sliding nearby and heard her scream.

The ice was so rotten that she had gone through on the first footfall, right at the edge. She was screaming and crying as I skidded down the bank and grabbed her hand. She pulled, I slipped, and we were both thrashing in the mushy ice water together, clawing at the bank for leverage. I managed a handhold and dragged us out as the other kids arrived and made a chain of hands.

As I pulled Barb up the hill and along the street home, kids scattered everywhere to shout news of the miraculous rescue. I was a neighbourhood hero, and kids everywhere sang my praises, for at least a day or two, all except Barbara. She was unimpressed that I had so daringly risked my life to save hers. Her lack of gratitude was inexplicable. She seemed to labour under the misconception that I was assigned to look after her and that by calling her scaredy-cat and shooing her off because she was afraid to slide on the steepest part of the hill, I in fact had created the problem.

Fame is fleeting and mine slipped away swiftly. Before the year was out, I was no longer the hero of the Prospect Hill. A combination of circumstances led me into another incident that earned me the name Fire Bug.

The grass was high, brown, and dry along the hill that fell off the Dawson Street cliffs and into McVicar Creek. We were playing in our pueblos as usual when I made an incredible discovery. I found in the rocks a perfectly good, unused wooden match. One of those stick matches about two and a half inches long with a fat red head topped with a white cap. Sometimes the heads were blue and white, but the ones my parents kept for the old stove were red and hidden away in a sturdy cardboard box with red birds printed on the cover.

You have to understand the times to understand the significance of the match discovery. In an age of wood-frame houses filled with flammables such as untreated heavy fabrics, straw insulation, cracks packed with coal dust, matches were dangerous; definitely adult things. Children did not play with matches — ever. "Never play with matches" was among the most holy of the prohibitions, right up there with not talking to strangers.

My little friend Brett, a couple of years younger than me and awestruck by the find, immediately advised me to bring it to my ma. His big brother Earl wondered if the match was any good. That got me thinking. I had seen my father take such matches and scratch them across the side of the matchbox and had always been mesmerized when they burst into flame. What made them do this? Could they be scratched anywhere and made to explode?

I suggested that we might have a campfire, catching my breath at the boldness of the statement.

Brett, becoming visibly nervous, said kids don't know how to make campfires. Only dads did.

I knew he was right. The consequences of a campfire would be enormous and I really didn't know how to start one. But the match. Was it any good? I made a lightning-quick decision, sweeping it across the rocks, watching it explode into flame. The explosion of flame was so startling that I tossed it away in fear.

The chances of a wooden match, barely struck when thrown into the breeze, landing still lighted in the grass were tens of thousands to one. My match rode the breeze over the cliff, gaining flame as it fell onto the rocks and bounced into a patch of high grass. Within seconds, the patch was ablaze, sparks blowing into other patches. We stood on the cliff spellbound as the breeze whipped the flames from patch to patch into the high grass. Within minutes, the valley was ablaze and we ran off the cliff and up the lane to our secret hiding spot in the loft of the garage at the rear of Earl's house.

Grass fires normally are not a big deal. Many people started them in those days to clean the vegetation and green up for spring. This grass fire, however, had the makings of a major catastrophe. Two dozen old houses lined the west side of the McVicar Creek valley. The breeze was from the east and the fire marched quickly to the backyards filled with sundry outbuildings and dry fences. If it hit the backyards, the fire would be blown into the houses and we would have a neighbourhood conflagration of Biblical proportions.

We could hear the scream of the fire trucks as we hunkered down in the loft's bed of old straw, dust, and dried pigeon shit. It was dark there except for the light spilling through cracks in the weathered barn boards. The cracks also let in the sweet smell of burning grass. We had heard fire reels, as we called them then, many times before but never to this extent. It seemed the fire departments of both Port Arthur and Fort William had arrived, and there were sounds of urgent activity and shouts everywhere. My friends' reaction to all the commotion was the same as Trixie's had been that day at the creek. They looked at me as if someone had just planted on me the kiss of death and fled, abandoning me crouching alone in the dark and peering out through a crack in the garage siding.

Courtesy of Jim Poling Sr.

Four generations of Polings gathered in the back yard of Robert and Eva's house at 331 Van Norman Street, Port Arthur. Left to right: Veronica, Robert, Ray, Barbara (baby), Eva, Jim (the author), and Grandma and Grandpa Desilets, Eva's parents from Superior, Wisconsin. This picture was taken circa 1948 and the Desilets would have been well into their eighties.

My father, called home from work as were other fathers in the neighbourhood, found me and led me to the scene of the crime. Earl and Brett, under light questioning, had given me up, adding how they had warned me not to do it. Dad and I stood on the hill overlooking the blackened valley. Firemen with sooty faces rolled dirty hoses while others checked for hot spots in the charred grass and along some of the fences that had caught fire. There was no "oooh, nooo!" or "Jesus Mexican Murphy!" this day. I had not seen my father so wracked with emotion but regretfully would again, many years later when another mistake changed our lives forever. I absorbed the scene of my destruction, then received a spanking on the spot and a lecture on the seriousness of my actions. Dad explained that only a superhuman effort by the firemen and volunteers had saved the houses.

Veronica and Barbara waited at the door when we arrived home. My mother's face was pale and drawn. Barbara's was round, shining with glee. She saw this as superb payback for the Prospect Hill incident. She referred to me as the Fire Bug. My parents' disappointment with me lingered for a long time. The neighbourhood had received a serious scare and they were at the centre of it.

I learned later that fire created a special fear in the Poling family. Fire was part of the reason the family had moved to Canada from Minnesota. The Great Fire of 1918 wiped out Cloquet, Minnesota, where my grandfather worked at the paper mill and where my father was born. Family lore told of how my grandmother held her babies in her arms as she waded in the St. Louis River as the fire consumed the town. My great-grandparent's house burned down and the lack of future work in the Minnesota woods and mills influenced my grandfather's decision later to take the family to Sault Ste. Marie, Ontario, where a new mill offered steady work.

The Cloquet Fire started October 10, 1918, as a smoulder at a Great Northern Railway siding called O'Brien's Spur. It spread under a pile of cordwood and crews tried to extinguish it over two days but left it because it didn't seem serious. On October 12 it erupted into a full fire. It marched across the Fond du Lac Indian Reservation and headed for Cloquet where more than 100 million board feet of dried lumber made the town a potential bomb.

The fire was part of fifty to seventy-five separate fires that merged, fanned by winds of seventy miles an hour. Within a fifty to one hundred-mile radius of Duluth, two thousand square miles burned. The fire left four hundred dead, two thousand injured, and thirteen thousand homeless. It was an incredible disaster. Cloquet suffered heavily. Five people died and most of the residential and business areas were destroyed.

Phil Bellefeuille, my Grandmother Poling's nephew, remembered the Cloquet Fire. As of September 1998 he was still living in Seattle at age eighty-nine when he wrote the following description:

> I was staying with them [Grandma and Grandpa Desilets in Cloquet] and going to school. Grandma took me to a show and coming out in the afternoon the sky was smoky and the sun was like the yoke of an egg. After supper all the whistles blew. Grandpa went to find out and came back then we had to go to the [rail] depot. There we had to climb up and into a gondola car [flat car with sides]. Ladies climbed up, the youngster was handed to her and buggy cast aside.
>
> While waiting I remember seeing a burning branch or something floating through the air. I suppose the heat of the fire kept it up, then it would fall and start another fire. The depot was on the river flats and the town was on a hill.
>
> And I remember after we got going one lady had several kids that got sleepy. One laid down, another on him and so forth as that the standing area made the sleeping area. The train was so crowded that we could not have fallen down.
>
> Dad found us with some friends of theirs. [He came] to take me back and while waiting in Carlton this nosy kid [Phil] had to open this door in the depot, looked in and there on the floor covered with cheesecloth were several black corpses. This kid shut that door quickly.
>
> In Cloquet, the depot was next to a sawmill and where they had lumber stacked high, air drying, it was

now but a black prairie. The concrete block buildings had some of the walls standing. Grandpa had some rifles and guns in the woodshed — their barrels were now pretty crooked.

The only buildings saved were on the island in the St. Louis River and that was mostly saloons and maybe another business?

I will never forget Oct. 12, 1918. It was a school holiday they called Columbus Day. [It was in fact Columbus Day, but it was a Saturday.]

Phil said the Desilets moved to Superior, Wisconsin then. When he arrived there he had only a shoe in one pocket and a statue of St. Anne with the Virgin Mary in another.

In my grandmother's house, there was an old photo of two women holding babies in arms while wading in the river and watching the flames. I heard that that was my grandmother holding my dad and his sister. The picture is long gone and we'll never know all the truth now. Certainly fire was burned into the family memory, and I couldn't look at the picture without imagining my mother and my friends' mothers standing in McVicar Creek while the fire I set consumed the neighbourhood.

Later that summer we again heard the scream of an emergency vehicle on an urgent mission. This time it was an ambulance and it came directly to 402 Dawson Street. Inside, Isidore LaFrance felt ill after dinner and began pacing between the living room and dining room, rubbing his left arm and left chest with his right hand. I paced behind him, thinking it was a new game. Down to the walnut cabinet that contained the radio receiver around which we gathered at night, then back past the dining room table and down to the Queen Anne chair from which I had taken my first steps. He was grey in the face. The pain took his breath away and suddenly he collapsed from what we later learned was a stroke.

He had retired less than a year earlier, walking away from the big black locomotives that he had tended or drove for just weeks short of fifty years. His railroading days were replaced by sitting and talking at Louise's bedside and taking us kids out for car rides to Boulevard

Lake. The grey-striped engineer's cap and overalls were set aside for suits and shirts and a fedora. No matter what he wore, he always looked massive, a neatly-dressed Paul Bunyan. And, whatever the clothes, one pocket always carried treats: hard candy for the grandchildren, Sen-Sen liquorice mints for himself.

Now he was on the floor, a huge immovable bulk. The big man who had lifted me so effortlessly into the cab of the hissing locomotive only months previous for his retirement run from Fort William to Port Arthur refused to respond to my little hands shaking his shoulders or my pleas for him to wake up. The ambulance took him away, and I never saw him again. Within a day, Isidore LaFrance was dead in a hospital at sixty-six.

For Veronica, it was more than the death of a father. It was the end of a fairytale existence in which a once childless couple devoted their lives to shielding their unexpected treasure from life's cruelties.

5 — CURRENT RIVER

ISIDORE'S DEATH OPENED A STRESS FRACTURE IN OUR LIVES at 402 Dawson Street. It widened as the reality of his death took hold over the following months, then became an abyss that we struggled to cross every day. He had been our bridge to a better life.

Louise's condition worsened, partly because Isidore's support was gone. She was no longer able to come downstairs to join us for meals on holiday occasions or to listen to a special radio broadcast. Her trips down the hall on crutches to the bathroom became more painful and use of a bedpan more frequent. At night, she cried out from her bedroom next to mine. I could smell wafting down the hallway the sweetness of wintergreen mixed with the sharpness of rubbing alcohol and other potions used to alleviate her pain.

The car with the Bourkes Drug Store logo came to the house more often. So did the doctor, hustling urgently into the wide front bedroom where Isidore often had stood at the windows staring into the street when Louise slept. Veronica became a full-time nurse, receiving some help from the Victorian Order of Nurses, saints who came a couple times a week and made life easier for us all. She had a second child now, Barbara, who was three when Isidore died. The heavier workload strained the household and created tension that pushed aside the easy living atmosphere our family had enjoyed.

With Isidore's full pension gone, Ray became the only breadwinner for the household. He worked as a grease monkey on the streetcars and new electric buses at the municipal transit barns on Cumberland Street near the lake. He was not certified as a mechanic and the work was not permanent or well-paying enough to support an extended family.

The pleasantness of family life dissipated. We missed my grandfather for the Sunday afternoon car rides, the nostalgic trips to the CNR roundhouse, the candies that appeared magically from his pocket and the humorous strength that pulled us together as a family. He had helped care for my grandmother and when he wasn't actually physically helping, just his presence helped to ease her pain. He was an anchor that held us in a calm, safe, and comfortable harbour well shielded from the misfortunes that touched other people. That's what he had always been for Veronica, and that's what he was for her family.

The strain of his absence showed on my father. He became irritable and did not eat well. He was impatient and one Christmas week when we were decorating a magnificent floor-to-ceiling balsam, he blew up and began throwing things. Not long after the doctor told him he had ulcers. The halcyon days at 402 Dawson Street, which included sitting around the radio at night listening to Lux Theatre, turned into times of worried looks and thin tempers.

More bad luck arrived not long after Isidore's death. Veronica became pregnant and miscarried. A doctor injected her with penicillin and she reacted violently. Her throat swelled shut, and she nearly choked to death in bed. I watched as a doctor slammed his car door shut on College Street and raced into the house and upstairs to her bedroom. I followed and peeked through the doorway as he worked on my mother and talked to my father. Doctors did house calls then, and this one was a regular visitor to our place because he looked after Louise. He had come once for me in the middle of the night, thrusting fingers down my throat and pulling loose a suffocating blood clot that formed after a tooth extraction.

My father, looking relieved, escorted the doctor from my mother's room and down the stairs. I crept in to look at her and ran from her room, terrified by what I saw. She lay on her back atop the bed sheets, a huge walrus-like figure with her eyes swollen shut. She had become slightly plump over the years but now appeared to be two to three times her usual size. I ran down the hall to my grandmother's room where she sat on the edge of her bed, saddened by the agony of not being able to help her only child.

A year or so later, there was another pregnancy. This one was successful and brought Mary Jane into our lives. I was ten and a half and didn't know what to make of it all, but I didn't have much time to think about it because another shock followed close behind. My father arrived home from work one day and announced we were moving. It seemed inconceivable. Dawson Street was the centre of our lives. We knew every person in every house up and down the Dawson and College Street blocks. The children played together and the adults watched out for all the children. People walking the streets stopped and talked and patted us kids on the head. I walked every day to St. Andrew's School where my mother had gone. Coming and going, I stopped at 331 Van Norman Street where Grandma Poling took something fresh from the oven and gave me pop bottles to trade for candy at Archie's corner store and soda fountain at the bottom of the hill.

We were not going far. The new place was up over Prospect Hill, not much more than a kilometre west of 402 Dawson Street, but out of the immediate neighbourhood. I would still go to St. Andrew's, although it would be a longer walk and not through the old neighbourhood.

The new neighbourhood was a miserable place. The house was a squat, square bungalow on Pine Street, on the edge of the northwest residential areas. It was dark, damp, and cramped. My parents and the two girls and my grandmother squeezed into three tiny bedrooms on the main floor while I descended to a homemade room in a corner of the musty basement where natural light never reached. Living there after 402 Dawson Street was a shock.

Why we left the elegant comfort of 402 Dawson Street for that backwater shack was a mystery. Perhaps it was a matter of money. Isidore's pension left with his death. My grandmother required more and stronger drugs. There were no drug plans, and my father's income was less regular as he quit the transit company and took up selling life insurance for Metropolitan Life. It was a painful uprooting for Veronica. Her homes had mostly been in the Dawson-Peter Streets neighbourhood and moving up, over, and beyond the Prospect Street Hill was not progress.

Not only was the housing rougher, but so were some of the neighbourhood kids. I met a couple of boys my age and during one visit to their house listened curiously as their father instructed them in the best ways to convince girls to have sex, a term I didn't quite understand yet. Worst of all from Veronica's perspective, there was water directly across the street. Not the clean, clear water that blessed so much of the Port Arthur area. It was a swamp, a real swamp with bullfrogs, snakes, reeds, and a gagging stench of wet rot. Malevolent mists shrouded it every evening after dark.

I set to work building a raft to explore the swamp. This set me up for a confrontation with Veronica, who banned me from going anywhere near this little northern Everglades. She soon realized that with caring for her mother and the two girls she couldn't keep an eye on me all the time. Her next best effort was to see about having the swamp drained. She called the city and made a fuss, but apparently the land was private. She called the health department, and one day I saw a worker arrive with high rubber boots. He stood at the edge of the swamp and lobbed some kind of disinfectant hand grenades at it.

Pine Street was depressing. I exhausted myself walking back and forth to the old neighbourhood, coming home to collapse in my room in the hole downstairs. Everything seemed to go wrong at that place. I built a rabbit hutch but one of the rabbits grew so huge, it broke out and spent the next two weeks eating everything in sight in our neighbour's garden. Then some of my friends visited from Dawson Street, bringing a couple sets of new boxing gloves. We boxed ourselves silly, with me taking a pummelling from which I began bleeding profusely from the nose and mouth. Some parents finally came out and stopped the bleeding, but the incident left me with a delicate nose that bled regularly for decades afterwards.

Even Christmas was an unhappy time on Pine Street. I prayed and begged for a pair of hockey skates for Christmas. I had seen them in the window of Laprade's sporting goods store downtown. They were the newest style with tendon guards that were actually part of the skate, not sewn-on attachments. They were the best skates a boy could have, and I knew that because Edgar Laprade, who was a Port Arthur hero playing for the New York Rangers in the National Hockey League, wore them.

Christmas morning came with much anticipation. Veronica watched nervously as I opened the box. Skates! Then came the realization that these skates had no tendon guards, were the old-fashioned style, and to my absolute horror had instep straps and buckles for support. They were baby skates! I overheard Veronica talking with my father that night about how they had made a terrible mistake in picking those skates. I was devastated.

Veronica was not apologetic with me. She was practical and mentioned offhand one day that she had heard that Laprade's sold special tendon guards that a shoemaker could attach to the back of the skates. If I saved money from selling newspapers and collecting pop bottles, I might be able to buy a pair. I went to Laprade's and saw them. They were tall tendon guards and you could see the protrusions of the protective bone inserts. They were fine though and I saved and bought them, had a shoemaker sew them on, and then I took a knife and cut off the support straps and buckles and had myself a reasonable set of real hockey player skates.

Veronica knew I was hurting in other ways from life on Pine Street. The kids in the neighbourhood were different, and I had a hard time fitting in. I often went alone into the bush beyond the swamp where I staked out a trapline for rabbits. She tried to occupy my time with chores then showed me how to plant a vegetable garden out back. No one would expect a garden to be a priority for an eleven-year-old boy, but life on Pine Street was so bleak that radishes and beets and green onions, all things that I had lovingly planted and nurtured throughout the spring, became a consuming interest that summer.

One evening at dusk, I was harvesting the fruits of my labour when I saw my parents walk toward me from the end of the driveway. My mother was carrying that blanket again and smiling. My heart sank. She'd gone somewhere and got yet another kid, I thought. I prayed it would at least be a brother. When she reached the edge of the lawn, she knelt and put the blanket on the grass. She lifted a fold and from it spilled a black shadow that was all ears and paws. It was a cocker spaniel puppy, and she tumbled into the garden and ran up my knees and onto my chest and began licking my face. It was the beginning of a long, loving friendship. We called her Dixie.

Dixie and I gardened together and explored the swamp. Later, I guess still not convinced that I was out of my Pine Street depression, my parents bought me a Red Ryder BB gun, and Dixie and I spent all our spare hours off in the woods, exploring and play hunting. We ate together and slept together, and the only times we were not together was when I was at school. I grew into manhood, and she grew old and content to lie in a warm place where she could dream of our days together in the woods.

Pine Street never brought complete happiness, however. When something good happened, there always was an offsetting complication or problem. So it was with Dixie. My mother insisted that Dixie be spayed and took her away in the car to a vet somewhere. When she returned, Dixie seemed fine until in the middle of one night, she jumped up on my bed and stood over me whimpering. I woke to find myself staring into the open cavity of her gut. Her stitches had all pulled loose.

The vet came and my mother spread a sheet on the kitchen table. The vet laid Dixie on the blanket and restitched her with butcher twine that Mom kept in a kitchen drawer. Veterinary medicine obviously has come a long since then.

Television had come to Port Arthur and for something to do, I would walk downtown and stand on the sidewalk watching the TV sets flickering in the shop windows. I could not hear the sound but the pictures were fascinating. Veronica had driven down to Bourke's Drug Store after supper one evening and saw me on the main street, standing and staring at the TV in the window. She went home and told my dad, who had vowed there would never be one of those things in our house, that it was a shame to have me standing on the main street staring through a shop window every night. A few weeks later, we had a TV and it was a wonderful thing. We gathered as a family each night in awe and sang along with some of the programs and laughed ourselves silly at others. *The Ed Sullivan Show* and *The Honeymooners* became never-miss family favourites.

We settled into our very different life on Pine Street, and after a year, it seemed like it would become permanent. Then came the news in 1954 that the Gateway Supply and Development Inc. was building a new subdivision in Current River, Port Arthur's far east end, on the other side of Boulevard Lake. The new houses would be family bungalows located on the east side of Hodder Street on the wooded slope overlooking Lake Superior. Most of the houses in Port Arthur were older, except for the one-and-a-half-storey wartime houses that had sprouted in many areas. This new subdivision would have the latest styles in postwar bungalows. There would be brick and stucco exteriors, kitchens with pink and gray countertops and breakfast nooks, and pink or blue bathroom fixtures.

My father shocked us all when he announced that he had put a down payment on one of these fine new places. We would all have to work hard to build a fence and put in lawns and gardens, but we would have a new home, something undreamed of in those days.

The Pine Street swamp grew smaller in the car rear window as we drove off to our new place. My parents had taken the plunge and bought the house at 42 Strathcona Avenue for $10,700. It was a one-bathroom, three-bedroom, so sleeping space was still tight — my grandmother required her own room, Barb and I had another, and Mary Jane's crib was in my parent's room. The kitchen of the new house was as pictured in the brochure. The highlight was a pink leatherette dining nook where the five of us snuggled together for meals. Sometimes when she wasn't too stiff or sore, my grandmother joined us at a chair at the end of the table.

We moved in July 1955, my parents taking on a whopping National Housing Act mortgage of $8,700 over twenty-five years with payments of $75 a month PIT. It was the start of a new life. A new era in fact because the move to Strathcona Avenue marked part of the North America-wide transition from city centre life to subdivisions and growing suburbs. Where on Dawson Street and even Pine Street we had walked to many places, now the car became a focal point of family life.

Strathcona Avenue was far from downtown. You had to drive down Cumberland Street, which followed the Lake Superior shoreline northeast, then cross the Current River bridge below the Boulevard Lake dam, then over one of Port Arthur's famous hills. Spread out on top of the hill was Current River, a community of mainly wartime houses separated from the rest of the city by the river and Boulevard Lake, the river's man-made extension. It was a blue-collar neighbourhood; many of the men worked at the nearby mills, Abitibi and Provincial.

Hodder Avenue was an extension of Cumberland Street and it ran along the edge of the Current River neighbourhood until it turned into

Highway 17 East, which led down the line to Nipigon. The east side of Hodder was bushland overlooking the lake and it was there that Gateway decided to build its little subdivision, which consisted of two blocks of houses along one side of Hodder and a new section of Strathcona that dead-ended into a rock face.

Everyone on the street had come from somewhere else in the city. New friendships formed quickly. My best new friend became Don Blight, who lived two doors over and was a hell of a baseball player and had a three-legged dog named Sox who used to entertain us by jumping fences to fetch a ball. His parents, Al and Helen Blight, and my parents became good friends, partying together on special occasions.

Veronica was gloriously happy on Strathcona Avenue. The house was new and practical. It was a safe street with only local traffic. The neighbours were all roughly the same age, late thirties couples now getting established but over the toughest years. Ray blossomed in insurance, his honest personality exuding the trust potential insurance buyers wanted from their agent. He bought us a new sectional chesterfield. It was black with gold speckles, and unlike Pine Street, we had a real living room in which to put it. We sat on it many nights, laughing and munching celery while watching the TV and the black china panther lamp with green eyes — something recommended for the top of your TV to ease the strain of watching this new magic box.

People began to come to our house as they had at 402 Dawson Street but had not at Pine Street. Louise LaFrance had been active and prominent in church and politics in her prime and some people had not forgotten her. One day a commanding-looking man with silver short hair and wearing a power pinstripe suit walked through the front door and into my grandmother's room. Veronica was flushed and excited as she prepared tea and cakes in the kitchen.

"It's Mr. Howe," she whispered to me. "C.D. Howe!"

C.D. Howe was the minister of practically everything during the federal Liberal dynasty that ran Canada throughout the war and into the late 1950s. He was the Member of Parliament for Port Arthur, and my grandmother had been part of his riding association. All this meant nothing to me, but when I grew up, I concluded he was the last politician to get anything useful done in Canada.

Wonderful as life was at 42 Strathcona Avenue, there was one gnawing discomfort for Veronica. It was the river, the Current River, and a tributary called the North Branch. Bad enough that she often lost her husband to the seductive charms of the numerous local waters, now she had moved to an area from which her only son could reach some of these waters by bicycle or foot. The Current River flowed from the Onion Lake country north of the city. It spilled out of the rough bushland at the city's northeast limits as a serious stream before falling into Boulevard Lake, the man-made effort created by the Current River dam just above Cumberland Street. The North Branch joined the main stream well out of the city and was smaller than its mother stream, in fact not much more than a creek at its farther reaches.

You could reach the North Branch by walking up Hodder Avenue until it became Copenhagen Road. A rough track followed the North Branch until the bush swallowed the track and the stream. In the 1930s and 1940s, it was a speckled trout factory available to anyone willing to hike.

Veronica knew from the beginning that Ray would spend a lot of his free time up there, throwing flies into dark little pools where the water stopped to catch its breath after running the rocky slopes toward Lake Superior. She also knew that their son would follow him there.

My first trip up the branch was just after I started walking. I remember tall, thin men with small round spectacles and brown fedoras and suspenders over their rough bush shirts. I remember bouncing in the back seat of a boxy car and the sickening crunch of the bottom hitting a rock, followed by a short but sharp, "Oooh, nooo!" I remember my father crawling on his back beneath the car and having his buddy, Bud Barnes, hand him a bar of soap. It seemed odd that he would crawl under a car to wash his hands, then emerge with hands covered with black stuff. I learned later that a bar of soap and a can of oil were critical items on bush roads because the soap could plug a hole in the oil pan temporarily.

Later they set me down by the stream and I had my first look at the masters at work. They waded into different parts of the stream, men still so thin from the Depression years that they looked like pencils wearing hats. They raised their long rods like batons, fly lines looping softly behind their backs before being thrust forward and sent flying at a tiny target area beside a log or just below a break in the rapids before a rock. They had a beautiful rhythm and laughed and kidded each other. They were gentlemen who could be tough when the toughness of bush life demanded it, and I knew early that I wanted to be like them.

I saw my father's toughness a few times, once when he became so angry I thought he would end up in jail. I was an altar boy at Our Lady of Loretto Catholic Church in Current River, a parish that served the mental institution at the edge of Boulevard Lake. That included holding Mass there occasionally for the inmates and staff.

One day en route to serve Mass at the mental home, I stopped to fish a pool close to where the Current River became Boulevard Lake. I caught a beautiful speckled trout and lingered too long. I pedalled madly down the Boulevard Lake trail to the big brick institution sprawled on a lawn at the edge of the bush. I tore into the makeshift sacristy and jumped into my cassock and surplice. Mass was about to start, so there was not time for the stern lecture that I was to receive and we filed out into a large room where an altar had been set up.

The inmates were well-behaved during Mass. I had expected to see people squirming in straitjackets and ranting and raving and running madly about. They were mostly calm and prayerful and orderly as they streamed in single file up to receive communion. Altar boys had strict orders to hold the patina closely under the chins of communicants for fear that crumbs, or God forbid, the entire host missed the tongue and fell. Communion was moving along nicely when a full-faced young man with eyes pointing in different directions and a head full of cowlicks stepped forward and offered his tongue. The host had barely touched his tongue when his eyes snapped open, and his hand flashed up and grabbed it while I held the patina but paid no attention to what he was doing.

Before anyone could blink, he was off and running, holding the tiny wafer in his hand high above his head. The temporary church erupted in chaos.

The priest roared to stop that man in the name of God, then bolted in pursuit, chalice held high in his hand, robes flowing in his wake. Patina raised in one hand, my own robes flowing, I raced behind, soon overtaking the much older priest, and closing quickly on the errant communicant now fleeing through the hallways. The command to stop in the name of God echoed off the hallway walls as our circus-like procession of altar boys, priest, nuns, and nurses and orderlies jogged through the hallways.

The hospital was large — it took in the mentally unbalanced from all of northwestern Ontario — but not large enough to escape for long. The fugitive hit a dead end, put his back to the wall and faced the mob. His face filled with terror, and he began trembling, lost control of his fingers, and dropped the host to the floor. There was a gasp followed by silence and stares of disbelief. The priest dropped to his knees and with one professional swoop scooped the host into a white cloth.

I knew from religious instruction that we now had to return to the church and burn the host and the cloth. What about the floor? Some priests said that if the host fell on a rug, the spot of rug must be cut out and burned. I stared down at the terrazzo floor where the host had been and wondered what would happen now. Terrazzo would not burn. Would they call in guys with jackhammers? I didn't find out because back at the church I received a tongue-lashing. Did I see now what can happen? Horrid things could befall us when we didn't pay attention. I would need to be diligent in future if I wanted to continue on the altar. The priest, a visiting missionary, was beside himself, unreasonably. He carried on so much that I left for home thinking he needed a room at the mental home. A couple of days later, I was at the church to serve morning Mass. The same priest arrived in the sacristy as another altar boy and I clowned about, lifting a capped bottle of Mass wine to our lips and pretending to drink it. The priest, a picture of anger in forbidding black robes with a flaming Sacred Heart embroidered on the chest, flew across the room. He slapped the other kid to one side then backhanded me full across the face.

I had been hit before in schoolyard fights, but there was something especially humiliating about being hit by a priest. He threw us into line before him and we marched onto the altar to begin Mass. My head spun and my face stung, but not as much as my pride. Defiance welled up, too much to control, and I walked off the altar and back into the sacristy. I pulled off my surplice and cassock and threw them on the floor. I ran out to Marion Street and down the hill to home.

I had planned to hide the incident from my parents because I was ashamed. My father was in the backyard, however, and saw me coming up the lane, wiping away the tears. I had reached the age when boys didn't cry, and he knew instinctively that something serious had happened. He had it from me reluctantly and within minutes, we were in the sacristy waiting for the priest to end Mass. What happened next is seared into my mind.

The priest arrived off the altar crimson with anger and demanding to know of my father if that insolent boy was his son. My father didn't answer but stepped forward and stared into the priest's eyes. Both were big men, my father over six feet and two hundred pounds. He asked the priest if he had struck me. The question seemed unnecessary since the welt was still swelling on my face and there was a cut where his ring had caught me.

The priest began to bluster and then my father, the gentle man who could drop a fly on the water as lightly as an angel's kiss, turned into a man I had never seen before. He grabbed the priest by the throat and pushed him against the wall. His big right hand flew up and slapped the priest's one cheek so hard the other cheek hit the wall, a slap heard out in the church proper. When the priest started to protest, my father backhanded him on the other cheek and pushed him to the floor. It was the last time I was ever in the sacristy of a church, although I have continued to attend Mass all my life. As we left, I peered over my shoulder to the incredible scene of a fully robed priest sitting, legs spread in front of him and a hand nursing his jaw.

My father did not speak on the ride home and we never spoke of the incident. I'm sure Veronica never knew what happened in the sacristy that day. For my part, I was bursting with pride that my dad stood up for me. On the other hand, what I had seen frightened me and I knew I would never tangle with this man. Other boys my age grew up challenging and even physically fighting with their dads. I never did, not just because I feared his hidden explosiveness, but because I respected him. That was a blessing because as it turned out, our days together were numbered.

We always attended Sunday Mass, often dropping in to see my dad's parents on Van Norman Street afterwards. I loved Sundays because the men, Robert Poling and his sons, would talk hunting and fishing and life in the bush. I sat quietly soaking up tales of being lost in the woods, of meeting bears, and of struggling through amazing adventures. We often ate Sunday lunch or Sunday dinner there, a huge gang crowded around the dining room table.

Grandpa often took meal opportunities to lecture on the virtues of eating light. He boasted of being 110 pounds soaking wet and said he could go days without eating because he never stretched his stomach by overeating.

He lectured me on always pushing away from the table hungry. Some day I would be hungry and having a stomach that was not stretched by overeating would help me bear the hunger. It didn't make much sense to me. I was already so skinny that Grandma was always pushing extra food at me. Besides, I thought the idea of eating was to stoke up, so it would be a longer time before you ran empty.

My grandfather's words came back to me one time up the North Branch. It was a time in my life to meet the challenges of the bush face to face over an extended period. Day trips were fine, but a man couldn't really know the bush until he went out and stayed in it a few days, living off the land, so to speak. My friend Bob Milne and I decided we would do this. We would head out on a Friday and come back on a Sunday, fishing for food, sleeping under an old boat we knew sat by a pond many miles up the North Branch. We packed up. Sleeping bags. Fishing tackle. Open-fire cooking gear but little food. My father drove us to the trailhead, and while making a cursory inspection of our packs during the unloading noted that we were travelling without food. We said we intended to catch trout and make bannock, pioneers' bread made with flour, water, and salt, then baked on a stick over an open fire.

We waved and set off into the bush, with father driving off with instructions to pick us up at the same spot late Sunday. We felt completely liberated. Go where we pleased, do what we pleased when we pleased. We walked and fished the river until almost dark, then crawled into a dilapidated cabin where we ate a snack and went to sleep. The next day we moved deeper into the North Branch country, fishing and exploring before reaching the pond where we were to make our main camp. We had sharp hand axes for cutting poles, which would prop the boat up on edge. We would fill the open sides with balsam branches and have ourselves a comfortable lean-to for Saturday night.

The boat was not there. We searched around the pond and in the bush beside it. Surely someone had simply stashed it, but we couldn't find it. We were without shelter, so started building one and before we knew it, it was getting dark. An afternoon planned for filling our creels was taken up building the lean-to. We had no fish to eat, no food to cook. We put the finishing touches on the far too elaborate shelter in the dusk, then set out our sleeping bags and crawled in.

The thunder and lightning arrived before we were asleep and was accompaniment for our rumbling stomachs. Rain arrived in sheets, blowing this way, then that way. We rigged a ground sheet at the lean-to's entrance to stop the wind-pushed rain, but within twenty minutes the roof began to leak. We had rubber-bottom sleeping bags and turned them over but the water seeped through the stitching in the bags. By midnight, we were drenched, as well as the clothes, bags, spare clothes we carried in our packs.

In the morning, sleepless, hungry, and stiff from the wet cold, we packed out. Two teenage boys who hadn't eaten anything substantial for thirty-six hours. Our stomachs hurt, then flipped excitedly when we encountered a bear on the misty trail. He seemed as hungry as we were but showed no interest in us. Farther along, we saw two other shapes in the mist. They were early morning anglers just starting out, and in the fashion of the day, we greeted each other and sat down on some stumps to chat. We explained that we saw a bear and left our packs but would go back for them. While we talked, one of the guys pulled out a can of sardines. My mouth watered with anticipation. True to the code of the woodsman, the guy took one sardine and then passed the can. Bob took one and so did I. Just one for now to be polite. When the offering made the full circle back to its owner, he took another then tossed the can over his shoulder. Then they wished us good luck and carried on down the trail.

Bob and I stared at each other tensely, waiting for the two to clear our sight. When they did, we hurled ourselves into the bush and found the spilled can. We clawed at the ground, picking up leaves, dirt, and sardine pieces together. Not a morsel remained for any raccoon. Sardines never tasted so delicious. I licked the can and noticed they were King Oscars and they became my favourite. My granddad's words came to mind: always push away from the table hungry because some day you really will be.

We had many better trips up the North Branch. The absolute best was the day we walked to the pond where we survived the overnight monsoon. The boat had not reappeared, but someone had lashed together a makeshift raft. I got on it and was poling about when up ahead a huge trout broke the water. I raised my fly rod and started looping out the line. At the end was a large Mickey Finn streamer that I had been using in the fast water, which was the most unlikely lure to be using on the pond. I rolled it through the air back and forth to get the line out and to dry the fly for a softer landing. It dropped dead centre on the widening circle left by the trout's splash. The hit was instant. The waxed line whizzed between my fingers until it was gone and the rod tip pointed down like a witching stick over hidden water. I knew I had the fish of a lifetime on. It plunged to the pond bottom then reversed course and came splashing above the surface, shaking head and tail in an effort to throw the Mickey Finn. "Wow," I heard one of the guys exclaim from shore.

This was the biggest speckled trout I had ever seen. It tail-danced across the water, then dived again only to resurface in another explosion of water. I kept working the line one finger over the other, gaining one inch at a time on him then losing a couple feet when he dived and ran. I prayed not to lose this fish.

The line went slack and my heart sank. I quickly pulled in a few inches. Nothing. I pulled a few more and the rod tip dipped again and the fight resumed. He'd tried the old trick of running at me to loosen the tension and increase the chances of throwing the hook. Thankfully, I knew Dad's trick of retrieving slack line quickly, and not long after that the monster trout flopped in the grass beside the pond, with my friends watching bug-eyed. I hadn't basked in this much glory since the day I pulled Barb from the Prospect Hill pond.

We didn't weigh or measure our fish. We fished for food and fun and gave little thought to the trophy aspects. It was better that way because you could allow a fish to grow over the years with nothing but someone else's memory to challenge you.

My pack that day was one of those army shoulder bags made of brown canvas with a top flap secured by two canvas straps inserted into buckles. It contained my sandwich and a couple of thin fly boxes. When

I stuffed the fish into it, the tail and a good third of the body protruded from under the flap. This was not a good thing because fish and where they come from are special information you do not share. You don't want anyone to see any fish unless you absolutely have to show them. I tried different ways of stuffing the trout into the bag but there was no room for that big tail.

On the way back down the trail we met a lone fly fisherman. I recognized the brown fedora and granny glasses from a distance. It was Bud Barnes, my dad's buddy. Fly fisherman unequalled by any other, except for my dad. We paused on the trail to chat and he asked about the fishing. I lied shamelessly, not wanting to divulge any information about the pond. He was not fooled and craned his neck to see how low the pack might be sitting on my back. I shifted so he couldn't get a view.

He walked off and I shuffled backwards, keeping the pack concealed until he was past. Then I faced the trail and peeked over my shoulder to see if he was gone. He had stopped and turned around and was pushing up the brim of his fedora with his thumb in a display of complete amazement. I could feel the big tail swaying behind me and when I looked again, he was hotfooting it up the trail trying to tie flies to his line as he went.

The North Branch was a happy and healthy place for a teenager to spend time. It was away from the temptations and dangers of city life. I walked it and climbed it, biked it and skied it. I hunted it and fished it and built little cabins along it. Veronica knew there were risks up there — the water, getting lost, wild animals — but she grew to accept that you can't protect your children from everything.

I knew she had accepted the North Branch as an important part of my life when early one December she asked me to go up the North Branch and cut a Christmas tree. Dad always had got the trees — towering balsams that had to be trimmed and re-trimmed to get them into the house — and I was determined that my first tree would measure up. I walked up one Saturday and knocked down a winner and dragged it down the Copenhagen Road, then along Hodder Avenue to home. I stood it in front of the living room window and she laughed when she asked me to turn it around. One side had worn away during the three-kilometre trek. We put the bare side against a wall and it became a special tree, not just because I got it, but because it was our last family Christmas tree. By the time the next Christmas arrived, the North Branch country that had provided so much happiness, particularly for my dad and me, would be the symbol of our living hell.

6 — THE BIG LAKE

THE NORTH BRANCH SHOULD HAVE BEEN THE LEAST OF Veronica's family safety worries. It was off in the bush behind Boulevard Lake. Out of sight, out of mind. However, she only had to walk to the height of land at the end of her street to see the mother of all water worries: Lake Superior.

At 82,000 square kilometres, Lake Superior is the world's largest freshwater lake by surface. Its average depth is 147 metres to as much as 407 metres deep and contains 11 quadrillion litres of water. With all that water and all that depth it is said to never give up its dead. All that water just doesn't sit there. It rolls back and forth in a gigantic granite bowl, grinding Olympian-size rock formations to pebbles. Whipped by winds, it can split rock, pile house-size pieces of ice atop each other, and fling spray hundreds of metres inland onto shelters built against it by humans. Its power is so fearsome that it tosses and sucks down huge ships like bathtub toys, the mighty SS *Edmund Fitzgerald,* or the *Big Fitz*, being the most famous modern day example. It took twenty-nine men to the bottom during a screaming Lake Superior storm on Nov. 10, 1975. The *Big Fitz* was the largest ship on the Great Lakes during the 1960s. She was longer than two football fields laid end to end. She weighed 13,632 tons and was the first ship ever to carry one million tons through the Sault Ste. Marie locks.

The *Big Fitz* had life rafts larger than Grandpa Poling's boat, an unnamed four-metre cedar strip capable of carrying all the beer and whisky a couple of guys would need for a day or two. It was small but mighty in its ability to fill with fear the hearts of our family's woman folk. For my mother, both grandmothers, and some of the other Poling women, it was a hated little craft that surely someday would take one or more of their men to doom. The problem was not the boat itself. Indeed, it was of such a dinky size that it was perilous to be out on the Big Lake except in the finest of weather. And yes, the little cabin Robert Lee added to it for foul weather travel certainly did not meet naval architecture and engineering specifications. In fact, the cabin made the ship somewhat top heavy. But the real difficulty with this boat, in fact, was the captain. He was completely fearless — some would have said reckless — on the lake.

Veronica could not spin through the rosary fast enough whenever my father came home and announced he was going out on the lake with his old man. Many a night I sat with her in the dark beside a radio turned low as she waited for a pounding on the door or a deadly ring of a telephone. Some of the most tense times of our life were when Robert Lee and one of his boys were somewhere out on the lake at night. In Poling homes, the women paced and kneaded their hands. Grandma Poling, with her gentle but defective heart, polished the floors with her late-night pacing while waiting for her overdue husband.

One wild night when horizontal rains bent big trees, Veronica gathered us three kids from bed and stuffed us into the back of the old car. She drove south on rain-lashed roads toward the U.S. border, then turned onto a bush road and arrived at Lake Superior's shore in some isolated spot. It was 3 a.m. and we were greeted with a flashlight signal stuttering through the stormy blow. Anyone watching this night scene would have assumed they had stumbled into a smuggling operation. Old gangster-style car, dark figures lugging gear up the lake embankment. A skiff from a lighthouse dropping Robert Lee and Ray off on the shore. They had been returning from Pigeon River, which forms part of the U.S.-Canada border, and had encountered motor trouble so they pulled into the lighthouse.

Grandpa Poling knew every manned lighthouse along Superior's shore on either side of Port Arthur. He also knew the keepers, especially those who appreciated breaking the loneliness of their work by sharing a bottle of Captain Morgan with Lake Superior's version of the Old

Man and the Sea. The old man fished at all hours and in all weather, his hardened little fingers running out copper wire line from wide wood or metal reels on stubby homemade lake trout rods. Every fish he caught seemed to turn into a Hemingway-inspired struggle. One time he landed an eleven-kilogram lake trout while fishing alone off his cabin not far from the paper mill.

Fishing, however, was not the only reason to be on the lake. There were explorations to carry out, and incredibly, trips by boat to Minnesota. He would take a buddy or a son, fire up the little Peterborough, and cruise down to Pigeon River, a run of seventy kilometres, a good three hours, across the open waters of the world's largest lake. The object of the trip was to enjoy refreshments at a hotel either at Pigeon River or Grand Portage, the place where the voyageur fur traders used to begin the far west leg of their travels. He was still an American citizen so felt it unnecessary to check in at Customs and Immigration where he no doubt would have been arrested for whisky running.

Navigating the waters between the Port Arthur harbour and the border is no insignificant achievement. The coast is spotted with islands and shoals, not to mention drifting deadheads from the logging operations that brought pulp logs to the mills. I cannot recall a compass or chart ever being in the boat.

Sometimes the taking of refreshments down the lake would take longer than expected and the trip home was in the dark. Drinking out on the lake was a deadly pastime. Our men received a chilling warning one time when the guy with the camp next door to Grandpa failed to return from fishing one night. He had taken off with a load of alcohol and fishing gear and disappeared beyond the horizon. They found his boat, but never his body. He had two kids the ages of Barb and me and I remember playing with them while searchers criss-crossed the lake looking for him. Veronica said the family would have to wait seven years to get the insurance money if the body was not found. They never did find it, and I often wondered over the years what happened to those people, a poor family to begin with and then left without a breadwinner.

Before he moved up to the outboard cruiser, Grandpa Poling did his water adventures in the *Undertaker*, usually on smaller inland lakes but sometimes on Lake Superior. One time he got it into his head that he would visit Nanabijou by canoe. The *Undertaker* had all the sailing characteristics of an empty pork and beans tin, so it was a shock when he announced his intention of paddling it across Thunder Bay to the mysterious rock cliffs of the Sleeping Giant. Canoeing that twenty-five-to thirty-kilometre stretch of treacherous water is somewhat comparable to gluing feathers to your arms and leaping off a cliff.

Grandpa made it back, albeit a different man. His hair had turned even whiter and his eyes reflected distant vistas and he seemed to have developed an inner calm. I lived with him later for two years but never worked up the nerve to ask what happened out there. I suspected he had seen the *Maemaegwaeshi*, mischievous little men the Ojibwe said lived among the rocks beside the lake.

The trip out to Nanabijou did not, however, end his yearning to do crazy things on the Big Lake. I have technicolor memories of the family hysteria when he announced the great adventure to mark his retirement: Circumnavigation of Lake Superior. No, not in the *Undertaker*. This finale of a lifetime of near-death experiences on water would occur in something much more substantial — the little cedar strip powerboat.

It was the summer of '56. I didn't see the launch because Veronica would have thrown herself in front of a train to stop me from witnessing "such craziness." I did see the preparations. The little cedar strip had been fitted with the homemade cabin. Gasoline drums filled much of the open floor space. Even my young mind was able to discern the potential for disaster here. Gas drums in an area not much larger than an overturned phone booth. Absent-minded grandfather. Grandfather's silver Zippo with the blow-torch flame. Grandfather's crumbling roll-your-owns trailing sparks like a shooting star. Yes, it was clear why the women were inconsolable; why the men wore deeply troubled frowns. No one could talk him out of the trip, however, and Robert Lee, sixty-five years old, set off one clear and calm morning before the sun rose over Nanabijou.

This quest to navigate twenty-four hundred kilometres of coastline ended prematurely. Not, however, in the fireball I expected would be seen from Port Arthur, Wawa, the Soo, Duluth, and points in between. Grandpa was gone one week. Then the phone rang, setting off another family frenzy. He was ill and put in at Marathon, three hundred kilometres down the north shore. Happily, he returned to good health and to a relatively more sedate life of sailing closer to home.

Grandpa Poling was as fearless in the forests as he was on the water. My dad had a dozen stories about the old man's crazy feats in the woods. The all-time favourite was the time Grandpa rode a moose. The two of them were paddling a faraway lake, fishing for trout, when an antlered bull was spotted swimming toward shore. The old man set course for the moose and ordered Dad to paddle full speed. When they got alongside, the old man announced his intentions to jump onto its back while Dad was to keep the *Undertaker* under control. Dad recounted many times how he tried to reason that riding a wild animal is not a sane way to enjoy nature. There was no reasoning with Grandpa, who sometimes took a nip of Captain Morgan against the northern cold. Dad watched incredulously as the old man steamed off down the lake, antlers gripped tightly and laughing like a lunatic until the moose hit shore and rightfully pitched him into the birches.

My father also told of the time that he, brother Bob, and the old man were sleeping under a spruce bough lean-to. My dad awoke to a pressure on his chest and a foul stench. He opened his eyes to see a mass of black fur above his head. A black bear had one paw on his chest and was sniffing for food. Just as Dad was about to scream he felt a pressure on his arm, squeezing tighter and tighter. It was the old man's fingers warning him to lie still and keep quiet. The bear helped itself to a backpack that contained some sandwich makings and wandered off.

Every year, the old man and the little boat made a dangerous run around the feet of Nanabijou and across the open water down to Rossport near the east entrance to Nipigon Bay. This was an incredible journey in a tiny boat, close to 160 kilometres by my estimation and it took a good chunk of the day just to get there. It is an area that has taken many bigger boats, including the *Gunilda*, a New York millionaire's yacht that struck a reef August 30, 1911, and sank in two hundred metres of water. Some believe the millionaire's treasure remains on the boat. One of my childhood acquaintances on Strathcona Avenue, Charles "King" Hague, drowned August 8, 1970, while trying to explore the wreck. The *Gunilda*'s top foremast and a plaque honouring King Hague still stand beside the Rossport Inn today.

Courtesy of Jim Poling Sr.

Robert Poling guided part-time in northern Ontario to help feed his eight children. Much of his fishing was done in a tippy little canoe nicknamed the *Undertaker*, pictured here. He once paddled it to the Sleeping Giant, roughly thirty kilometres across Lake Superior from Thunder Bay.

I don't know what treasure lay in the *Gunilda*'s grave but for our family the real treasure at Rossport was first prize in the annual Rossport Fish Derby. The Rossport Fish Derby was an amazing phenomenon. How a dinky village with only a few streets could attract thousands of anglers from all over the Canada and the U.S. is beyond comprehension. It did and I guess one of the reasons was the first prize: a brand new car. In the 1950s, not many people had what it took to buy a new car and the chance to win one was a powerful draw.

Rossport at derby time was a gold rush town. People walked shoulder to shoulder on the town footpaths and the few tiny streets. Boats floated gunwale to gunwale at the docks and at anchor in the harbour, one of the prettiest along the north shore. People cooked on open fires and on portable barbecues. They slept in boats and in tents in yards rented out. Folks with money stayed at the Rossport Inn, which was still operating a nice little dining room as of a few years ago. The excitement tingled in your nostrils as you pushed through the crowds. Any one of us thousands of fishermen could be the winner. No matter who you were or what friends or money you had, if you knew how to work a lure at the end of a rod, you could win the Rossport Fish Derby. The tiniest boat could be the biggest winner and we were among the tiniest.

On my first year at the Rossport Fish Derby we were out with our trolls set long before dawn. The motor purred at trolling speed and we worked our copper lines between our fingers, tugging slowly then letting the line drop back to make the silver or gold lure flutter like a crippled bait fish. In my sleepiness, I heard the ping of metal line going taut and saw my father reef hard on his rod.

"Got him!" he shouted, but we had no idea of size because my father always shouted "Got him!" with equal enthusiasm whether the thing on was monster, or minnow, or rubber boot.

Soon it became obvious that this was a really good fish. Grandpa kept the motor at steady troll to keep tension on the fish, although the strain was breaking my father's arms. The excitement built as he strained and reeled, then strained and reeled some more. Even in the wan predawn light I could see the sweat running from his forehead and down his nose. The angle of the line into the water steepened and there was a clatter as someone scrambled for the landing net. My father stood, put his foot on the transom and held the homemade rod high. Below there was tremendous splash followed by exclamations of unbelief. The fish was bigger than Grandpa's twenty-four pounder! We were going to win the Rossport Fish Derby! I'd have my picture in the *Port Arthur News Chronicle,* standing there with Dad and the fish and Barb would never dare to call me Fire Bug again.

I saw the landing net go over the side but didn't see what happened next. I was bowled aside during the netting chaos and fell backwards into the cabin area. I did hear clearly those famous phrases float out across the fishing grounds: "Jesus Mexican Murphy! Oh, no, oooh nooo, nooo, nooooo."

7 — BIG BEAR LAKE

VERONICA SHRUGGED OFF NEWS OF OUR LOSS OF FAME and fortune at the Rossport Fish Derby. New car be damned. All that mattered to her was that none of us had drowned. None of the Poling men involved ever recovered from the loss of the Rossport Fish Derby. How could they? They had seen the winner with their own eyes, just inches from the gunwale. In the net it had been. In, then somehow back out, down into the black depths and taking with it all the glory and fame, and a new car.

There were no recriminations. How could there be when no one really knew what had happened? In the excited jostling, the net had slipped, turned, and given the prizewinner an escape route. They just didn't talk about it and whenever someone raised Rossport in conversation, their eyes drifted upward and locked onto some invisible horizon. The women, who pried the news from the subdued returning fishermen, said nothing about the incident. Grandma Poling and Veronica considered themselves big winners every time a husband or son returned home alive from the Big Lake. They suspected too much Captain Morgan had been involved in the Rossport Fish Derby and they might have been right.

The Rossport area gave Veronica other reasons for worry. Just east of it was the railway town of Schreiber, home of Bud Alcorn, another insurance agent and my father's long-time fishing pal. Bud had two cabins on Big Bear Lake, far off in the bush behind Schreiber. He had grubstaked a prospector, and in return, the old rock hound had built two log cabins at Big Bear, one on a point at the south end of the lake and one on the far shore.

In the '40s and '50s, Big Bear and the surrounding lakes teemed with native speckled trout. With their iridescent red and blue spots and salmon bellies, they were the prettiest fish in the world and among the best fighters, especially on the end of a fly line. Dad and Bud usually went after them twice a year, on the Victoria Day weekend just after the snow left and in the autumn just before the season closed. Both men were virtuosos with fly rods. They were a joy to watch, each working the dark shoreline waters from his own end of the canoe. They fished with drop leaders of three flies and often fought more than one fish at a time.

Veronica's worry about these fishing trips was the amount of canoeing involved, often in bad weather. She also fretted about the drive from Port Arthur to Schreiber, which included a stretch along Lake Superior called the Moose Gauntlet. Here the moose came out onto the highway at night, creating a hazard for traffic and sometimes charging the car headlights. To get the most fishing time in, we drove the two hundred kilometres at night, both coming and going. During his many trips to Schreiber, my dad had hit moose twice, both times with not too severe results. One night we came across a car that had struck a moose and my father had to drag the driver from behind the wheel. The big dead beast was sprawled across the hood of the car and blood streamed from the driver's face.

Veronica worried about Big Bear trips with good reason. A canoe to my dad and Bud Alcorn was just something to fish from and to carry from lake to lake. They gave little attention to proper equipment or canoe safety. Lifejackets took up space better used for fishing gear and never were carried. My mother feared they would drown on one of these trips, and that fear heightened to panic when my dad started bringing me along, starting at age eight.

On one early trip we arrived at Hays Lake, between Schreiber and Terrace Bay. On the far shore of Hays was the trailhead for the long trek to Big Bear. The canoe that would take us across the lake was the infamous *Undertaker*. Hays Lake was a sullen stretch of water with snow flurries blowing across a nasty little chop. It was the first trip of the year and we had extra supplies for stocking the cabins for the season. I watched nervously as they loaded the *Undertaker*. These two guys combined weighed 160 kilograms and we had a huge pile of gear. I wasn't sure the *Undertaker* was going to like this three-kilometre paddle on big water exposed to the north wind, but I was sure I was going like it even less. It was cold and the snow intensified, but I knew there would be no question of not going. Many months had passed since the last trout had been finessed into a landing net.

A mournful "Oooh, nooo!" interrupted the launch preparations. I jumped and looked around to see if I had done anything wrong. My father muttered something about missing paddles. Indeed, the paddles had been left in the driveway in Port Arthur. Typically, my father stopped everything to make an urgent check of his fishing gear. His sigh of relief was clearly audible through the wind driving the snow. It was all there. One could walk around the lake, but one couldn't fish without gear.

We could have driven the few miles back to Schreiber to get paddles, but that was an unnecessary waste of good fishing time. Dad went to the trunk, produced two iron shovels and we set off. It was a ridiculous sight. Two men with snow shovels paddling an overloaded four-metre canoe into the teeth of a spring snowstorm. The *Undertaker* sat so low the water splashed up to my fingers gripping the gunwales. We made the far shore after some terrifying lurching that sent water into the bottom of the canoe where I sat. The trip had barely begun and already I had a wet ass, one of the worst discomforts of bush travel, and one not happily suffered so early in an adventure.

Trailhead is a misnomer for the head of the trail into Big Bear Lake. There was no trail, at least not one that I could discern. In early spring with patches of snow on the ground the trees and undergrowth barren of leaves, a trail is hard to find. We didn't really need a trail at first because we diverted to a falls on Ansell Creek where big trout swam. I watched Bud Alcorn work a fly up the river and into the falls, letting it slip along the current to the edge of river foam as thick as the frothy milk on top of a good cappuccino. The fly disappeared immediately and after a long struggle in fast water a spectacular rainbow trout lay on the bank. I remember how it bled a deep red that blended with the red stripe along its body and the red hackle of the Mickey Finn. When I got older and had my own fly gear, I always carried a Mickey Finn.

The falls at Ansell Creek was a short, happy diversion. We reshouldered our packs and within minutes a deep and scary bush consumed us. We followed the general course of the creek on a trek that would cover five to six kilometres before we arrived at Big Bear. Ridges of deciduous trees — birches and poplars — rose to as high as four hundred metres above sea level then gave way to spruce lowlands with black muck that grabbed at our boots. Some areas were so low they were flooded and we had to skirt them.

We stopped for lunch at an abandoned prospecting site where a company had once drilled for gold. It was like the movies in which the characters stumble across ruins in the jungle: Two buildings beaten up by the weather, doors hanging at crazy angles and undergrowth creeping through broken windows. There were racks on which rested the long and narrow wooden boxes where lengths of grey-black drill core samples were stored. I examined the rounds carefully but found no telltale gold or silver glitter. I loaded my pack with some for souvenirs. Dad watched my little packsack sag as I filled it with the pieces of treasure, but he didn't say anything. Minutes after setting off again, the weight began to slow me down. Still he said nothing, but pushed on ahead as I fell farther and farther behind.

This was my first time so deep in the heart of northern Ontario. Everything appeared dead and the only sounds were the whisper of wind in bare branches and the trickle from water running through any spot low enough to carry off the melting snow. On later trips, I would be amazed at the thickness of the forest, the dense walls of tag alders, the sweet scent of the balsams, and the wetness of moss so thick at the base of tall dark trees that you could bounce in it.

I began shedding the core samples then ran a bit to catch up with Dad and Bud. They made no comment. They were like that. They could have told me not to pack the cores in the first place, but they believed that in the bush you had to learn things yourself.

Because my legs were much shorter and my lungs much smaller, we stopped often, sometimes at a brook where a tin cup hung from a branch and remained there year after year. People passed by here only a few times a year. The cup remained where it was because that was the rule of the bush. No one removed things that others might need. Cabins were left unlocked for those who might need shelter and all that was expected in return was that goods used be replaced if possible, and that things be left as they were found.

The cold water from the stream made my teeth ache. It was clear and sweet, like no other water I had tasted. We drank our fill and I think back now on how wonderful that was. Water was so pure and plentiful even just fifty years ago, yet today we dare not drink directly from most lakes or streams. Since then we have gone from drinking from a tin cup left beside a stream to the horrors of Walkerton, Ontario, where seven people died and hundreds of others were sickened by bad water. Boil orders for bad tap water are a common occurrence in Canada today.

Big Bear Lake was still wilderness and everything that I expected. The skies had cleared allowing it to reflect the beauty surrounding it; white birches in contrast against the vibrant green of balsams and the darker shades of spruce and jackpine. Blueberry bushes grew thick and tight to the water's edge, the only breaks being where beaver or deer had their trails. On the points and at other spots along the shore, grey granite chunks grew out of the water as if placed there on purpose by some superior being. The water was crystal when you scooped it into the palm of your hand but tea-coloured when you stared over the side of a canoe and straight down into it.

One cabin was on a rocky point that we could see across the bay from our arrival point. The other was at the far end of the lake, perhaps a kilometre farther. Both cabins were similar: one-room log construction with two sets of bunk beds, a table, chairs, a wood stove, and a shelf for storing foodstuffs. There was a washbasin outside and a latrine back in the bush.

The lake was about one kilometre by one kilometre, but it seemed much bigger, perhaps because it had a couple of long bays. Why they called it Big Bear I could only assume and didn't really want to know. Directly behind the far cabin was the trail to McCuaig Lake and to the right less than a kilometre down the shore was the trail up the creek to Little Bear. I wasn't allowed to wander the bush, because it was thick and vast but I was allowed to paddle a canoe out front and was left to my own devices to learn how. I was shown in detail, however, how to pull it ashore, turn it over, and dry and patch with glue and canvas the holes I punched in it whenever I hit a rock.

We fished in one canoe, thankfully not the *Undertaker*, which remained at the trailhead because we had canoes stashed at Big Bear.

Dad and Bud took turns fishing the stern while I occupied my usual position on the floor in the middle, a bait rod dangling over the side and a can of worms between my knees. I pined for the day when I could leave the worms behind and join in the elegant symphony of fishing with flies. No one will believe it, but we sometimes fought five or six trout at a time. Dad and Bud used the drop fly rigs that allowed them to offer three different flies at time in the hope that the trout would have interest in at least one. So we had seven baits in the water, and I recall at least one time when I fought a fish while Bud had two on a drop leader and Dad had three.

I don't know if it is correct to call these trout true Lake Nipigon natural brook trout, but they had all the characteristics. They had full firm girths of salmon colour that flashed red when you reeled one through the tea-coloured depths. They averaged roughly one kilogram and usually were in the thirty-five centimetre range.

Success in Big Bear was spotty, but the fish there were a good size. McCuaig was two kilometres behind the north cabin and was roughly one kilometre long and less than a kilometre wide with a shoal in the middle that produced the biggest fish of all. Little Bear was a one kilometre uphill hike along a creek that we sometimes stopped to fish. The fish in Little Bear were the smallest of the three lakes, but fishing there was hot when the bite was on.

When it was too dark to fish we sat in the cabin and talked, about fishing and firefighting and exploring new lakes and sometimes about Al Cheesman, the famous northern Ontario bush pilot. My dad had flown with him and told how he once dropped him on a lake that he and Bud Barnes were prospecting and found it too small to fly back off. They tied the plane to a tree on shore and Cheesman revved the plane to full power and gave them the signal to cut the rope with an axe. The plane shot forward and jumped into the air, rope brushing the treetops as it lifted over the bush lining the lake. Cheesman was a legend and flew for the Ontario Provincial Air Service soon after its formation in 1924. He also flew in the Antarctic with the famous explorer Sir Hubert Wilkins.

Many years later, I wrote the obituary of Al's son, Dr. Ken Cheesman, the flying dentist. Ken dropped out of high school in Thunder Bay and became a pilot like his dad, but at age thirty-six, his medical examiner told him that bush flying was stressful and dangerous and he should find another line of work. He returned to school, became a dentist, and set up a practice in Sault Ste. Marie. He was winding up his dental practice, retiring after twenty-seven years, when he got a call to do a freelance flying job for Batchawana Air Service. Another pilot had unexpectedly booked off and the service asked Dr. Cheesman if he would take the flight to pick up a party of American anglers. On his way to make the pickup, he crashed in high winds and rain.

I don't know if the story about Al Cheesman tying a rope to his plane was the bush equivalent of an urban legend, but I heard it many times, along with other bush flying stories that convinced me that when I grew up I would be like him. I would be a bush pilot.

We made many trips into Big Bear, trips often punctuated with the famous "Oooh, nooo!," a most memorable one occurring along Little Bear Creek. Dad was standing midstream, tying on a new fly because the ones he was using weren't garnering any interest. It was late spring and blackflies were horrendous and gnawing at his ears. He took a swat that caught the corner of his spectacles and sent them spinning into the swollen creek, never to be seen again.

I was fishing downstream when the "Oooh, nooo!" floated by. The sound was a clipped and urgent utterance, so I walked up to see what was happening and found him stranded helpless in the stream. He couldn't see enough to get back to shore. I guided him out and back down the trail to the canoe. I learned two very important lessons that day: guys suddenly left blind on the river develop a colourful vocabulary and, when someone takes you into the bush, always pay attention to where you are going because you never know when you might have to lead the way back.

More than once a loud and painful "Oooh, nooo!" rolled through the woods when he forgot a rod or reel or some other piece of equipment.

"Oooh, nooo, noo!" boomed out across the lake, lifting a flock of early ducks and startling me equally. His eyes immediately went to the manual wind reel I was attaching to the bamboo rod. He had forgotten his new reel. My graduation to fly-fishing had to wait until another trip.

I learned a lot about my dad at Big Bear Lake. I saw his anger surface once again on the trail up to McCuaig Lake. He had two friends along, one of whom insisted on carrying a .22 rifle because it was September and hunting season had just opened. My father felt there was a time for fishing and a time for hunting and you didn't try to do both on the same trip. He asked that the rifle be left behind, but the friend insisted on carrying it.

Halfway up the trail, we encountered two large coveys of partridge, ruffed grouse, and some spruce grouse. I counted twenty-five. The guy with the rifle went nuts, shooting into the birds without picking a precise target. He wounded a couple and kept shooting at the others that probably had never heard a gunshot before and ran about stupidly. My father was furious. He tore the rifle from the guy's arms, aimed it, fired five times and killed five partridge, the legal limit for one person. He tossed the rifle back at the guy, then stormed up the trail.

Another time at McCuaig Lake, I saw him at his gentlest. We were fishing the shoal and catching beauties, but the weather was foul, with rain and increasingly high winds. We were blowing about and he made for shore, but a gust of wind caught the canoe off balance and we capsized. It was near shore and the wind blew us to where we could stand and drag the canoe and gear ashore. We found a protected spot in a stand of jackpines and broke the dead lower branches for a fire. I was young and wet and cold. The jackpine forest was black and ugly and the sky was charcoal grey. I was suddenly afraid. Dad boiled water and threw a tea bag into the open pot then poured some out for me into a metal cup. I remember seeing soot and needles in the tea and I was fighting back tears. Dad sat beside me and put his arm on my shoulder and explained how the woods were not always sunny and safe and fun, but real bushmen who kept their heads and looked after themselves had little to fear there. It was a lesson not just about the bush; it was a lesson about life.

The best Big Bear expedition was the final one. I was a teenager then and took my turn carrying the canoe up the trail. Dad had not forgotten anything this trip and I had my own fly rod and reel. We put a canoe into Little Bear from the rocky point where the creek falls out and fished the shaded shore on the left. It was a dull day but a magical one. We worked together, me in the bow covering the black flat water just ahead and to my left, Dad paddling and working the areas that I missed. Despite working the water all along that shore to the end of the lake, we couldn't coax a rise. It began to rain, lightly but steadily, and Dad turned the canoe and started paddling back. Off to our left, there was a splinking sound, louder than the raindrops on the water and the little circle on the surface was heavier than a raindrop could make. Dad said to start working my rod; the bite was on.

Before I could cast a fly, I heard, "Got him," and soon I was repeating those words. Rises began appearing all around the canoe, moving gradually toward the point at the end of the lake. We fought fish one after the other. I caught my first double, and at one point Dad had three on but couldn't net them all. Salmon bellied specks flopped everywhere along the length of the canoe. We grinned at each other and fished the school right into the point. When we landed, we had exactly fifteen each, the daily limit. With what we already had back at camp packed in moss, we would go home with five dozen fish, which was good because money never came easy to our house and a basket of fish or a haunch of deer always made life a bit easier.

We shook hands and congratulated each other. We had worked well together as a fly-fishing team and I knew he was as proud of me as I was of being his son. It was a fine day, but it was the last time we would ever fish together.

Book Two

TRIALS

8 — LAKE OF THE WOODS

THE SUMMER OF 1960 HELD MUCH PROMISE.

Our family was maturing with two teenagers, a six-year-old, and Mom and Dad with a few early grey streaks in their hair. Dad excelled in the insurance business. He had found his niche, something he liked, something that he believed in, something that he was good at and which earned him respect. We were comfortable in our new house on Strathcona Avenue, where we ate most of our meals together and talked. After dishes were done, we watched television and sometimes, when her pain was not too severe, Grandma LaFrance would hobble on crutches to the living room to join us. We were like one of the families we used to see on television in the fifties. Happy, comfortable, and nice.

Veronica had everything she wanted: a good husband, fine place to live, the satisfaction of caring for her mother, and the joy of watching her children stretching out for adulthood. Soon the two eldest would be off to college, and she could pause to reflect on family rearing well done. It is still hard to accept how quickly that classic family portrait cracked, then shattered. How a whirlwind of tragedy picked up our placid lives and our dreams and hurled them against a concrete wall.

Our family had never taken a trip together, mainly because someone always had to be at home to look after Grandma LaFrance. So it was with great excitement that we jammed ourselves into our new Meteor station wagon late in June and headed west. We were going to Kenora, the outdoor recreation capital of northwestern Ontario. It was a day's drive and the family would drop me off to start my summer job in the Ontario Junior Rangers program. They would carry on for a little holiday into Minnesota to visit some of Dad's relatives and friends and see Cloquet, the town of his birth. Friends and relatives had agreed to look after grandma for a few days.

I waved goodbye to the family as they drove away from the Kenora float plane dock, the assembly point for the Junior Rangers. Standing there caused me some pain, and not because my family was leaving. I would miss them, but, like every seventeen-year-old, I was straining the leash and ready for some independence. Being there reminded me of how one of life's little cruelties had denied me the chance to make docks and float planes an integral part of my life.

Airplanes had been my obsession since I was a child. I loved the stories of bush piloting adventures — Wop May and the Mad Trapper manhunt — and stopped to watch the sky whenever I heard an aircraft engine. I browsed Green's Hobby Shop frequently. I saved some money, and I began buying my way into the hobby of building and flying hand-controlled model airplanes. I became good at it, and Mr. Green spent much time with me and encouraged me to become a pilot when I got older. In high school, I joined Air Cadets. Veronica thought I looked grown up and handsome in my blue uniform. Dad said little but made it known he was against the idea. He feared that belonging to a military organization made young people more likely for military draft if there was another war.

Air Cadets offered chances to fly and I grabbed them. Twice I travelled across the Prairies to the Sea Island cadet summer camp on the West Coast. I won a flying scholarship, which offered me flying instruction at no charge. At the end of the course, I would have a private pilot's licence, all for free. All I needed was a medical fitness certificate and I found myself inhaling and exhaling deep breaths for a doctor in the low-slung, yellow-brick medical building on Cumberland Street in Port Arthur. The medical examination would be routine. I knew the doctor personally, even chummed with his son. He was tall and urbane with premature grey hair and best of all, he had been a pilot in the Royal Canadian Air Force. He listened to my chest with his stethoscope then hooked the ear pieces behind his neck and looked at me with eyes as blue as an Indian summer sky.

"Son, you'll never ever fly with a heart like that." I looked over my right shoulder, then my left, to see who he was addressing. Surely it wasn't me. He said I had a very serious heart murmur and asked my parents to call him.

My bush piloting dreams dissipated like lake mist in a hot morning sun. Instead of flying, I found myself at the Mayo Clinic in Minnesota where doctors diagnosed aortic stenosis, a narrowing and stiffening of a main valve that controls blood flow from the heart.

I still wanted to take the scholarship even though medical certification for a pilot's licence was impossible. Dad said to face reality: I could never fly and it was waste of time taking a flying course that would lead nowhere. He talked to some friends about the Junior Rangers and suggested that I apply. It would be clean and healthy outdoor work and at the end of the summer, I would have a few bucks in the bank.

So I stood at a Kenora float plane dock — not preparing to fly, but waiting with a group of guys for the Lands and Forests bus to take us to the Junior Ranger Camp at Sioux Narrows. By nightfall a dozen of us were in camp — a collection of bunkhouses and tents on an elevated point overlooking Lake of the Woods.

The lake is a massive body of water speckled with hundreds of islands and bays. It straddles Ontario and Minnesota and is an outdoor vacation paradise for people in both Canada and the U.S. The Junior Rangers worked on the lake every summer girdling unwanted trees, brushing roadsides, and hauling garbage out of Sioux Narrows Provincial Park. Part of the program was to learn some bush skills. We worked hard during the days and slept hard at night in the plywood shacks overlooking a small bay not far off Highway 71, which connects the Trans-Canada Highway and Kenora with the Fort Frances area to the south.

We had been in camp two weeks and were just getting used to the routine: wakeup siren after dawn, washing in the lake, huge breakfast including pie at the cook tent, then assembly for the day's orders. Whoever installed the siren must have had much experience with teens. We were a tough bunch to get up in the morning but the wailing siren did its job.

On the morning of July 13, I inexplicably awoke before dawn, long before the wakeup siren sounded. This was unheard of because I was a champion teenage sleeper, capable of doing twelve- and fourteen-hour super sleeps and never waking on my own. Despite our cabin being dark and silent, I could not fall back to sleep. I lay back on my pillow and recalled a pleasant dream that I'd had about my Grandmother LaFrance just before I awoke. It had left me with a warm glow of good feelings, almost like a satisfying meal after several days of hunger.

I got up, slipped out of the cabin where my three roommates were fast asleep and went down to the lake to wait for the morning light. When it was bright enough, I pulled out my shaving kit and knelt at the shore shaving and washing. I liked using the water as my mirror and a totally accurate reflection wasn't necessary because I was only shaving advanced peach fuzz. As I finished up, a face appeared in the water above mine. It startled me, and because it wasn't fully recognizable, I turned quickly and found myself looking at the chief ranger. He asked if I was Poling. I wondered if he had found out about some of my antics in camp, like floating across the little bay at night to meet girls at the park, but I told him yes.

He hesitated, then stiffened and gave me the news that my grandmother had died during the night. My father wanted me home.

I was shocked and so confused I didn't ask immediately which grandmother, although the dream held the answer. When I did, the chief ranger didn't know her name but said it was the one who lived at my house — Grandma LaFrance.

It was a long trek home. First the truck ride to Kenora, the wait at the station, then the train ride to Port Arthur. I had a lot of time to think about my grandmother and to reflect on how I had dreamt of her the night of her death. She was a remarkable person who seemed to be able to raise herself to a plane above her pain. Her body had long been broken, but her mind was powerful. She had a remarkable ability to calm people and to make them stop and think things through. She could be brutally frank when she felt she needed a hammer, rather than a feather, to drive a point through a harder than usual skull. I was shocked one time when she applied her frankness to me.

"You're self-centred, Jimmy, and you have to get beyond that," she told me several weeks before I left for the Junior Rangers.

I was shocked, hurt to core. It hurt all the more because I was the son she never had and she was a goddess to me. It took years for me to realize that she told me that because she loved me and didn't want me hurt by a character fault. Her assessment was right and although I never fully corrected that fault I continue to at least recognize it decades later.

Louise LaFrance truly was a portrait of courage. Never did she complain or question why she had been chosen to bear the pain of the crippling that attacked her not long after my birth. It advanced quickly, twisting her fingers like pretzels, then deforming her ankles and knees. You could see the pain in her eyes and from my bedroom I could hear her moaning in restless sleep, sometimes calling out crazy things like "bottle green, bottle green" when the drugs she took against the pain grabbed control of her mind.

It was not just the physical pain she suffered. There was the awful humiliation of a strong, independent woman reduced to

Courtesy of Jim Poling Sr.

Louise LaFrance was a true portrait in courage. She was stricken with crippling arthritis in the 1940s and lived with Veronica and her family until her death in 1960. The severity of the arthritis can be seen in the left hand that is gripping the crutch.

a near infant lifestyle, dependent on others to fulfil most of her basic needs. She often needed a bedpan to relieve herself and relied upon her son-in-law to strip her and lift her into the bathtub. Hour after hour, day after day, year after year lying back or sitting on the edge of her bed.

To pass the time and ease her pain, she took up smoking. Late into the night I would hear her stir, then listen for the scrape of a wooden match against the side of a box of Redbird matches. Then the acrid odour of sulphur drifted into my room, followed by the sweetness of smoke from a Sweet Caporal. Sometimes I would get up and go to her door and see the red tip of the cigarette glow brightly as she inhaled, and I would go in and we would talk in the smoky darkness. Mostly the talk was about growing up and sorting through the conflicts between a teenager and his parents.

Occasionally she would ask me to reach down into her bedside cabinet and pull out the bottle of brandy my father placed there for when she had trouble sleeping. She would take a drink, smoke another cigarette then tell me to go back to bed because I needed my sleep if I was to do well in school.

Mostly I remember her voice, sweet and powerful, inconceivable that it issued from such a broken reed of a body. I remember it from the Christmas Eve before she died, a magic night in which I heard her singing as I walked home after midnight Mass.

Fresh-fallen snow protested beneath the crush of my gumboots breaking trail down the unploughed lane. Dry, sharp squeaks, not unlike the cries of cheap chalk cruelly scrapped against too clean a blackboard.

Skuur-eek, skuur-eek.

The boots ignored the sounds. They moved on, ribbed rubber bottoms and laced high leather tops creating a meandering wake in the ankle deep snow. From each side of the trail, drifted snow leaned tiredly against the backsides of the bungalows, dropped there to rest by an impatient blizzard just passed through. Their crests were indistinguishable against the white stucco walls but nearly reached tufted piles of fluffy snow clinging nervously to windowsills and eavestrough lips.

The squeaks flew through the still night air, dodging fat flakes that fell heavy and straight onto my cap bill, but occasionally splashing into my face flushed warm from the walk. I could have ridden back home from Mass with the family, but the teenage mind always prefers independence, and it was a chance to visit friends along the way.

Faint strains of music joined the squeaking as I approached our back fence. I stopped to hear the music more clearly, now identifiable as singing voices escaping through an open window. I shuffled forward and listened to the notes float out crisply and clearly, then mingle with smoke rising from the chimneys. Notes and smoke rose together into an icy sky illuminated by frost crystals set shimmering by thousands of stars and the frosty moon the Ojibwe called *Minidoo Geezis*, the little spirit moon that appears small and cold early in winter.

I held my breath to hear better and determined that the music was "O Holy Night," and the notes came from the window in my grandmother's room. It was open to the cold because most people smoked cigarettes back then and at gatherings cracked a window to thin the smoke. They sang the first verse, and, when they reached the sixth line, the other voices ceased and one voice carried on alone:

"Fall on your knees! Oh, hear the angel voices! O Niiii … iiight Diii…vine! …" That's the part where the notes rise higher and higher until the singer reaches an awesome note.

The solo voice belonged to my grandmother, and I knew she was hitting that high note while sitting on the edge of the bed that had been her prison for sixteen years. The others had stopped singing to listen to her. The second time she hit the high notes at the words "O Night Divine," a shiver danced on my spine.

When she finished singing "O Holy Night," the other voices started up again, this time with "Silent Night" and other favourite carols. I went into the house and found Christmas Eve celebrants — my mom, dad, and some neighbours — crowded into the ten-by-ten bedroom that was my grandmother's world. They sang long into the night, mostly in French because the neighbours were the Gauthiers who seldom spoke English to my grandmother and mother.

After the singing ended my mother served tourtière, which I slathered with mustard. Then we gathered at the tree and opened our gifts. I have long forgotten what I got, and it doesn't matter, because my real gift came many years later: the gift of realization that those high notes were not solely the products of the lungs. They were driven by something stronger than flesh — an unbreakable spirit. They came from strength far beyond anything that a mere body can produce.

They came from the will to overcome.

My grandmother was not a burden in our house. Just the opposite. While she couldn't cook or clean or babysit, she was our family's spiritual leader. Not just in religious terms. She was strength. She was the will to overcome. We all brought our problems to her and she comforted and advised us. When we hurt, we ran to her and she draped her twisted arms around us and absorbed our pain because she truly believed it was better for her to have it than us.

When I grew older, my respect for my parents deepened when I realized their sacrifices in looking after her. Bedpans and disrupted nights. The lifting and bed stripping and lifting and massaging. Bathing. The drug bills to pay out of pocket because there was no medical plan. Never could they plan a trip without making arrangements for her care.

Those were times when people didn't put their parents in nursing homes. Duty was held above personal satisfaction. Our family, my parents in particular, suffered because my invalid grandmother lived with us, but it was never an issue. I have difficulty with the concept of confining parents to nursing or retirement homes. That said, my parents did not live to be old, so I faced no difficult decisions. Also, we live in faster times in which both spouses usually work and there is little time to think, let alone time for caring for someone else. I cannot condemn people who choose not to care for their parents at home. I do condemn a system that promotes pushing older people into homes where they spend the rest of their days smelling the stench of each other's urine, listening to each other's cries in the night. When my grandmother wet herself in bed, my parents were there to change her. When she screamed at night, we were all there to hear her, and I think our world was a better place because of that.

Not having her with us anymore was incomprehensible at first. Especially for Veronica. She had an unusually powerful bond with her mother, for reasons we would discover later. We moved on. We buried her beside Isidore in a sunny patch at St. Andrew's Cemetery and were thankful her pain was gone. As the years and decades passed, I thought many times about the dream I had the night of her death.

9 — THE MISTAKE

VERONICA STRUGGLED WITH HER GRIEF AS SHE CLEANED Grandma's room and stored the remnants of her strongest lifelong relationship. She cried a lot. She was fundamentally a happy person, someone who lived to laugh and enjoy life. Sadness did not suit her. It turned her into someone else: someone older, quieter, and somewhat removed from what was going on around her. Gone was the smile, so wide it stretched to the edges of her eyes to include her entire face. So were the humming and the happy chatter with the dog or a bird that might light on the kitchen windowsill.

I felt helpless, not knowing what to say, or how to react. I was relieved when she said I should return to Sioux Narrows soon after the funeral. The quiet beauty of the Lake of the Woods country was a world away from the confusion and family strains back home. It was easy to leave the sadness at Port Arthur. Life moved along at the Sioux Narrows and each day was a new adventure. We cleaned, dried, and rolled water hoses used on forest fires. Once we trucked out to a forest fire where we did mop up duties, dousing embers and hot spots with water from backpack pumps.

Each of us had to take a turn manning the fire lookout tower that stood high on a hill and made me dizzy whenever I looked up at the steel ladder I had to ascend. It was a terrifying climb up the metal ladder, but once safe inside the lookout, the view was magnificent. Rugged green hills pockmarked by pieces of blue water.

Lake of the Woods is spectacular bush country, an incoherent jumble of granite, pines, rivers, lakes, and ponds. It imbues a sense of independence in anyone who spends time there, and when I returned home after two months I was wilder for the bush than ever. In September, I found it hard to stay around the house when I wasn't at school. I wanted to be up the North Branch, fishing, hunting, and exploring.

We could get to the North Branch bush country by walking a couple miles to the city's edge, then up the Copenhagen Road or along a number of foot trails. I spent Saturdays there fishing and hunting partridge and looking for deer sign for the upcoming deer-hunting season. Dad appreciated my fondness for the bush, but did not encourage me to hunt anything other than ducks and partridge. Something had turned him off deer hunting. He wouldn't say what it was except that there were too many crazy people in the bush and it had become a dangerous pastime. I had hoped he would take me deer hunting, but he ignored the subject even though we had done some duck hunting together.

Had he wanted to take me deer hunting it would not have been possible that fall. My father suffered from phlebitis, an inflammation of the leg veins. He had been drafted by both the U.S. and Canadian armies for the Second World War, but was ruled medically unfit because of the condition. It worsened over the years, and in his early forties he was troubled by varicose veins. His doctor, a friend, said it was silly to suffer when surgery was a simple option. Doctors did the surgery, which included removing the knotted veins, just after the deer season opened in October.

I intended to hunt without him; however, I didn't have a deer rifle. I dreamed that one of the family rifles, which hung on racks in the Van Norman Street summer kitchen, would be passed along to me. That didn't happen, so I bought, at a Lands and Forests Department auction of confiscated hunting and fishing equipment, a .303 army rifle. You didn't need gun permits or testing to buy guns then. There were no hunter training requirements, no special requirements to buy firearms or to hunt. You just had to be sixteen to obtain a gun and to be able to hunt on your own.

A high school chum, Ed Blady, was keen to hunt deer, and we laid plans to hunt the North Branch territory and talked about how we would get our deer. When the season opened, we were up the North Branch every weekend and sometimes after school.

One warm late October Saturday, we walked a hilly slash line just before dusk. The sky on the west side of the narrow line was crimson. On top of a rocky hill, silhouetted against the red sky, our dream deer appeared. It was a good-sized buck, its rack visible even at a couple of hundred yards. We wanted to move closer but knew that he had only paused while crossing the slash. We adjusted our sights and let fly, shot after shot. I hit him in the antlers spinning him, and Ed's final bullet from a seven-shot carbine caught him through the neck. We were shooting through iron sights, and it was pure luck that any of our bullets came anywhere near him.

Dark descended as we climbed the hill and saw our prize. It was full dark by the time we realized that we had to do something with him. We lighted a fire and gutted him the best we could by firelight, because being inexperienced hunters we travelled light and didn't have a flashlight. We also didn't have any transportation. We were two kilometres off the road and had another seven-kilometre walk back into the city. Ed decided he would walk and I would wait with the deer.

It was an unnerving night. Darkness sealed off the rest of the world outside the campfire light and I felt far from civilization. Animals snapped twigs and scurried in the surrounding bush. Perhaps a brush wolf waiting for the fire to die down. Perhaps the doe that had been with the buck when we shot him. I tried keeping the fire up, but without an axe I was reduced to leaving the carcass and walking farther into the bush to find scraps of dead wood. After six hours, the fire was almost gone and I figured Ed had got lost getting out so I did a foolish thing. I left the deer and started walking out. Fortunately I had an illuminated compass and knew how to use it, and after an hour and a half I heard a car door slam then a bit later saw bright lights over a knoll. They were searchlights and when I walked into them, Ed and a knot of police and search-and-rescue people greeted me.

Two weeks later, we were back in the bush not far from that slash line. That morning, which was to become the most horrific in my life, the rolling hills wore the mist like a dirty white woollen sock. The sun, which had risen three hours before, had given up trying to burn away the thick overcast. There wasn't much more light than when we had entered the woods at dawn.

I suggested we find a place to rest. Ed nodded agreement and we climbed a steep rise and walked into a small clearing. It had been tough slogging even for two keen and slender seventeen-year-olds, and we sprawled on a sloping slab of damp granite where we ate our breakfast of sandwiches and soft drinks.

Few words were spoken. Ed and I hunted often together and a lot of talk was not necessary. Below, at the edge of the tilted clearing, stood a high pine, its tip shrouded in fog, its wide and heavy boughs bent to the ground to form a doorless evergreen tent. Something moved enough to make one of the boughs tremble. I stopped eating and watched intently. Another movement. Then another. Silently I signalled Ed and snatched up the Enfield, whispering that he should take the left and me the right.

We spread out. Five seconds and five steps later, a grey-brown object moved across an opening in the boughs. I saw the haunch of a resting deer that probably had scented our approach.

"I see it," I said.

"Where?" Ed asked.

"There it is," I replied as the brass butt plate of the Enfield contacted my shoulder and as I saw the centre of the haunch cover the open sights. That deer was ready to bolt. I didn't have a clear shot that would kill, but I had to stop it before it jumped away into the dense bush. I couldn't see if it was a buck or doe, but I didn't feel I needed a positive identification because we had never had a bucks-only law in our area. I squeezed off the trigger and the woods exploded.

"I got it," I cried with exhilaration.

We ran to the tree, Ed a few steps ahead. I can't recall the exact words that came out of Ed's terror-stricken face.

"It's a man!" I vaguely recall him screaming. "You've shot a man!"

Beneath the boughs lay a man of about sixty, his face white and twisted in pain. He squirmed horribly as a circle of deep red widened quickly just above the knee of his thick grey bush trousers. He cried hoarsely that I had shot him, shot him in the leg.

Ed was beside him instantly, tearing off a belt for a tourniquet and yelling urgent instructions. I heard my rifle clatter across a rock ledge where I had flung it with all my strength.

My mind screamed for help. I took one more horrified look and began to run.

My recollections of the next few hours run in triple speed. I recall a wild two-kilometre run through the woods, a startled motorist flagged down on the Trans-Canada Highway, sirens from an ambulance, and the man's pale features as he was wheeled urgently through the hospital's emergency room doors. Then I recall the interrogation at the Ontario Provincial Police building. Giant fingers, cold and invisible, squeezed my lungs as I sat there. My breath came in gulps and my stomach fluttered as I gave the two police officers my statement. I knew nothing about rights and lawyers and was too heartsick to care. I told them everything without thinking of getting legal help or even of calling my parents. They wrote my statement on long sheets of white paper and I signed the last sheet.

Not until the black-and-white cruiser stopped in front of our brick-front bungalow did my head begin to clear. I thought of my father inside, recovering from varicose vein surgery and how angry and hurt he'd been when I bought that army surplus rifle. The money I had spent on the rifle was supposed to have helped us buy new fishing gear. I knew I was about to break the heart of the man I loved and respected. I wished desperately to avoid him and to run to my mother's arms and cry like I had never cried before. Something told me that I could ease at least part of the pain by going to him and breaking the news like a man. The house was quiet. He was alone on the sofa in the living room, unable to move about much because of the surgery.

"Dad," I whispered, fighting to keep my voice from breaking. "I shot a man in the bush. He's hurt bad and the police are outside."

He stared in disbelief, his mouth vainly trying to form words. I sat beside him. He murmured something about his world falling apart. I saw the anger erupt in his face. Then he grabbed me around the shoulders and pulled my head into his chest. We both cried a long time, but he never chastised me or looked down on me. I believe that because he didn't, I was able to find the strength to survive the difficulties ahead.

The days that followed were tougher for him, my mother, and my two sisters than for me. There were reporters at the door, and our name was constantly before the public as the condition of the man I shot fluctuated. Things were to get much worse. My father was well-known throughout the twin cities because he met many people through his insurance work. I recall seeing his wastebasket filled with aborted letters in which he tried to explain to friends and associates why he would not be able to carry through with certain activities.

The victim's leg was amputated and that increased the pressure on our family. One Sunday we were at Grandma Poling's house after Mass and the telephone rang in the kitchen. Grandma shuffled into the living room, hand over the heart beating through the same hereditary valve defect as mine, face ashen, other hand trembling as she told us the man I shot was dead.

His name was John Alexander Irvine Bowie, age sixty, of Fort William and he was a railway car brake tester. He died of a blood clot resulting from his wound.

The funeral was in Fort William, and in what had to have been one of my father's toughest moments, he announced that he and my mother would escort me to the funeral home where we would pay our respects. We walked together, one parent on each side of me, up the carpeted aisle to the coffin. Family and friends sitting and standing stared at us as we approached the coffin and knelt to pray. I remained conscious of those surroundings but remember nothing else after reaching the coffin.

After the burial, the police charged me with criminal negligence causing death, a crime that carried a maximum of life in prison. For our family, it was like being struck by lightning. We were dazed, but began to realize slowly that this was real life. We were facing catastrophe. There was a good chance I would be sent to prison. Without question, I had pulled the trigger and any defence seemed impossible.

10 — REMEMBRANCE DAY

WITHIN A WEEK OF MR. BOWIE'S FUNERAL, MY PARENTS and I sat in a second-floor legal office in an old building downtown, just off the main intersection of Arthur and Cumberland Streets. Across the desk, a smallish man with thinning hair leaned back in his chair, listening intently. He exuded confidence and energy. Tom Callon was well-established as a lawyer in 1960. He was roughly my parent's age, early forties. He had a general practice and was known as an excellent civil litigator with a strong social conscience. He also was one of the only Port Arthur lawyers doing criminal work. He took the case, and we began meeting in his office and at his home, preparing for trial. A preliminary hearing of my case was set for early December. This hearing would determine if there was enough evidence to send me to trial.

It was incomprehensible that I faced life in prison. Hunting accidents were common then and were considered unfortunate mishaps that simply happened. Times were changing, however. Society saw too many tragedies in the bush, many related to carelessness, and there was a movement to have the legal system reduce the deaths and injuries.

Vic Ibbetson, the tall and stern Crown attorney in Port Arthur, was determined that a conviction or two in hunting accident cases would be a start to reducing the slaughter in the bush. Some serious jail time would send a message in block letters to anyone stepping into the woods with a gun. Ibbetson had tried for convictions in three other hunting deaths but lost all the cases at trial. The reason, he believed, was that he had used the more serious charge of manslaughter and juries probably felt this was using a sledge hammer to drive a finishing nail. My case was his fourth, and he decided he had a better chance of convicting me on the lesser charge of criminal negligence causing death.

For Veronica and Ray, this was the crisis of their lives. Ray with his crutches and bandaged legs was the image of a defeated man. Veronica wore the pain of serious worry. Life was not supposed to be like this. The family dream was for me, the eldest Poling grandchild, to become the first Poling to enter a university and go on to a life beyond paper mill or transit barn work. Instead I was headed for penitentiary, although I wouldn't be the first Poling to take that route. My great-grandfather, Robert Lee's dad, Isaac Ellsworth Poling, had been there because of drinking and gambling, although on what charges I never did know.

Our lives became a blur. The only image I was able to focus on for more than a few minutes was a prison transport bus taking me through the gates into Stoney Mountain Penitentiary in Manitoba. There I would join the criminal class and expectations for my life would end. Plans for my education were now shattered. Even if I escaped conviction, which seemed unlikely, the cost of my defence would leave no money for university. I now wore the mark of one of society's losers. The attitude of the day was that decent citizens didn't end up before the courts. If you got there, the police and the Crown felt you deserved to be there and few people ever questioned their judgment.

Two weeks after the accident, Dad wanted to go out somewhere and asked me to drive him. It was the first time that he had asked me to drive the car, a reversal from my constant pestering for permission to drive. Although I had come first in my driver education course at school and had a driver's licence, he never asked me to drive. He seemed afraid of me doing anything that moved me out of childhood. He had opposed my deer hunting, had become angry when I bought an old motorcycle, and had not favoured me joining the Air Cadets. It was as if he didn't want me involved in anything in which I could get hurt.

Driving him that day — November 10, 1960 —was a big deal. So was the fact that as we left he said it was cool outside and asked if he could wear my red wool jacket with the Junior Rangers crest. I was delighted to be driving him and having him wear my jacket even though he appeared to be stuffed into it because he was a much bigger man than I. When we got back home, I helped him out of the car and into the house. He was unsteady, which was unusual because his recovery to date had been excellent. There were three steps up from the side door landing to the kitchen. He hesitated on the second, then put his hand to his eyes before falling headlong like a tall oak cut at its base. He hit the floor with a crash and was out cold. My mother and I tried to move him, but he was too heavy. We called an ambulance, which took him to St. Joseph's Hospital where he regained consciousness and settled into a room for observation overnight. Veronica went to visit him that evening, and they joked and had tea together before she came back home.

I watched a late-night television movie down the street at the home of my pal Donnie Blight. His parents turned in early and at about 1 a.m. we heard the telephone ring. Don's dad, Al, ran out from his bedroom in his pyjamas, face ashen like my grandmother's a few days earlier when she had taken the news of Mr. Bowie's death. He told me to get the hospital fast; my dad was very ill.

It was the early hours of Remembrance Day 1960 and a vicious early winter storm lashed the city. The snow fell thick as I ran home. My mother was not there but the car was. Tracks in the snow indicated someone had been there to pick her up. I found the car keys inside and took the car out for the first time alone. It slipped and slithered through the streets, and when I reached St. Joseph's Hospital, I left it running on the street and ran into the hospital and up the stairs to my dad's floor. I passed a cubby hole near the nursing station when a voice called my name. Sitting in semi-darkness, nervously massaging his prematurely grey temples was John Nickerson, my dad's friend and physician. He got up wearily and placed a hand on my shoulder. He had been crying. He said he was sorry; he didn't know what happened but maybe it was a blood clot.

For a second time within two weeks, my heart began hammering roughly, taking my breath away. My head spun and I felt like I would pass out, but I turned and ran down the hallway, down the stairs, and into the car. I spun it around and turned up the hill to Grandma Poling's house. Every light in the place was on despite it being 2 a.m. I ran through the front porch and fell through the front door into a clutch of uncles and aunts holding onto Veronica who was wailing hysterically.

My mind now can only wander through patches of memories of that Remembrance Day and the days that followed. A tailor fitting me for a rented suit. Staring into the coffin and touching his waxen hand. Holding my mother as she collapsed at the church. Uncle Jack crying and shivering in his wheelchair at the bottom of the church steps. He had been in an accident and smashed both legs, those same legs that had survived the crash of his bomber. There was no way he could negotiate the steep steps.

A day after the funeral I still hadn't cried. One night I walked out of the house and up to Current River outdoor rink where the boards were up waiting for colder weather and more snow. I stood beside the rink boards and gripped them with all my strength trying to hold back the sob that was exploding inside my body. I breathed quickly a couple times, but it erupted. I cried as only devastated youth can cry. I cried until I vomited, then I cried again until I fell beside the boards too spent to move.

11 — ON TRIAL

WHILE WE MOURNED OUR LOSS, THE CROWN PROSECUTOR worked diligently preparing a solid case against me. He had an opportunity to test it before a preliminary hearing in which a magistrate would consider the facts of the case and determine whether they warranted putting me on trial. The hearing took place in a little courtroom inside the Port Arthur courthouse that sat on the hill behind St. Joseph's Hospital and overlooked downtown. Witnesses, relatives, reporters, police, and general busybodies packed the hearing room. It was dark and crowded and I had difficulty seeing who was who, but that probably had more to do with my fear than with the lighting. The police officers recited the facts, showed exhibits, and gave details from my statement.

Ed Blady, always steady and never questioning our friendship, told his part of the story. Members of the dead man's hunting party filled in the details. They explained that Mr. Bowie had been a member of a large deer hunting party. He had a game leg for some years and could not walk far without resting. He had been walking a trail, but he tired and had hobbled off to find the shelter under the canopy of a bushy pine.

The magistrate listened and took notes. He then said there was enough evidence to support the charge and ordered me to stand trial at the spring assize of the Supreme Court of Ontario, set for February 1961. The trial would take place in the larger courtroom down the hall. The magistrate freed me on one thousand dollars bail, because I was a student and not considered a major threat to society.

At school, I endured strange looks from my schoolmates. Teachers said nothing about the tragedy. School life moved along much as before, but my marks slid as my fear of going to prison increased. While other kids worked on homework in their bedrooms or at kitchen tables, I sat in Tom Callon's living room as he instructed me on the case. He went over and over the details and coached me how not to fall into the traps laid by the prosecutor. He told me not to offer any more than I was asked — yes or no were the best answers — but always to tell truthfully what had occurred.

On February 16, 1961, three days after my eighteenth birthday, two guards escorted me into an oak-panelled prisoner's dock in a cavernous and frighteningly formal courtroom. A balding and stern judge, resplendent in dark blue robes with a red sash, stared down at me while the lawyers fought over selection of twelve jurors. He was Mr. Justice S.N. Schatz, the judge who, a year earlier, had ordered fourteen-year-old Stephen Truscott to stand trial in adult court for the murder of twelve-year-old Lynne Harper in Trenton. That decision left Truscott open for the death penalty. He was convicted, but his sentence was commuted to life in prison and he was released after ten years. In 2004 the federal government sent the Truscott case to the Ontario Court of Appeal for review, saying, "There is a reasonable basis to conclude that a miscarriage of justice likely occurred in this case."

My trial began as another bad dream. Parts are vivid. Other parts I do not remember. I remember my borrowed dark suit and how it used to be wet from armpit to elbow. I remember the polished brass rail in the witness box and how I nervously twisted my fingers around it. I remember choking back tears and anger as the tall, aging prosecutor in black robes pounded me with accusing questions. He was scornful of the distance involved in the shooting. How could I have shot another human at fewer than fifty yards? Yes, it was true he was partially hidden under the tree. Yes, it was true that he was wearing dark grey trousers and a red and black checked hunting shirt that showed more black than red on a dull, misty day. Yes, it was difficult to imagine why he would hide under a tree. But how? How? How?

He told the jury he could accept that I believed I saw a deer. However, he contended that it was unacceptable for any hunter to shoot someone and then say in his defence that he honestly thought it was a deer.

Tom Callon argued that it was an honest mistake. He challenged the jury to find any evidence of wanton or reckless disregard for others and produced character witnesses who said I was thoughtful and cautious.

My heart sank when Mr. Justice Schatz summed up the case, with two chilling statements: Good character was not a reason not to convict me and honest negligence was not a defence for the shooting. The jurors listened to this intently, then filed out to decide my fate. The police took me to the district jail to await my fate.

Veronica always said to be careful what you wished for because you might get it. As the police car pulled up to the old stone jail on the hill overlooking the Big Lake and Nanabijou, I thought back to all the excitement of the last hanging at the jail when I was a child and how I had wanted to see the jail. Now here I was, walking up the stone steps and into the entrance where a guard turned the keys on the huge steel gates.

Jail confirmed all my fears accumulated over three and half months. The gates crashed closed behind me with an ominous metallic clang. The guards stripped me, showered me, and dusted me with powder, then marched me naked to see a doctor. He looked at me, asked me if there was anything wrong with me, then scrawled the infinity sign beside my name when I said I didn't think so. I was too confused to tell him about my heart condition, which he would have discovered had he given the stethoscope a cursory run over my chest.

I can still feel the cold of that place. The chill of the X-ray machine placed against my chest to check for TB. The thin prison cloth and the rubber boots worn without socks. The metal dinner plate and drinking cup absorbed the cold and immediately turned cold the meal of bologna, bread, gravy, and greasy coffee. Within a day or two, I could be on my way to Stoney Mountain Penitentiary and I knew I couldn't take it. I began to formulate a boyishly impetuous plan to escape from the courthouse if found guilty. The guards had never handcuffed me and I would make my break from the courthouse steps. I knew the neighbourhood like my hand and if I could get away for a few seconds, I would be gone. I realized the seriousness of my plan, but if branded a criminal, I would behave like one. My jailers seemed confident about keeping me. They didn't return my personal belongings when the police marched me out to their car again and drove me downtown to hear the verdict.

The courtroom was crammed with onlookers. The buzzing of tense and excited voices stung my ears as I stepped into the dock. People fidgeted. Veronica, surrounded by anxious relatives, appeared on the verge of a nervous collapse. The silence was total as the jury filed into the courtroom through the tall padded jury room door. The judge asked a man in the back row, the foreman, to stand and face me. I could feel the pulse beating in my head and the world stopped when the foreman spoke.

"We find the accused not guilty as charged," he said steadily.

People sighed and whispered loudly. I heard my mother crying, then the judge speaking. Someone unlocked the door of the dock and I stumbled out in a daze, not knowing which way to turn. Then I did what I wanted to do since that first day the police brought me home to face my father. I ran to my mother, fell into her arms, and cried without shame as the entire court watched.

Almost fifty years later, I still wonder about the trial and the accident. I was found not guilty and yet I killed a man. It was my fault; I pulled the trigger. Should the jury have found me guilty and sent me to prison? My life would have been much different. Instead of the opportunities found later in journalism, I would have found despair. Would I ever have had a wonderful wife and four great children and grandchildren? The system would have made me into a person much different from the person I became.

Still, I took a life through carelessness. A man who was a father, a husband, a respected human being, was dead because of me. My actions brought untold grief to other people. I sometimes wonder if I have demonstrated the sorrow and contrition equal to such an act. On the other hand, can any amount of sorrow ever be enough? My survival instinct told me to push ahead or become another casualty. I moved on, but I think often about that day in the bush and wonder whether it was just that I was found not guilty and not legally punished.

In 1960 roughly 150,000 people hunted in Ontario. There were 118 accidents that year in which 36 persons died, according to the Ministry of Natural Resources 2001–02 hunting regulations. In the year 2000, there were 423,000 hunters, only 4 accidents, and no deaths.

The dramatic improvement in hunter safety statistics is because of intense hunter training and government laws requiring hunters to wear blaze orange. There is no question that had Mr. Bowie been wearing blaze orange, and if I had received formal hunting training, there would have been no accident. Regretfully, the most important human learning experiences always seem to come from mistakes.

There was little question that Tom Callon's vigorous defence of my actions saved me from prison. Ibbetson was hungry to put me away. It wasn't personal, strictly business. Tom Callon was just as hungry to see justice done; he didn't see it as just for a boy to be locked up among criminals for years because of what he called an honest mistake. He told me many years later that Justice Schatz felt the outcome was just.

Tom Callon became an even better lawyer over the years and later a judge. He had a distinguished career as Mr. Justice Thomas Callon of the Ontario Supreme Court, donning the same kind of robes that Justice Schatz had worn during those horrible days of mid-February 1961. I talked with Mr. Justice Callon more than four decades later. It was a pleasant meeting and helped me add perspective to that terrible chapter of my life. The meeting also reminded me how lucky we are when intelligent and compassionate people become involved in our lives.

12 — FAREWELLS

VERONICA HAD A POCKETFUL OF FOLKSY WISDOMS AND witty sayings into which she could dip on any occasion. "Talk to my face, my ass is tired," was her favourite expression when we kids ignored any of her suggestions or orders. Or, "You can fool some of the people some of the time but you can't fool all of the people all of the time." A favourite for when things were not going well was: "Bad things come in threes."

She was wrong about that. There is no rule limiting bad luck. We proved that not long after I walked out of the Port Arthur courthouse with my unexpected freedom. We hadn't yet emerged in the spring of 1961 from the serial shocks of the previous ten months. There had been no time to assess the impact on our lives of the tornado of miserable events. We were too traumatized even to begin grieving properly. At night I would hear Veronica crying in her room. Once I passed her door and saw her standing in the darkness staring out the window and whispering tearfully, pleading with Ray to come back. The nights that I did sleep deeply I had nightmares, waking once to see a witch's face on the wall, and another time seeing my grandmother, leaning on her crutches, framed by my bedroom doorway.

By day we were consumed with gathering the pieces of our lives. Veronica had to figure out the estate, tombstone, money, and how she would support three children. We kids had to get focussed on school because all of us had been distracted from studies far too long. My marks had slid into the danger zone.

The Victoria Day weekend was approaching, a tough time for Veronica because it was Dad's favourite time as he prepared his fishing gear for the first spring trip to Big Bear Lake. Barb's fifteenth birthday was May 20 and Veronica allowed her to have a mixed teen party, perhaps as a way of beginning to restore some normalcy to our lives. The basement was decorated, a record player moved down, and the house took on some cheerfulness for the first time in almost a year. Veronica asked me to stay home that night and unobtrusively oversee the proceedings. My bedroom was in the basement, off the party room. I would stay there, monitoring any teenage nonsense, but would not interfere with the party as long as it remained sensible. Barbara smirked at this. Imagine, the Fire Bug left to oversee the party.

I stayed in my room reading with my ear tuned, as Veronica told me. The party room pulsated with 1950s rock and roll and the excited buzz of young teens. Inexplicably all went quiet. Not a sound. Silence among a dozen or so excited teens who seconds before had been dancing and chatting. I rolled to the end of my bed and swivelled my head to peek outside the doorway. The kids were frozen like statues, as if playing a game of Stop the Music. Their faces were stony in fear. Among them, off near the staircase, I could see another frozen figure, an older stranger holding his arm straight out. His face cracked when he spoke, telling everyone not to move or he would kill them.

His eyes were wide with a desperate look, and his stare was unfocussed. He was crazed. I couldn't see what was at the end of his outstretched arm but assumed it was a gun. I glanced at the bedroom wall to my gun rack. My fingers reached up, then stopped and began to tremble. My mind went mushy when I realized I would never again be able to point a gun at anyone. The worst thing I could do was enter the room with a gun and get into a gunfight with a madman holding a bunch of kids hostage.

Behind and above me was a basement window. I jumped up on my bed, unlatched it, and crawled through. I ran like crazy to the house next door. It was in darkness and empty. Then to the Blights'. In darkness. Then the house next to the Blights'. Darkness. I was desperate. The next house had a light on and I pounded at the door. The people were home and they called the police. I met the police on the street and guided a sergeant to the window from which I had escaped. We peered down into the bedroom below where the madman was sitting on my bed with one of the girls and he was tickling her throat with a hunting knife.

What happened next was one of the sorriest police actions I ever witnessed. The sergeant signalled others to storm the basement. They clumped down the basement stairs, burst into the party room, and when one of the boys pushed a girl aside to clear a path, the cops mistook him for the intruder, grabbed him, and pummelled him to the floor. The kids screamed and pointed, "In there! In there!" Luckily, the invader was so spaced out he didn't hear the commotion. The cops went in, pounced on him, and took the knife away. The wonder of the evening was how he didn't slit the girl's throat during this Keystones Cops episode.

The man, a twenty-four-year-old paroled convict from Stoney Mountain Penitentiary, had been released a few days before and was travelling east. He was hitchhiking on Hodder Avenue when he inexplicably walked over to the next street, ours, saw the lights, heard the music, and walked in. He had a history of mental illness but had been released back into society. He was tried and sentenced to return to Stoney Mountain for another two and a half years.

The incident was the last straw for Veronica. We were caught in the vortices of an evil wind, unable to break free as it blew us from one tragedy to another. Grandma LaFrance, the hunting accident, Dad's shocking death, the trial, then the madman breaking into our home. When school broke for the summer, Veronica packed up Barb and Mary Jane and took off for a car tour of southern Ontario to visit relatives. I stayed behind for a job as a bellhop at the Prince Arthur Hotel. In Sault Ste. Marie, she visited her cousin Rene Aquin and his wife, Cass. Rene had been the federal Indian agent in Port Arthur and had transferred to the Sault. She confided to them the agony of trying to create a new life without her mother and her husband.

Later, somewhere around Sarnia, a car T-boned her car. No one was hurt, but her car was badly smashed and it was just another example of the ill wind that continued to push her along. She was fed up. She just wanted to run, fast enough and far enough to escape whatever it was that was blowing her through wall after wall of bad luck. When she got back to Port Arthur, she called Cass in the Sault and asked her to find her an apartment for September.

She sold the house on Strathcona and turned her back on her lifetime in Port Arthur. I did not know why. I just stood on the curb, waved goodbye then rode my motor scooter, carrying a box with my few possessions, over to my grandparents' house on Van Norman Street.

Too much had happened in too short a time. Maybe she was broke and had trouble maintaining the house. My father's death left us some insurance money but not enough for us to live long without Veronica working. There had been my legal costs and two sets of funeral costs. Veronica had no employment prospects. She had not worked a day outside the home since she had been a telephone operator, an occupation that no longer existed. The last twenty years of her life she had devoted exclusively to caring for her mother and her husband and children.

Someone confided to me years later that she felt abandoned. She was stunned and confused. Others had always sheltered her from life's harshest realities — her dad, mother, then her husband. The only family she had left were the Polings and she was an in-law, not especially close to them. She told someone that more than one of the male friends who offered comfort were looking for more than friendship from her after Ray died.

All she ever told me was that she had to do whatever was necessary to raise the girls. I could have gone with them but refused. My life was in Port Arthur: my friends, my school, the North Branch. My grandparents took me in and set me up in one of the back bedrooms on the second floor. It was comforting to go there because I felt that in a way I was reliving my dad's life.

The house was huge and had been elegant in its day. A wide oak staircase descended from the second floor, stopping at a spacious landing with a sitting bench before entering the main hall off the living room. Two heavy brown wooden pillars guarded the entrance to the living room that had at least nine-foot ceilings and thick natural wood trim. Thick wooden doors pulled from the inside of the walls to close the living room off from the dining room, which was occupied by my grandmother's 1920s era walnut dining table and buffet, a floor model radio, a cot where my grandmother napped and the old rocking chair with wide wooden rockers and armrests.

My grandparents treated me like their sixth son. It was amusing observing the antics of two retired people constantly in each other's hair. Robert Lee was a heavy smoker and asthmatic. He would sit in his rocking chair smoking and coughing until I thought his lungs would turn inside out. Eva wanted him to quit and had devised a plan that required my co-operation. Grandpa smoked Export plain tobacco that came in tin cans with a dancing Highland lass painted on the outside. He rolled it in a cigarette-rolling machine that made one long cigarette that was razor cut into several normal sized cigarettes. Grandma ordered that I would be in charge of rolling the cigarettes as part of my keep and secretly instructed me to roll them so tight the old man could draw little smoke from them.

I remember him starting into my first batch. Out came the trusty Zippo, and he drew in hard then expelled only a small amount of smoke. He drew again and again until he caused himself a coughing fit. Out of the rocker he leaped and headed directly for the kitchen sink where in the cupboard below he kept a bottle of Seagram's 83 whisky, the clear one with the dimples in the glass. He poured himself a shot, cleared off his coughing, then announced that whisky was the only damn thing that would cure that cough. Before long he was breathing in less smoke, but coughing more and making numerous trips to the kitchen sink. Grandma decided that more smoke and less alcohol was the best compromise and ordered me to loosen up on the tobacco rolling.

Grandpa Poling was always a source of some commotion. He had bad eczema, especially on the elbows. While he was still working at the paper mill, he tired of the itching and scaling, so he went to the sulphuric acid vat and dipped his elbows. His elbows were swathed in bandages for days afterward.

One day I arrived home from school to a huge commotion on the street and in the backyard. Grandpa had been rocking and smoking when he glanced out the rear window and saw to his amazement, a moose standing on the lawn. It was an incredible sight considering the house was only a couple of blocks from downtown. Ignoring my grandmother's pleas not to do anything rash, he ran to the summer kitchen where the old .38-55 rifle was hanging, then walked out the back door and shot the moose dead. This display of urban hunting skills did not amuse the police and conservation officers, but they didn't press the matter, probably because of his age.

Sometimes Grandma dispatched me to walk down the Van Norman Street hill to meet him when he was returning from a trip to the beer parlour. She worried about him crossing streets when he had been drinking because he wore hearing aids that distorted his hearing in traffic. She would have walked to meet him herself, but her deformed heart valve prevented her from climbing the hill.

One day he was late and Grandma sent me to the beer parlour to fetch him for supper. Twenty-one was the Ontario drinking age and I was eighteen but looked twelve. I entered the Waverley Hotel downtown and peered through the doorway of the men's side (beverage rooms were separated into Men's and Women and Escorts' in those days). He was sitting alone. I tried to get his attention and finally did. He waved me in. I signalled him to come out, but he was insistent that I come to the table. I approached cautiously, watching for waiters, and he ordered me to sit down. No sooner than my butt brushed the chair than a waiter was all over us, saying that I would have to leave.

Grandpa had had a couple and I could see his stubborn streak stiffening the grey bristles of his crew cut. He shot back belligerently that I was Ray's boy and he wanted me to join him. The waiter protested but the old man held firm, noting that I had been old enough to bury my father the previous fall. His eyes moistened behind the thick-rimmed glasses that had the hearing aids built into the sides.

The waiter scanned the room. It was an hour before evening shift change at the paper mills and grain elevators and the place was near empty. He dropped four glasses of beer and told us to drink them fast, then get out. The glasses were the ones with the narrow bottoms and fluted tops where the white "hit" line was painted. This was the line mandated by the government to ensure bartenders did not serve patrons short beers. I took my first gulp. I had never tasted draft beer, which was wonderful with a tangy taste and a salty bite. There I was drinking beer in a beer parlour with a bush legend, my grandfather. Wait 'til the guys heard that I had been drinking at the Waverley!

My grandmother was happy to see me back with him for supper but was suspicious about why I had been gone so long. She had a habit of stepping up close and breathing in deeply when she thought any of her boys had been drinking. I had tried to conceal the odour with peppermints, but judging by the looks she gave my grandfather that night, I think she suspected that I had been officially initiated into the Poling branch of the John Barleycorn Society.

A few months later, I arrived home from school and the house was empty and deathly quiet. This was unusual because with boarders someone always was around. There were no supper preparations in the kitchen, no tantalizing dish simmering on the stove. I shrugged and sat down at the dining table to do homework, and not long after a procession of uncles and aunts arrived holding grandpa. I thought for a moment they had picked him up at the Waverley, because he was unsteady on his feet and was weeping. Then they told me that Grandma had taken a spell earlier in the day and had died in the hospital just down the hill.

The big house on Van Norman felt hollow and empty of the sounds and smells of her presence. Never again would I smell the golden sweetness of homemade batter steaming in the double waffle iron, nor hear the wet hiss of the steam table she used for pressing sheets and pillowcases and my slacks. She had been the epicentre of a gentleness that filled every corner and crack of the house.

After she left, our lives fell into a numbing routine. The boarders came and went, pretty much minding their own business. Grandpa woke me early every morning for school and I put out bowls of cereal and he made coffee. On Sundays he made his famous Mulligan stew in a ridiculously huge aluminium pot. When the dishes were washed, he set the pot out in the unheated summer kitchen where it sat in the cold until the next day when I removed it and reheated it for supper. Then I put it back until Tuesday and so on until it was finished.

For Fridays grandpa would order a piece of lake trout from Wilmot and Siddall, the little grocery store where all the Polings still bought their groceries. Grandpa fried it and served it with boiled potatoes. We had our choice of canned corn or canned peas and for dessert there were canned peaches, pears, or cherries. Some Fridays he forgot to order the fish and we had kippered snacks with boiled potatoes and one can of vegetables, but I could not get that smoked fish anywhere near my mouth and ate only the vegetables.

It was my final year of high school, but the prospects of a university education were looking slim. My mother wrote that she didn't have the money. I was awash in hopelessness as I sat at the grand walnut table in my grandmother's dining room, filling out university applications perhaps thinking the tuition fees suddenly would appear. I had ten dollars from an uncle and ten dollars from my grandfather to support the applications. But submitting the applications was futile and deep inside, I knew it. There were promises of help from family, but I knew no one could support me through years of university. I knew what everyone was thinking: there had been some tough breaks and there was nothing to do now but go out, get a job, and live life like everyone else. Dad never would have accepted it. He saw in me his dream of a university education. The fact that I would not surely worsened the aching emptiness that I felt and still feel more than four decades after his death.

In the meantime, I needed to work through the summer. The Prince Arthur Hotel, then Port Arthur's version of the Park Plaza and overlooking the Big Lake, rehired me. I had worked there the previous summer as a bellhop, but all they could offer me was pool attendant, a huge drop in prestige and money. The tips were terrific as a bellhop — the Four Aces, in town for a concert, once gave me five dollars for carrying their luggage. Then there were the side businesses, supplying booze after hours and women. I was too naive to be brought into the hooker business, but I did turn a few bucks bootlegging booze that I obtained through cab drivers.

The pool job was boring. I opened and cleaned the pool just after dawn each day. It took a couple of hours to vacuum, clean the filters, do the chemicals, and scrub down the scum ring. The rest of the day was spent keeping the pool furniture organized, running errands for guests and of course acting as lifeguard. I still hadn't learned to swim and the management knew it, but I had instructions on how to fish a drowning person out with a pool hook or pitch them a life ring.

Working the pool had some special fringe benefits. Often families would check in with teenage girls and I got to meet them at the pool. Later in the summer, one of the grandstand acts for the Canadian National Exhibition moved into the hotel for the week. The act was the June Taylor Dancers from the Jackie Gleason TV show. Most of the girls were in their late teens, gorgeous, loved the pool, and wore bikinis. I fell over every piece of furniture at the pool while scrambling to fetch them Cokes, towels, suntan lotion. Their smallest wish was my command.

After they left, a tall and handsome guy in his late twenties began coming to the pool. He was a professional diver in town for a salvage job. He spent a lot of time at the pool and we talked, he telling me stories about dives around the world and how he almost drowned one time in an accident off Jakarta, a place I had never heard of. I told him I would love to learn how to dive, but never mentioned I didn't know how to swim.

One morning he arrived at the pool with diving gear, mask, snorkel, fins, wet suit, and a lead diving belt. He geared me up, showing me how to use all this stuff. Then he showed me how to wear the lead belt and told me to jump off the diving board. I was now well over my head in this charade. I duck-walked onto the diving board, took a deep breath, and jumped. My fins hit the pool bottom and I stayed there. I tried thrashing my arms and kicking my feet, but the weight belt anchored me to the pool floor. The belt had a quick release and I found it and popped to the surface like a cork. I told him that was great, but now I had to get back to work. I feigned an attempt to enter the water to retrieve the belt, but he dived in and picked it up, saving me the embarrassment of revealing that I couldn't swim to the bottom and bring it back.

Later in the week, I brought him a sandwich and sat chatting with him when he tapped my shoulder and pointed to the pool. A little girl had left the shallow end and was drowning under the diving board. Her mother had left her in my care and the diver, the girl, and I were the only people at the pool.

"Go to work," the diver said, pointing to the pool.

I ran to the pool's edge. The girl was now in the middle, too far out to reach with a pole. Throwing a life ring was no good because as I approached she went down for a second time. I leaped and dog-paddled to her. She came up and grabbed me around the neck and I started to go down with her. We thrashed about, me trying to break her stranglehold on my neck but not succeeding. We went down and I gulped water. I broke one arm free and thrashed toward the edge of the pool. As we went down again, a hand caught my wrist. It was the diver, and he pulled us both out.

He admonished me for not telling him I couldn't swim. We gave the little girl artificial respiration. She was okay, but I was embarrassed.

The near tragedy at the pool reflected the low expectations I was developing for my future. It occurred during the final week of the summer when I was absorbed in trying to decide what was going to happen with my life. The summer mail had brought news that I failed two subjects and was two Grade 13 credits short of university entrance requirements. I also was short the pile of money needed for tuition and board. My grandfather had reached some kind of an agreement with my mother for room and board while I lived there. My mother had not been paying it and I had been trying to put something against it through my little salary from the Prince Arthur Hotel.

I wasn't the only one with low expectations for myself. My teachers did not express any hope for my future. Youth who have been in trouble are troubled youth, so the thinking went. Even Tom Callon seemed hesitant about my prospects. After the trial, I said that perhaps I could go to law school and become a lawyer like him. He explained that not everyone could become a lawyer, but I could train as a law clerk.

The tag of a person who has had troubles is hard to shake. I saw this clearly one day late in that summer of 1962. I made a U-turn on my motor scooter in front of my grandfather's house and did not notice an approaching car. I wheeled in front of it and it came to a screeching halt. Two angry men emerged and began berating me for being careless. One was a well-known and respected clergyman. He reamed me thoroughly explaining that there was a child in the backseat of his car. It could have been thrown forward and injured. He demanded my name, and when I gave it, he nodded knowingly that I was the Poling who was in all that trouble.

He ordered me to report to him twice a week. These meetings would help me back onto the straight and narrow. I was humiliated by the dressing down, but frightened by his threat to call the police, so I agreed to the meetings. Another visit to a police station was the last thing I needed. As he slammed the door on his car, I yelled out my real answer, which was not a nice thing to say about a man of the cloth, but what would you expect from a troubled youth?

The incident nudged me over the edge and into a scheme I had been mulling over for a couple of weeks. I decided I would leave Port Arthur like my mother. I would head for Sudbury, where Gerry Poling, the youngest of my uncles and aunts, worked as a reporter for the *Sudbury*

Star. I reckoned that he could get me a job as a reporter, if I could pull together enough money to make the trip.

I had few possessions, but I took two guns and a Mexican gold dollar piece to a pawnshop on Cumberland Street and got enough money to stake myself for some serious pool shooting. The Mexican gold piece had been a fob on my Grandfather LaFrance's Hamilton railway watch. The plan was to parlay that cash into a bigger stash by playing pool at Hanson's. I wasn't a terrific pool shot but pool can be like golf, a head game that played right can sometimes cover weak skills. I knew who I could not beat and who I might beat.

Hanson's Pool Room was on St. Paul, a stubby little street at the heart of downtown. It had operated there for decades, a hangout and meeting place for generations of young men. It was blindingly dark when entered from the sunlit street. The only light came from under the green cones that shaded the bulbs above the soft green velvet table lights. Cue racks, many with hasps and locks, lined three walls. The front of the hall was a newsstand and snack bar, where Edgar, a man with salt and pepper hair and rimless eyeglasses served up the world's best hot dogs. The buns were steamed and the mustard, relish, and diced onions were fresh. A Hanson hot dog melted in your mouth and there was no equal to it anywhere.

Edgar and a diminutive assistant racked the balls at the end of each game and collected the twenty-five-cent payment tossed onto the table surface, scooped up and deposited into the grimy grey cash aprons they wore. That was the price, two bits a game, but the play had better be reasonably quick or you got shouted at.

Hanson's was an institution. My dad and Bud Barnes had played there, skinning lesser players for cash during the Depression years. Pros or would-be pros always made a stop here during their cross-country wanderings. You could tell one when he walked through the door with a breakdown pool cue case under his arm. Guys watched a stranger play a game or two, like gunslingers sizing up the competition and deciding whether to make a challenge.

It was also a place for bad guys to hang out. The cops visited it regularly looking for one suspect or another. Often on a Friday or Saturday night they would come in, round up some of us guys and march us to the police station only steps up the street. They held us in a cell area before parading us out into a line-up before the witness of some recent crime. They genuinely needed line-up fodder, but I think they also rounded some of us up as a warning of what can happen when you slide off the straight and narrow.

The bad guys often talked in Hanson's washrooms about their heists, and sometimes there were fights around the pool tables. Toughness was part of the atmosphere, and if you didn't know how to avoid trouble, you quickly found yourself in it.

I did well at Hanson's with my pawn money. I picked my matches carefully and walked away with a small roll of bills in my jeans. As I left, I bought a hot dog from Edgar and told him I was leaving town. He looked at me, sizing me up through those rimless glasses, and growled that the only place I would end up was Stoney Mountain.

Actually I was headed in the other direction — east. I walked the block down to the waterfront and booked passage on one of the passenger ships still working the Great Lakes. I hadn't been on a big ship before, except when I was a child and our family toured the SS *Noronic*, moored at the Port Arthur dock. I was six then and someone snapped a picture of me, blond curls tossing in the wind, standing beside the deck rail. It was one of the last photos taken on the *Noronic*, a passenger ship built at the Port Arthur shipyards in 1911. A few days after our visit, it burned at Toronto's Pier 9 leaving 118 people dead. Polings on boats always seemed to bring on some disaster or other.

After booking my passage, I went to my grandfather's house and threw some clothes into a packsack and said my goodbyes. I returned to the pawnshop to retrieve my grandfather's Mexican gold piece, but the proprietor laughed and said I had sold it to him, not pawned it. There was no use arguing; the ship's whistle was blowing a few blocks away.

The ship steamed directly east out of Port Arthur on a crystal blue-sky day when the Big Lake was flat except for its ever-present swell. I looked back at a young lifetime of memories rising in its wake. Some of them weren't nice memories, but memories can't be sorted into piles of keepers and discards like photographs. You have to take them all with you, and I did, as the big ship, pistons pounding harder and harder in her belly, sailed past Nanabijou's feet and set a course for Sault Ste. Marie and for me a new, if somewhat uncertain, life.

Book Three
JOURNALISM

13 —THE GREAT DECEPTION

EXPECTATIONS FOR MY FUTURE WERE NOT GREAT WHEN I walked down the gangplank and off the boat at Sault Ste. Marie with five bucks in my pockets and one change of clothes. Veronica was joyous when I knocked on the door of her apartment atop the hill that overlooked the St. Mary's River. She had settled in well and both Barb, sixteen, and Mary Jane, nine, were back in school after their second summer in the Sault. She was ecstatic about my arrival, but anxious about my future. She didn't feel she could afford to support me for long and wanted to see me established and earning a paycheque.

My immediate prospects were thin. I was a high school dropout in a new city and without connections. I did have some work experience that might count for something. Veronica recalled my work experience in two hotels back home, the Prince Arthur Hotel as bellboy and pool attendant and the Hodder Avenue Hotel as a general basement slave who organized the hotel stock and kept it clean, dry, and away from the mice. The Hodder Avenue Hotel, owned by Carmen Sisco and his siblings, was a going concern with a booming beer parlour frequented by mill workers, a decent restaurant, and some rooms. As well, it added a swank cocktail lounge where couples could go for an evening of entertainment and a Dairy Queen across the street. Carmen liked me and one time fetched me from the basement and brought me up behind the bar in the beer parlour. As I stared wide-eyed at the guys sitting at small tables sipping draught and smoking cigarettes, Carmen placed a big hand on my shoulder and announced to anyone who could hear that one day I would be in charge of all this. Carmen died unexpectedly shortly after and my future as a hotel mogul evaporated.

Veronica fantasized about me making it in hotel management. She announced immediately after my arrival that it would be wonderful if I became a hotel manager in some exotic place where she could visit. I said that I was just passing through. My plan was to move along to Sudbury to become a reporter there with Uncle Gerry, my dad's youngest brother. She was not impressed, no doubt because my plan was so youthfully vague and because I had not yet even talked with Gerry.

She suggested I forget about Sudbury and get a job at the *Sault Ste. Marie Daily Star*, a suggestion that was the opening line of a deception that changed my life. I protested that I didn't know anyone at the *Sault Star*. Veronica's reply was swift and assured: they might not have any jobs in Sudbury, but they certainly did at the *Sault Star*, where they were looking for young reporters. She had seen an ad in the paper.

Since Veronica sometimes played loose with details, I asked to see the paper with the ad for reporters. She thought she had thrown it out, but why not go there in the morning and inquire? I did, unaware that she had worked her trick of taking a smidgen of truth and rolling it into a bigger-than-life fact.

I found the *Sault Star* building on Queen Street. It looked like a telephone exchange and might have been before the newspaper took it over. There was a telephone switchboard just inside the glass front doors and a white-haired lady with a sunburst smile directed me to the second-floor newsroom. I shifted nervously at the double-door entrance to the newsroom, waiting for someone to notice me. No one did, of course. The room was a chaotic scene in which typewriters clattered urgently, reporters shouted into telephones, and editors slapped layout rulers on the dummy pages urgently needed by the composing room as the morning deadline approached. I shuffled a few steps inside the newsroom, edging closer to a desk where a middle-age woman checked page proofs. She glanced up, taking my measure from head to foot with a look of stern kindness. I explained that I wished to apply for the advertised reporting job. She looked at me as if I had just stepped off a lake ship, which of course I had, and said I was the wrong gender. The *Star* had advertised for a reporter, but a Women's Page reporter.

My face coloured with mortification, reflecting embarrassment, and anger with my mother who had deliberately not told me the job advertised was for the Women's Page. In those days, women wrote news strictly for women and the change to lifestyles sections was still far off. I stammered that I was sorry; someone had told me they needed a young male reporter. I turned to leave and find a hole.

The woman was Nan Rajnovitch, the editor of the Women's Page, and more importantly the daughter of J.W. Curran, the founder of the *Star*. She and her siblings owned and operated the *Star*. Brother R.L. (Bob) Curran was the publisher and brother John Curran the managing editor who sat in the glassed-in office directly behind where I stood. She dropped her eyes back onto the page proofs as I backed up through the doors. Then for reasons that she could never explain, she looked up and motioned me back. She said the city desk just might need someone and that if I was willing to wait until the morning deadline passed, she would have that guy on the other side of the newsroom talk with me.

That guy was tall, thin, and balding prematurely in his midthirties. His face was red from the fast pace of getting the paper out and when he approached me later he scared the hell out of me. I didn't know it then, but Homer Foster, the *Star*'s news editor, was a shrewd judge of newspaper talent with a knack for training young reporters. His exterior was leather tough and he threw things when he became angry, but away from the news desk he was gentle and soft-spoken. He asked me a series of questions, none of which I remember except for how much money I expected to make.

I blurted the first figure that jumped into my head: $150. He turned even redder, exclaiming that even he didn't make that. I cringed, then leapt to set the record straight. I meant one fifty a month, not a week.

Foster stared incredulously at the 119-pound bone bag before him and muttered something to Mrs. Rajnovitch. She said for me to leave my number. Years later, I learned of the conversation that immediately followed my departure. Foster told Rajnovitch that he needed a junior reporter but that anyone willing to work for only $150 a month couldn't have much self-esteem. He noted that I had the appearance "of a scared little rabbit." She offered that I was just a kid and didn't have any concept of the working world, but I looked honest and bright.

I ran from the building, never expecting to return. It seemed hopeless that they would hire me after the way I performed. I talked it over with Veronica and she said maybe I should get a part-time job and enrol in high school to make up the two Grade 13 courses I had missed. I went out the next morning to think about my future. Veronica was beaming when I returned. She wore that "I-know-something-that-you-don't-know" look.

She teasingly offered that there had been a telephone call for me. This was a mystery because I knew no one in this town except her and my two sisters so who would be calling me? She said the *Sault Star* had called. Then, after some dramatic pauses, said that the *Star* wanted me to start as a junior reporter Monday morning.

I didn't believe her. I phoned a number she had scratched on a sheet of paper. It was Homer Foster. Sure enough, I was to report Monday. I would be paid $230 a month.

The journey from childhood adventures along McVicar Creek to the hard and cynical adult world of a daily newspaper is interplanetary. One is a world of youthful fantasies where all dreams are possible; the other is a field scattered with wonderful dreams sometimes fulfilled, sometimes lost on the road of life's harsh realities. I entered that world less than a week after standing on the stern deck of the ship and watching the horizon swallow Nanabijou.

The contrast between teenage life in Port Arthur and the newspaper world was never more obvious than during my first morning at the *Sault Star*. The editors assigned me a desk near the back of the newsroom, along the west side windows. The newsroom was large for a small-town operation, occupying the space of a medium-sized bungalow. It was at the rear of the second floor of the *Star* building, a modern three-storey concrete structure on Queen Street, the main drag. The west and south sides were all windows, the west ones looking into neighbouring buildings, but the south side providing an excellent view of the St. Mary's River and the U.S.A. Many newsrooms of the day were equipped with ancient furniture, dating before the Second World War and in some cases before the First. Our typewriters were relatively new and the desks were custom-made wood with plenty of drawer space. They were painted grey and had green Arborite tops.

I had plenty of time to examine my desk. I sat from 8 a.m. until about 9:30 a.m., when an editor approached and told me to practice my typing. I wasn't sure how to practice something I didn't know how to do. Almost an hour later, people stood up at their desks, then filed out through a side door. Unknown to me, morning deadline had passed and everyone was gathering to smoke and drink coffee in a lunchroom down the hall. Within a minute or two, I was alone except for one mournful soul bent over a desk in front of the clattering teletype machines delivering the news agency reports — the Canadian Press news on green paper and United Press International on yellow.

The newsroom smelled of the warm paper dust created by the rolls running through the teletypes. It mingled with the metallic smell of molten lead from the Linotype machines one floor below and the sweetness of the printer's ink on the basement presses. These

Courtesy of the Sault Star.

Sault Star newsroom late 1960s. At the main editing desk are Homer Foster (left), the author (on telephone), Jody Curran. Man with his back to the camera is the wire editor who handled copy from the news service teletypes. In the office in the background is Managing Editor John Curran.

were smells, sounds, and sights new and exciting to someone who thought newspapering was just about guys in porkpie hats trying to right the world's wrongs.

I strolled to the teletypes and glanced down into their chattering teeth, then sidled over to the man making pencil marks on the green and yellow pieces of paper. His back was bent like a comma, his forehead near touching the desktop as he pored over the copy through pop bottle lenses set in heavy black frames. I decided to break the ice. I introduced myself and asked how he liked working there.

The head, covered with wavy dark hair sprinkled with silver and far too long for the style of the day, turned slowly while no other muscle moved. It tilted and turned until the eyes pointed in my direction. They were two eggs in a Teflon frying pan, slipping unfocussed side to side, their whites rimmed with an angry red. They were unnerving and I dropped my glance down to a coffee cup that the man clutched tensely in one hand. The cup was half filled with a clear liquid I assumed was water, which was odd because it was decades before sipping water would become fashionable. As his face raised in my direction, I saw with horror that it was a mass of swollen red sores, some oozing small drops of pus. It looked like the face of a Dick Tracy character. Cracked lips, barely noticeable in the mess of inflammation, moved almost imperceptibly, emitting a mumbled stutter.

"Buh, buh, bu, bet, bet better," he stuttered miserably, "buh, buh, better than su, su, su suc-king cah, cah cah, co-ocks in a qwai, qwai, quiet cuh, count-ry stu, stu, store."

The head slowly turned back to its down position. A hand, veined and dried like a dying leaf, trembled as it raised the cup to the sore lips. The thick sweetness of exhaled alcohol wafted past my face. I backed away to my desk, shocked because I had never seen anyone trucking such a load of alcohol that early in the day.

They called him Coach, apparently from his days in sports. He was the wire editor, which meant he came to work well before dawn to sort the wire service copy and select what stories would be most interesting to the readers in the Soo and surrounding district. Starting early allowed him to quit early and by noon he was free to weave his way out of the newsroom and down the street to his favourite beer parlour. There he would drink into the evening, flop for a few hours in his apartment, and get up to scowl at a new dawn.

On my second morning, Dave Robertson, the jovial, big-boned city editor, took me aside and began filling me in on how to be a reporter. As he spoke, there was a tremendous roar, followed by a crash in the middle of the newsroom. At the news desk, Homer Foster was on his feet, red-faced and cursing some production snag, or perhaps a crank phone call put through at deadline.

"Jesus! Jesus! Jesus! Jesus!" he roared, sweeping away the pieces of the telephone he had just smashed into his desktop. Robertson put his hand on my shoulder and gave me his famous look of understatement: "Oh, and another thing you need to know about working here. Every day at this time we have prayers."

I rapidly figured out that oddballs filled the *Sault Star* newsroom and it was difficult to sort out who was normal and who was not. I guess none of us were normal. We were a mix of locals and vagabond reporters come from somewhere else and destined to move on to greener journalistic grazing spots. All were quirky. Some were alcoholics, Marxists, generally lost souls who for the most part did not have real lives beyond the newsroom. Many were young like me and yearning for the adventure and glory of setting the world right through daily newspapering.

One lost soul, named Davey, invited me out for a coffee on my third day. He held me captive telling me about his time as a commando in the Second World War. His favourite story was about sitting in a hayloft, somewhere in Europe, smoking and tossing a hand grenade back and forth. Another soldier walked past the barn door below and someone yelled: "Catch!" The soldier missed the catch and looked dumbly at the grenade by his feet, then up to the loft. By the time he returned his glance to the grenade, it exploded. Davey laughed.

I didn't know if this story was true or made up or exaggerated to impress me. I came to learn that Davey, like my mother, tended to stretch the facts. He once wrote a story about a child who miraculously survived a fall through a fourth-storey window. The child suffered only minor cuts and bruises and was treated and released from hospital. The child's mother phoned the paper to complain that although it was true the child had fallen through a fourth-storey window, it was a removable storm window that had been leaning against the house at ground level when the child tripped and fell into it.

An odd collection they were indeed, but many were determined, courageous individuals. I'll never forget young Peter Miller from eastern Ontario scanning a newspaper or a book two inches from his face, then lowering his head down to the flat of his desk to write notes. He was an albino with failing eyesight, but he was dogged in chasing a story and making sure it was accurate. He moved on to bigger papers and the last I heard he was working for the *Calgary Sun*.

Then there was Val McAdam who was married to one of the Curran girls. I didn't know his story and still don't. All I knew was that he showed up sporadically to work and when he did other reporters kept their distance, not only because he was tough and cranky, but because they had heard he was good and didn't suffer fools lightly. I first saw him one morning at a desk near mine. He was struggling to light a cigarette, so I leaped from my chair to offer my lighter.

"Bugger off," he spat.

The newsroom went as quiet as the woods on a winter day. An editor passed by and guided me back to my desk, whispering that the biggest faux pas anyone could commit in the newsroom was to try to help Val McAdam. McAdam had no hands and my first reaction, wrong as it was, was to feel sorry for him. Val McAdam despised people feeling sorry for him and with good reason. He didn't need pity or help because he got along just fine. He had a watchstrap on one arm stub and used it to hold a pencil. He took notes with the pencil then turned it around and used the eraser end for dialling the phone or turning pages. He smoked American cigarettes in soft packages and when he wanted a cigarette he bumped the package in his shirt pocket until one popped up and he bent his head and caught it between his lips. One arm was amputated just below the elbow and he would put a Zippo lighter in the crook, flip its cover with the other stub, then scratch the flint wheel. It was an amazing performance, but any person who stared suffered the heat of a McAdam tongue-lashing.

Most everyone in the newsroom had a thirst for alcoholic beverages and these were the dying days of newsroom drinking. If you needed a stiff nip to settle your nerves, you could find a bottle in most desk drawers. You needed to be twenty-one to buy liquor, and I was nineteen, so I had one of the older guys buy me a mickey for my desk. I never got the opportunity to use it because not long after, the publisher banned drinking in the newsroom. The ban had little to do with bad optics or the fact that some people were producing the news while half snapped. Publisher Curran laid down the ban the day someone, for the umpteenth time, ignored his rule that liquor bottles were not to be tossed in the wastepaper baskets. This day one smashed and a cleaner sliced his arm open from elbow to fingertips. R.L. was outraged and when R.L. was outraged, you took cover. He was a little man with dark hair closely shaved at the sides and hard dark eyes that glowered through wire frame spectacles. He had a smudge moustache like Hitler and was much feared, as were most publishers in those days.

R.L. did allow booze in the newsroom on special occasions, such as Christmas Eve. One Christmas Eve a reporter got roaring drunk and stood on the filing cabinets reading Ann Landers letters that had been mailed to the paper by readers with problems.

Most of the drinking occurred several blocks east of the *Star* at the most famous drinking spot in northern Ontario, The Victoria House. Owned and operated by John Chow and his brothers, The Vic was famous throughout the province and beyond. The Chows were amazing proprietors. They had incredible knowledge of their clientele and regularly surprised them with their amazing memories. Someone who had been gone from the Soo for years would show up during a visit and one of the Chow brothers would bring him a beer without asking. It would be the brand the person drank when they frequented the place in years past.

I once returned to the Vic after a two-year absence and Jimmy Chow recognized me immediately when I strolled in and took a seat. He sped to my table with a bottle of beer on his tray and greeted me with his delightful accent.

"Ord Wienna, Jim?" he asked.

I protested, reminding him that I drank Crystal. I hated Old Vienna beer because it turned my head green and gave me the runs. Jimmy had already snapped the cap on the bottle, but his hand had carefully covered the label. He dropped the beer and turned it with the label facing me. It was a Crystal. He put his hand over his mouth and chuckled all the way back to the bar.

The *Sault Star* gang gathered regularly at the Vic to wash away the tensions of daily newspapering. Dave Robertson, the city editor, would hold court, regaling everyone with stories in his Scottish brogue. After last call, everyone adjourned to his apartment, where dark rum flowed among a clutter of musical instruments, music stands, sheet music, and 78-rpm opera records well worn from Dave's research for his weekly opera column. How an opera column lasted so many years in that rough-and-tumble steel town is another of the *Sault Star* mysteries.

The late-night drinking sessions usually produced a catastrophe of some sort. Someone would take a tumble over a French horn and split their head. Dave fancied himself a gourmet cook late into the evenings and became famous for setting fire to his place. I often skipped the sessions at Dave's to join Veronica and her friends at one of the other beer parlours. She loved an evening with draught beer, cigarettes, jokes, and stories.

One of her favourite stories was one that she got from me and it involved the time Dave Robertson introduced me to the Queen. Queen Edith. She arrived at the newsroom door one morning carrying a shopping bag in each hand. My desk was closest to the door, so I got up and asked if I could be of help. Yes, she said, she was here to see Sir David. Sir David Robertson, the prime minister. She was elderly, kind, and quietly well-spoken, but I figured she was a whacko and was about to send her back through the doorway when a ham-like hand swept me aside. The same hand extended forward to usher this diminutive woman into the newsroom. Robertson led her to a chair near my desk, close enough that I could hear the conversation. The government was not doing something it was supposed to do and the Queen was seeking the prime minister's assistance. He nodded gravely then gently took her by the elbow and guided her in my direction.

He explained softly that young Mr. Poling was one of his newer people but quite reliable. He introduced me to Her Majesty Queen Edith and asked me to take copious notes on her problem so we could produce a story that would solve her problem.

The interview and note taking lasted forty-five minutes. The woman was completely coherent and explained her problem, which I can't recall in any detail, clearly and rationally. When it was over, she rose, shook my hand regally, said goodbye to Sir David, and departed. She appeared a couple times more over the next year or so and was ushered to the desk of the newest reporter, where she explained her problem and gave instructions on how the story should be written before gliding from the newsroom with royal waves to Prime Minister Robertson and other members of her government.

We didn't know who she was or where she lived, but somewhere back in time, she had first appeared at the newsroom door and Robertson's quick mind and kind heart decided that joining her fantasy was better than the kicking and screaming that might occur if she was subjected to the standard heave-ho given visiting whackos.

The visits of Her Majesty accented in my mind two of the realities of the *Sault Star* operation: quirkiness and uncommon fairness.

14 — DEAD PEOPLE MAKE NEWS

THE WEIGHTY BLACK PHONE RANG SO SHRILLY THAT IT rattled on the glassy green Arborite desktop. It always seemed especially shrill when delivering something big. I cradled the receiver and pulled a pencil from behind my ear. An excited female voice blurted news of an explosion. Sounded like a bomb. On James Street, right behind her house.

The voice belonged to Emma Tadashore, my mother-in-law. She and Art, my wife's dad, lived on Queen Street West, thirteen houses down from Algoma Steel No. 2 gate, but their back yard opened onto a laneway leading into James Street, the main drag for the Soo's Little Italy.

My marriage to their daughter Diane had given me the edge on anything that happened in the west end. The Tadashores and the Sanzostis, Emma's maiden name, were related to everyone. Art and Emma were young elders in the Italian community that had developed at the end of the 1800s when immigrants moved in to staff the new steel plant built where Lake Superior dumps into the St. Mary's River.

The James Street area was an olive patch of Italian culture dropped into Sault Ste. Marie's southwest corner. By the early 1960s it was firmly rooted and had spread many blocks east and north of the Algoma Steel Corp. plant. James Street itself was only three blocks long, two of them packed with Italian businesses — two grocery stores, two pool halls, two hardware stores, and an assortment of clothing establishments and other businesses. Above the brick storefronts were black wrought iron balconies where people occupying the apartments could step out, take the night air, and shout at friends below, "Eh, Rocco, come va? Che cosa fai?"

The street was alive with shouts and bustle and the colourful sights and smells of Italian market life. Walkers on the sidewalks below the balconies had to dodge baskets of Bacala, dried codfish that stood stiffly alert and waiting to be taken home to be stewed with prunes. Most of the people on the street spoke in Italian, although they could speak English. Mangiacakes, the cake-eating non-Italians from east of Gore Street, the unofficial dividing line between cultures, were viewed with suspicion.

I met Diane in the *Sault Star* newsroom during my first week as a reporter. She was the payroll clerk and hurried up to my desk to get my vital statistics. Within the year we were engaged.

One of Art's first duties as my future father-in-law was to introduce me to Jimmy Street and the Italian community. He walked me up the lane out back, along the street and to the door of a pool hall where a husky young man leaned threateningly against the doorframe. If I had gone there alone, he would not have budged, but with Art leading, he gave way and we entered a world previously secret to me. Men stood at a bar and drank aperitifs and coffee. Others sat at small tables and smoked little black cigars and cigarettes and talked with animated hands. In a back room, one group gambled with Italian cards. My entry into the pool hall's closed society told everyone that I was blessed by the Italian community and should be treated like one of them.

My plunge into this new culture did not impress Veronica. She remembered my dad's stories of growing up in the Soo and running with the Gore Street gang, who hung out at Therriault's Pool Hall. They were all Mangiacakes who occasionally ventured into James Street territory to fight with the Italian boys.

In Port Arthur we had little contact with Italians or any other ethnic groups. There were a couple of Italian kids at St. Andrew's. And the guy who ran the soda fountain near the school also was Italian. Many Italians lived and worked over by the coal docks in Fort William, but far removed from our neighbourhoods.

Veronica saw me pulled into the Italian society and away from our family. She didn't like it and would have preferred me to spend more time with her and my sisters. But sons often follow their wives' families and she slowly accepted it and Diane, although she continued to exert her influence in odd ways. When our first child was born, Veronica wanted him named Raymond, for obvious reasons, but we decided on James Raymond. Veronica put a birth notice in the *Sault Star* announcing the arrival of her grandchild, Raymond. She started calling him Ray, then settled into Jimmy-Ray.

Meanwhile, my mother-in-law's urgent telephone call had found me racing my Volkswagen Beetle into the west end where I stood and viewed with amazement what was left of James Street Hardware. Police, firefighters, and ambulance workers scrambled through the rubble left by what appeared to have been a bomb blast. Witnesses said there had been a muffled explosion on the street and the hardware store caved in. Incredibly, people inside escaped, except for one worker, Bobbie Fera, who someone recalled had been in the basement. The emergency crews worked like fiends clearing a path into the basement, but when they found him it was too late. They pulled him out, bloody and broken. His death was attributed to an explosion caused by a gas line leak. Gas had seeped into the basement and when Bobbie flicked on an electrical switch, or maybe even a cigarette lighter, the place went boom.

The explosion was national news and it had a major impact on my future. The Canadian Press (CP), the national wire service, wanted every word it could get on the explosion because initially it was feared that many more people were dead. I set up a command post in a store across the street and telephoned the latest details to CP. I got everything before anyone else because of my blessed status on the street.

CP is the news co-operative owned by the daily newspapers in Canada. It gathers news from around the country and the world and distributes it to its member newspapers and radio and television outlets. Membership in CP requires newspapers to provide CP with all the news from their coverage areas. Member newspapers were obligated under the co-operative agreement with CP, so I had to file my explosion reports to the CP bureau in Toronto. The coverage gained me attention among CP executives who took notice of young reporters out in the sticks and tucked the information away for future recruiting.

I discovered that day the exhilaration of doing news on the fly. Dictating stories composed as you talked into the phone was the ultimate challenge — telling the story as it happened, yet always straining to be completely accurate. It infected my blood that day. Getting fresh information that no one else had; flinging yourself onto the typewriter when under a deadline; riding the razor's edge between speed and accuracy. Nothing could duplicate the hot blood rush of getting the story and getting it into print. No drink, no drug was as fast and strong as the breaking story. Filing to CP heightened the exhilaration because CP's deadlines were every minute, not once or twice a day like daily newspapers.

The rush was short-lived, however. When the story was yesterday's news, there was a sadness accompanied by the realization that the story that had given you such a jolt had caused grief to others. I knew Bobbie Fera and his death was a shock, but newsroom life taught me one of the principal laws of newspapering: dead people make news.

There were lots of James Street Hardware–type stories. Other explosions, drownings, horrific car crashes, airplanes downed in the bush. We lived off the tragedies of the community, tragedies that people wanted to read about in detail. Some of those stories haunt me. Decades later, I still see a pair of little girl's empty mittens clinging to the edge of the ice out on the St. Mary's River. I can almost hear her cries for help and see her succumbing to the cold and slipping away.

The girl was eleven years old and her parents had split. After school each day she went to her grandparents' house, which faced the river on Bay Street. This day she became bored and crossed the street and climbed a high snowbank beside the river. She walked out to play on the ice but fell through.

I tagged along with a cop assigned to the search and we found little footprints trailing over the snowbank. We followed them onto the ice. They ended at a hole and a pair of blue woollen mitts frozen to the edge. The little girl had clung to the ice not more than a couple hundred yards from one of the busiest streets in Sault Ste. Marie. The snowbanks blocked a view of her from the street and deadened her calls for help. She clung for God knows how long, no doubt crying and calling until her little body succumbed and she slipped out of her mitts and into the icy depths below. I watched the police recover bodies over the years, often children with lifeless eyes and open mouths and often felt the urge to look at the sky and scream: why do you hurt these little children?

Bush searches were common around the Soo. One of the saddest was for a young man lost behind Devil's Lake. He was in his early twenties and was staying at his parents' cottage. He went off hunting alone and never returned. Searchers found a spent casing from his rifle and surmised that he saw a moose, shot at it, perhaps wounding it, then chased it into the bush. During the chase, he lost track of where he was and wandered in circles for hours, if not days. The temperatures were below freezing at night and the searchers fought against time to find him alive.

The search lasted a week, ending tragically when we found the body under a pile of brush. The young guy had clawed out a shallow hole in the ground and partially covered himself with brush to keep warm. In his hands was a partially chewed chocolate bar. He was so cold that he couldn't undo the wrapper and had tried to gnaw through the frozen bar, foil and all.

These were exciting stories that chewed at you when the action slowed and you were alone. They were easier when you had company, someone to talk to, especially a photographer.

One *Sault Star* photographer I always liked working with was Stan Stratichuk, a great shooter who tended to flush red and stutter when he got excited. One late winter day, we investigated city ditches that posed a danger to kids because they were deep, filled with runoff and lightly frozen over. We found a ditch where a child had almost drowned. It was five feet deep and crusted with a half inch of overnight ice. We found a wooden pole, which I was to ram through the ice to illustrate the depth of the ditch. Stan suggested I go to the other side of the ditch where I could hold onto a picket fence, lean out over the ditch, and get the pole standing straight up and into the ditch. What happened next was inevitable and had all the characteristics of a slapstick comedy routine.

Stan, peering through his SpeedGraphix camera, urged me to lean forward. A bit more. Just a bit more to get the pole standing straight up. I was almost horizontal to the ditch, my fingers gripping the top of one picket. I heard two cracks, one of the picket snapping, the other of the ice breaking as I hit it head first. My breath left me as if sucked away by a giant vacuum. I bobbed to the surface, fighting to breathe, but my lungs seemed frozen shut. I was about to go down again when Stan put down his gear, grabbed me, and pulled me out.

The woman of the house with the weak picket fence came out and rushed me inside where she ordered me to remove all my clothes. She gave me towels, then a pair of her deceased husband's pants and a shirt. They were XXL and at 119 pounds, I was virtually a pool cue with ears. I couldn't wear the offered belt and the widow found me a piece of rope to hold up the pants. I was some sight as we marched into the newsroom, shuffling with rolled-up pant legs and clutching the rope around my waist. At the news editor's desk, Homer Foster looked up, absorbed the scene, and growled a question. I struggled to talk and hold up my sagging clothes while Stan turned red and stuttered.

Foster growled again, ordering Stan into the darkroom to develop the photo of me drowning. Stan grew purple and was babbling out of control now. There was no picture of me drowning because he had dropped his camera to save me.

Foster roared. Did he understand this correctly? A professional newspaper photographer had stopped shooting to save a reporter from drowning? He looked incredulous, then mumbled something about drowning pictures being priceless; reporters were a dime a dozen.

Stan never lived down missing that photo, and I had to bear merciless teasing about the widow who had dressed me.

Stan and I were assigned to cover some scientific experiment out in Michipicoten Harbour, north of the Soo. We were to do stories and photos from a ship that was setting off depth charges in Lake Superior. Recording stations in both the U.S. and Canada would measure the shock waves. At the last minute, those in charge refused Stan permission to board the ship because there was not enough space. I had my own camera and Stan gave me a quick briefing on what pictures to look for before I sailed off into the black night.

U.S. Navy personnel were in charge of the explosives. They wired a giant crate — as big as a small bathroom — on the deck of the ship. A crane arm was to lower the package into the water after the final connections were made. These final connections were the responsibility of a U.S. naval officer expert in bombs, torpedoes, and other things that make a big bang. Everyone gathered at the crate to witness the last few minutes of preparation. The officer took a wire in each hand and slowly began to bring them together. The image told the story perfectly I thought, so I raised the camera and hit the shutter release. My camera equipment was not as up-to-date as that of the photographer waiting back on shore. In fact, my flash used old-fashioned bulbs, which produced a blinding light and sometimes exploded. This one did, illuminating the ship deck for yards around with a flash of white light and yellow flame.

The naval officer stood frozen in time in my camera, fingers joining the wires, eyes wide with surprise, face twisted in shock. There was a collective sucking in of breath from the assembled observers and helpers, then the officer leaned fully forward and spat through compressed lips, "Son, never ever do that again." He turned and walked to the deck rail to gather his wits before returning and making the connection.

Probably nothing illustrates better the differences between the 1960s and the new century than my dealings with two chiefs of police during my Soo years. The first was Chief Robertson, who had been there for years. I visited him every morning before picking up the police blotter of overnight occurrences and we often talked and drank coffee. He was nearing retirement and I was still a teenager, but we got on well and always had something to say to each other. He was the handgun registrar for the area, and when I expressed an interest in pistol shooting, he reached into his desk, took out a pad, and issued me a permit to carry a handgun. Not only did it allow me to carry a handgun to a shooting range, it also was a high-priority permit allowing me to carry on it my person at any time.

I got deeply into handgun shooting and often competed against police teams. I even gave range instruction to some of the Soo police officers, who were horrible shots. A couple of these guys were on duty the morning of a manhunt for three desperados who had committed an armed robbery. The robbers, still carrying guns, had fled into the bush in Korah Township on the northwest side of the city. I arrived at the edge of the bush as the police were starting the search. The area was large and there were only a few officers. Two detectives I knew from the shooting range saw me and asked me if I had my gun, and if so, I should join the search. I got my gun from the shooting box locked in the trunk of the car and we plunged into the bush. I was young and foolish and didn't think about the consequences. There were armed guys in these trees, armed guys chased by armed police, and there could be shooting.

We thrashed through a large tract of bush before emerging at a farm clearing. Off to one side was a working barn with a hayloft and a rundown one-and-a-half-storey farmhouse. The farmhouse was an excellent place to hide out — anyone who watched the movies would know that — and we approached it with stealth and from different angles. To get to it, we passed the front of the barn, then one of the cops kicked in the door and yelled for the bandits to come out. No one did and a search revealed nothing.

The cops caught the bad guys later and learned that they had been hidden in the hayloft when we walked through the yard. One had sighted us with a gun and could have shot us all. That news cooled my enthusiasm for police work and helped me realize another good reason why reporters should report the story and not be part of it.

I learned this again when I received a telephone call telling me to be at a certain street corner at a certain time.

I knew the voice. It was one of the police officers I dealt with at the Soo cop shop. I walked down to the corner, was pulled into the back seat of a big black sedan, and found myself sitting beside the new chief. He was a big cop with a stare that locked your eyeballs in place and he was all business as he told me in hushed tones that the head of the Communist Party of Canada planned to sneak into town to do some secret organizing. He planned to meet in secret with some union leaders. The Cold War was on and some parts of society still saw Communism as a serious threat to democracy. The police worried about the Commies infiltrating the biggest unions in the Soo, including Local 2251 of the United Steelworkers of America, which represented thousands of workers at Algoma Steel, the lifeblood of Sault Ste. Marie. The police planned to find out the date and place of the meeting and to expose to the public the union leaders meeting with the man working to overthrow the capitalist world.

The chief decided that I would go with a plainclothes detective and stake out the movements of the president of Local 2251. Following him would lead us at some point to the big meeting. It did. After supper, he went to a downtown motel where a check with the desk confirmed that one room was rented by none other than Canada's top Commie. The detective contacted the chief and we met at a restaurant across the street from the motel.

He sat at a table in the rear shadows of the place, drumming his big fingers impatiently on the table. He outlined his plan: the cream of Sault Ste. Marie union society was in the motel across the street, lapping up Communist dogma. The best way to expose it was for me to take a camera, walk up to motel room door, kick it open, and start shooting photos. Of course, the police involvement would be a secret.

Me kick the door in and start shooting pictures? Break and enter on a group of citizens holding a private meeting? I was too naive to ask what would happen if they decided to call the police. I could hear Homer Foster roaring across his desk at me: "You did what? You kicked in the door of a motel room because you say the chief of police told you to? Have you lost your mind completely?"

I feared burning my relationship with the cops, the chief in particular. I had the best access to police matters of any reporter in the Soo and I could see it evaporating if I backed out of the plan. I said I had to alert my editor to this big story so he could plan space and went to the phone. Walter Stefaniuk was the assistant city editor of the *Sault Star*. He was one of those rare journalists with fire in the guts for the story and he was experienced. He had started at the *Star*, gone to work in the competitive British newspaper market and now had returned. He would go on to the *Ottawa Citizen* and later the *Toronto Star*. He heard my breathless recitation of the day's events, then told me not to do anything. He would be there in a few minutes. Stefaniuk joined us at the restaurant and listened patiently to the chief's plan. He looked at the chief, then at me, then across the street to the motel. "Why don't we just go and knock on the door and ask them what they are doing?"

The chief was flabbergasted. He said they wouldn't answer the door or if they did, they would slam it shut and hole up and we would never get the story. Walter got up and signalled me to bring my camera and follow him. He was shaking his head as we walked across the street. "Kick the door in? Jesus!"

He walked boldly to the door, me and camera in tow, and rapped aggressively. The rapping produced no shouts of panic or scurrying inside and was answered in good time by a mild-mannered-looking man who I recognized immediately as the leader of the Communist Party of Canada. Over his shoulder, I could see the boss of Local 2251 and the leaders of some other unions such as the woodworkers. Stefaniuk, always animated and often excitable, especially around deadline, was completely cool. He introduced us and said we would like to talk with him and take some pictures.

The top Commie, who didn't even look evil like those pictures of Lenin and Joseph Stalin, was nonplussed. He readily agreed to the interview, in roughly forty-five minutes when his meeting ended. When we returned, we conducted an excellent interview in which the leader explained his visit and the fact that freedom of association was a right in our country. He was simply sharing his beliefs with others in hopes they would pass them along to others.

We ran the story of the meeting big — top line, page one. It created a major concern about Communist infiltration of the unions but that faded quickly and today in the post-Soviet era, the entire incident seems ridiculous. It was an important moment of my career. I learned the danger of being overwhelmed by the importance of a source and from Walter Stefaniuk's cool thinking, I observed that a common sense approach is often the best approach.

15 — WOLVES DON'T BITE

THE *SAULT STAR* HAD JUST CELEBRATED FIFTY YEARS UNDER Curran family ownership when I walked wide-eyed through the double doors of its newsroom. James W. Curran (J.W.) bought it in 1901 as a weekly called the *Sault Courier*. He took it daily as the *Star* on March 16, 1912, reflecting the growth of a town booming as loudly as the blast furnaces at the young and growing steel plant in the west end.

J.W. was a marketer well ahead of his time. He gained world renown for the *Sault Star* by offering one hundred dollars to any person who could prove he had been "et" by a wolf in the District of Algoma, the *Star*'s circulation area. He used the offer to promote shamelessly Algoma, the Soo, and the *Star*. He claimed that all Canadian newspapers and half of those in the U.S. reprinted his offer, first published February 14, 1925. No one ever collected the one hundred bucks and J.W.'s fascination with wolves put the Soo and its paper on the map. He promoted the wolf theme for years, publishing *Wolves Don't Bite* in 1940 as a collection of stories about wolves and the people of Algoma. To this day, a howling wolf is part of the newspaper's logo.

Curran invested his time and money in his community because what was good for the community was good for the paper. He built it into a respected Ontario daily, which he later passed along to his sons and daughters. The active family players in the 1960s were Publisher R.L. (Bob) Curran; Managing Editor John Curran; Women's Editor Nan Curran Rajnovitch; and her sister Catherine McAdam, who also worked on the Women's Page. They produced a variety of grandchildren, many of whom entered the family business as reporters.

The *Star* operated on old-fashioned values because it was a family paper with a lot of family history wrapped into the business. The family understood that the paper was not just a means of family support; it was a community service. As Ben Bradlee, the famous editor of the *Washington Post,* wrote in his memoirs, family papers operated as a sacred trust. The family put significant resources into covering the community. As city editor later, I had twelve city staff and six photographers. That did not include two district staff, several women's staff, plus the sports people, and two editorial page editors. We had a full library that consumed a large corner of the newsroom and staffed by two librarians.

We didn't have mission statements and corporate goals in those days, but everyone on staff knew the job was to inform readers and let them develop their own opinions. Our work was to gather information honestly and present it accurately and fairly. The newspaper's owners and the society of the time demanded fairness. In seven years at the *Sault Star,* I never was asked to slant a story or to do anything I thought went against the grain of good journalism. There were no special favours for anyone, including the judge who arrived at my desk one day and pleaded with me to keep the name of a relative out of the paper. When I refused, he went to the publisher. Bob Curran never mentioned the judge's visit and the name appeared in the paper the next day.

Publisher Curran was austere and demanding, but he never interfered to seriously compromise the editorial product. Except when he decided to write himself. He did not inherit J.W.'s storytelling and writing abilities. J.W.'s *Wolves Don't Bite* is filled with well-written images presented in a snappy newspaper style. The writing reflects a storyteller who paints his tales on the page, often with tongue-in-cheek and with good humour. R.L. was the dullest writer I ever edited.

R.L. sometimes took trips and wrote about them. Once he went to Moscow with a delegation of newspaper executives and this produced a massively boring series on the USSR. Several times, he went on vacation to Mexico, each trip producing long and detailed travelogues. I had the misfortune of having to edit much of the Mexico series, which the newsroom dubbed Mexico, Son of Mexico, and Return of the Son of

Mexico. It was brutal work because of the tormenting urge to slash-and-burn and rewrite what was before you. He detailed every living moment of the trips, including drinks at bars and dinners in restaurants. Airplane rides. Conversations with Camilla, his wife. However, considering that he was publisher, we held editing down to spelling and grammar although never once did he interfere with the editing of his own stuff.

Some of the third generation of Currans were bright and talented and would have been capable of carrying the torch that J.W. had lighted and passed along. However, in the late 1960s the newspaper business began to change. The small guys — papers operating in small and medium towns — often were family businesses that had plugged along until they found themselves confronted with rising costs and aging plants that required huge amounts of capital to upgrade. The *Sault Star* was one of these. Its three-storey concrete home downtown was cramped. Parking was a problem even though much main street activity was moving out to the shopping malls. Circulating with trucks from the cramped downtown lot was problematic. Plus, the paper needed new printing equipment, a major expense. The Curran family was aware of all this and struck a committee to look into a new location, new building, and new presses. It found a site out of downtown near the northern highway, but as the plan took shape the family realized that a new building, presses, and the move required huge funds.

Thomson Newspapers lusted after the *Sault Star*. Thomson was a large corporation that got its start in northern Ontario when Roy Thomson, badly near-sighted but with a sharp vision for squeezing nickels out of little newspapers, bought the *Timmins Press*, then began building an empire of small papers and radio stations. Thomson, who later went to Britain and became a lord, had a reputation of being stingy, not spending on news, and using his papers as bank machines — taking lots more out than he put back in.

The Curran family, faced with the physical rebuilding of the paper, began to think about selling it. There were eighteen family shareholders with opinions split on whether to sell or move on into a new era. None of them wanted to sell to Thomson because of fears that he would skim the gravy of advertising and leave the readers little worthwhile news content.

Eventually the family did sell, but not to Thomson. They sold to Southam, a growing family-rooted newspaper corporation with a reputation for its willingness to spend money on news. Thomson offered a third more money, but the family sold to Southam because they figured it would carry on the family tradition of newspapering not simply for profit. This was a fine gesture, but in the end it didn't matter. Years later the dark shadow of newspaper corporatization would move over the entire industry, blotting out any remnants of good old-fashioned newspapering where making money was not the only, or even primary, goal. Southam itself would be swallowed later by the would-be media baron Conrad Black, who would eventually become yet another master of corporate disasters.

The Currans sold the *Star* in 1975. But in 1969 there were no thoughts of it being anything other than the comfortable family operation it always had been. That presented a problem for me. Family newspapers meant the family members got priority in most things. I wasn't family and that was a huge obstacle in getting ahead. I had moved through the ranks — more and more senior reporting jobs, columnist, assistant city editor, then city editor. I could be city editor forever, reasonably happy in my small pond and close to Diane's family and mine. Or, I could think about breaking out, leaving the comfort of families behind and jumping into the big leagues of journalism beyond the Soo.

An event in 1968 helped me make my choice. I needed an assistant city editor. There wasn't anyone I wanted in the newsroom, so I suggested to John Curran that we bring the best person I knew from the outside. That happened to be his son Jody, who had been working for the *Kitchener Record*. He was a good newspaperman, and I did not think of the repercussions of having one of the family working beneath me. It was not long before I felt Jody's breath — real or imagined — on the back of my neck.

My progress during my seven years at the *Star* delighted and amazed Veronica. My work was stable and interesting and Diane and had produced two grandchildren — Marcella having arrived on Valentine's Day 1967, two years to the day exactly after her brother Jim. Veronica was starting to see some fulfilment in her life after those years of tragedy upon tragedy.

She also had moved on in her personal life. Not long after I settled into the *Star* and married, she was seeing Bill Brooks, a divorced Algoma Steel foreman. A month or so after my marriage in 1964, she phoned me and announced that she and Bill had gone over the river to Michigan to be married. Until my wedding, I had been living with her and my sisters in an apartment building on MacDonald Avenue, and she knew I would never tolerate Bill in the place while I lived there. Now that I was gone, she decided to marry him. I was not happy with her decision, but it wasn't my business.

The MacDonald Avenue apartment sat on the hilltop facing south, so it had a view of the St. Mary's River valley. The view became an important source of information in my job because on many mornings someone at the Canadian Press news agency in Toronto would call and ask me if there was fog in the St. Mary's River. At first, I thought it was a joke, but then realized that the fog held up shipping and delayed ships were news to other newspapers along the St. Lawrence Seaway. So when CP called to ask if there was fog in the river, I had to stop what I was doing, run to the back of the newsroom, and look out the window. Sometimes I would run back to my desk and shout into the phone that it was so foggy I couldn't see out the window!

To eliminate this frequent annoyance, I recruited Veronica to step out onto her balcony on grey mornings and telephone me with any reports of river fog. It connected her to my working life and gave us an opportunity to talk.

I had a lot of contact with CP beyond fog reports. I was responsible for ensuring that Soo news that was of interest outside the Soo was filed quickly to CP's Toronto office. When it wasn't, I heard from Jim Bastable, CP's Ontario bureau chief. Jim was elfish — he liked to joke and laugh — and during our talks, he often kidded me with the line: "So how long left in your sentence in the Soo?"

In 1969 I shocked him by replying: not long. The next day I received a call from John Dauphinee, who was about to take over as CP's general manager from the legendary Gilles Purcell, who was retiring. This began a long love-hate relationship between me and CP. Dauphinee, tall and urbane with a shock of white hair, cut close on the sides, and steely blue eyes, said there was a job in Toronto and someone had told him that

I might be able to cut it. His voice carried an inflection that he rather doubted I had what it takes. Whether I did or not was academic at that point. I was a northern Ontario boy imbued with a northerner's disdain for the asphalt jungle of Toronto and had no intention of living in the Toronto morass. Northern Ontario people had a different culture, a different way of seeing and approaching things.

A couple weeks later he called back. How about Edmonton? I was excited. Alberta. The West. I had visited the Prairies and B.C. through the Air Cadet summer program and was caught by the pioneer spirit of life there. I was definitely interested but wanted to visit CP in Toronto first to see how it operated and to discuss the deal. Wrangling over expenses started immediately and ended with CP reluctantly paying half my gasoline expenses to drive the seven hundred kilometres to Toronto.

CP's head office was on University Avenue in the heart of the Toronto jungle. It was a squat, compressed little building that inside reminded me of the contents of someone's stomach. It was a jumble of paper-strewn desks and homely grey teletype machines, the hum and clatter of which never ceased. The place had a Second World War look. A guy wearing a green eyeshade sat at a central desk barking orders to editors at desks around him.

Dauphinee quizzed me hard, probing for my weaknesses, and finally he found one. I admitted there were times when I got fed up working six or seven days a week directing people who often couldn't match me in terms of work ethic and talent. He replied that I likely couldn't hack it at CP then; it would be like jumping out of the frying pan into the fire. Zap. I had displayed ego, a mortal sin in CP.

He meant the barb to deflate my ego and I resented it. I said I would think about all this and walked out of his office. On the way out, I stumbled into a dark-haired, skinny man. He knew who I was and introduced himself. He was Doug Amaron, the chief editor, former war correspondent, and a great guy. He invited me over to a desk where we sat and chatted. During the conversation, I showed the resentment I carried out of the Dauphinee interview and told him I planned to stay in the Soo.

Amaron smiled and said that everything he had heard about me indicated I would make a terrific CP man. Dauphinee was just trying to test my mettle. I immediately liked Doug and trusted him. I decided to accept the job.

In the following years, Dauphinee and other CP people would stick more pins in my ego. Not long after I joined the company, Dauphinee showed up at the Edmonton bureau just after 6 a.m. No doubt he expected to sit there waiting for a sleepy head editor to arrive late to open the bureau. I was already there, only because our new twin babies had awakened me in the night and I decided to go to work early to escape.

He was surprised and seemingly disappointed to find me busy at the main editing desk. We made small talk and he mentioned offhand that there was a letter in my mail slot. My heart bumped across the back of my tongue. Now what? I had passed the probation period for new staff, but maybe they had changed their minds.

I sauntered over to the mail slots, a homemade wooden pigeonhole effort that was classic CP furniture. I opened the letter. It was from Dauphinee and announced I had won the CP Story of the Month Award for a feature on the Battle of Batoche in Saskatchewan. Dauphinee stood across the room watching closely for my reaction, which was downright joyous. In those days, CP's very best writers won the awards and I had nailed one in less than a year. He noted that it was "not a bad piece," but as one of the judges he had voted for someone else's work because it was much better. Zap. The hissing of my ego flowing through the dagger hole in my back was heard all the way to Red Deer.

The thought of leaving the Soo to work for CP in Edmonton was frightening. This would be an emotional upheaval of major earthquake proportions. The *Star* was the only real workplace that I had known. I entered the newsroom as a boy of nineteen and in 1969 stood there as a man of twenty-six. It had been my life, a place where I fit in after the turbulence of my teenage years. It had taught me to report and write, and most importantly, to think. My guts churned at the thought of not being there, of being somewhere else where I might not do as well as I had at the *Star*.

I had done well there, a pathetically naive and uneducated boy who had worked up to city editor. The Currans were good to me, paying me what I was worth, $160 a week in the end; sending me on courses; and creating an atmosphere for me to learn every day. Much had changed in my life: every day I learned immense amounts about newspapering and living. I had a wife, a house, and two kids. However, one thing would never change. I would never be a Curran, and it was obvious that only Currans would occupy the top spots at the paper while the family owned it. I was restless and had a yearning to move on, to live in other places, and experience other things. I knew I had to leave and take my chances.

In August 1969, we packed up our lives and prepared to begin a great adventure in the West. Homer Foster was sad to take my resignation but said he always knew I would leave and that my personality was a good fit for western culture.

A new job, new city, and a new life warranted a new suit. So, during my final week in Sault Ste. Marie, I strolled across Queen Street to Davis Clothing for a fitting. Davis Clothing was a family store on the northeast corner of Queen and Bruce Streets. The building with its apartments above the store was described by Morley Torgov in his hilarious memoir about the Soo, *A Good Place to Come From.*

Murray Davis, who ran the store with his brother and who was active in community affairs, measured me. As he moved his tape from point to point, we talked about journalism and his view of how it often can be a destructive force. He saw journalism as a negative business that did too little to help build society. As I was leaving the store, he shook my hand and looked at me over his tailor's glasses.

"Good luck, Jim. And whatever you do, be a builder."

Be a builder. Don't tear things down unless you plan to rebuild them better. Nothing worthwhile is built on negativism. That message reverberated often in my head, never louder than decades later when corporatization grabbed the newspaper business by the throat and began to rip the life from it.

I hooked up our fourteen-foot travel trailer to the car, settled the kids in the back seat, and honked and waved as we pulled away from the curb at Diane's parents' home in Little Italy. Relatives lined the sidewalk, weeping and waving a long Italian goodbye.

16 — CP: THE EGO BUSTERS

THE BIGNESS OF THE WORLD BEYOND SAULT STE. MARIE WAS obvious when we left the Ontario bush and crossed the Manitoba border. The Prairies stretched in a seemingly never-ending flatness, although we were surprised by the hills and valleys left by the ancient glaciers, then the rivers, and smaller streams. We camped in parks whenever it got dark and sat by fires, awed at the hugeness of a sky not blotted out by trees. After five days, Edmonton appeared as a smudge on the horizon, but soon we were into it, threading our way through its low-slung buildings, many with western fronts. There were few tall buildings then. The Chateau Lacombe, with its revolving restaurant top, was new, but it didn't look like a real skyscraper like the ones in Toronto.

I gave no thought to the fact that Edmonton was Veronica's birthplace. I recalled that my grandparents lived out West briefly. Beyond that, all I knew about her family was what she had told me in the shipwrecked ancestor story. I remained intrigued by why she told me the story and by the manner of the telling. And, of course, I had no inkling that I would leave Edmonton in a few years, only to return almost forty years later to comb its libraries and archives for information about her birth.

None of this was on my mind as I wandered Jasper Avenue, a historic main street of the former trading post and now provincial capital, oil town, and Gateway to the North. Its population had almost quadrupled since the 1947 oil strike at Leduc, just south of the city. In 1969 the population was nudging 425,000, many of whom had poured in from the

Alberta countryside and other provinces. I was fascinated by the people, the city, and the Prairies. Homer Foster was right; the place suited my personality. People were relaxed and trusting, filled with a pioneer spirit. Attitudes were similar to those in northern Ontario, where often we shot from the hip but always got the job done and done on time. The Prairies were excitingly different, overflowing with interesting stories. The politics were bizarre with Harry Strom's Social Credit succumbing to the new Conservative dynasty and Ross Thatcher ruling Saskatchewan like a pint-sized czar.

The CP bureau was in the Canadian National Railway's building on Jasper Avenue, kitty-corner from the Macdonald Hotel. A metal mesh screen was bolted across the windows overlooking the street to block the sun and to prevent distractions. The bureau consisted of a wire room, lunch room, bureau chief's office, and a wide-open newsroom space. The desks were tables with black metal legs supporting metal tops covered with a thick linoleum-like substance coloured dirt brown or bile green. The office smelled of paper dust and human sweat. When the people exuding the sweat spoke, they usually shouted over the constant thumping clatter of dozens of teletype machines lining the east wall.

There were about eighteen people on staff, supervised by a bureau chief and a news editor. There were correspondent points in Calgary and Regina, and Edmonton also was responsible for collecting news from and about the Northwest Territories and Yukon.

The work was brutally demanding. The bureau operated on shifts covering twenty-one hours a day, grinding out news and sports, taken in from member newspapers, radio and TV stations, freelances, and from direct reporting. Staff pounded out stories on old typewriters, then teletype operators punched them into the tape reading machines that fed the news wire. The pace was furious, accompanied by a relentless pressure to be accurate.

It was disheartening work at times. There was none of the public recognition and other glories I had experienced as a high-profile writer, columnist, and editor at the *Sault Star*. CP expected its staff to toil anonymously in the service of its member newspapers. This was a co-operative, a collective effort in which individual heroism was not encouraged. The newspapers that paid our salaries often viewed us with disdain, lower-paid hacks who wrote to a wire service formula.

The Edmonton staffers, like the people at the *Sault Star*, were interesting and quirky. One used to steal other people's lunches; one ran off with the bureau secretary, leaving their respective spouses stunned. They were a mixture of drones who did their work as directed and some smart, independent journalists who learned how to work around CP's style dictates and military precision and develop their own style.

The culture of CP from London, England, to Victoria, B.C., was railway-military nurtured by a management shaped by two world wars and the railways that initially held the monopoly on the nationwide transmission of information. The culture stressed the importance of the system and its mission, less on the individuals who made it work.

Outrageous individuals were not in short supply at CP, however. Gilles Purcell, who retired several months after I joined, was a legend as CP's top boss. The story goes he was watching a practice parachute drop in England during the Second World War when a bundle hit him, causing him to lose a leg. I can't remember whether the amputation was above or below the knee, a knowledge lapse that was a mortal sin at CP. Every CP story mentioning a leg amputation had to say whether the limb was lopped off above or below the knee, and if it didn't, the writer heard the wrath of Gilles Purcell.

Purcell was demanding and that attribute became a CP trademark. On social fishing trips, he demanded that schedules be met to the minute, toothpicks be placed on the camp table with all fat ends up, and cans be stacked on shelves with the label fronts all facing out.

I once saw a letter from him to a Vancouver bureau chief who wanted to add half a staffer to the Vancouver complement. The bureau chief supported his request with pages and pages of notes and calculations justifying the proposed staff addition. Purcell's letter crushed any hope for extra staff help. It said: "I want you to cease immediately these delusions of grandeur."

Purcell drank Mount Gay Barbados rum and copious amounts of it were available on fishing trips. During one ice fishing expedition on Lake Simcoe, north of Toronto, considerable Mount Gay was consumed against the cold, while the participants sheltered in a heated ice shack.

The shack had a large rectangle cut through the floor to allow several or more fishermen to dangle their lines into the lake. There is a story of how Purcell got up from his seat to exit the building for some outside relief. He stumbled and fell into the ice-fishing hole. His artificial leg, which he called Barney, became unattached in the thrashing and sank to the bottom of the lake. This was disaster of Himalayan proportions. Barney, Purcell's famous leg, lost at sea! Fortunately, they were fishing in shallow water and Barney was located and fished out.

One of the most memorable staffers in Edmonton was Lorne Bruce, an older staffer who suffered from either multiple sclerosis or muscular dystrophy, I did not know which one. Lorne hunted and pecked at keys at an excruciatingly slow pace. Papers fumbled and fell from his hands, his speech was sometimes incomprehensible as he stuttered and slurred his words. When he stood to walk away from his desk, he looked like he would topple over. But his eyes were afire with determination and there was nothing that could stop him from getting the story done.

Anyone talking to Lorne on the telephone and not knowing his condition would have been convinced CP was staffed by incompetents. This was always a problem at CP. Newspaper staff seldom saw CP staffers at work in their bureaus and did not develop an understanding and appreciation of their work. CP editors were good dogs to kick because the CP culture of service to its members meant that they seldom bit the hand that fed them.

CP-ers were tough and fast and competent, in some cases brilliant, and many had the spunk to move out of the small towns and test their competency in other places. There was an old saying that you could walk into any press club and immediately pick out the CP person. He or she was the one standing quietly at the end of the bar, the best reporter in the room, but the only one not saying so.

CP bashing was, and still is, popular. It sickened me when I first encountered it after moving to Edmonton, and over the years I would not tolerate it. One time when I had advanced to the executive ranks, I slammed the phone down on John Bassett Sr., the media czar, former owner of the *Toronto Telegraph*, and friend and confidante of important Conservative politicians. He was unhappy with something CP had reported and called me. He started the conversation by trying to push me around with many goddamns and other choice newsroom language. I asked him politely to stop swearing at me. His rage heightened and he delivered another stream of cursing through the phone. I tried to be diplomatic and asked him to stop swearing and tell me calmly exactly what his complaint was.

He screamed that no one told him to calm down and that he had been in the newspaper business before I was born. I asked him again to quit being abusive or I would hang up. The last I heard of his voice was something along the lines of "Do you know who the *&#! you're talking to?" The crash of the telephone receiver hitting its cradle, then bouncing off the desk and into the far wall was heard in the newsroom down the hall. Homer Foster had been a mentor in more ways than one, and I had learned to smash a phone with the best of them. I wrote Bassett a note saying I was sorry to have had to hang up, but they didn't pay me enough to listen to abusive language. He wrote back:

> December 7, 1989
> Dear Mr. Poling:
> Thank you for your letter of December 6 and as the holiday season looms, you should give thanks for the fact that I am no longer a Publisher or Director of Canadian Press.

Overall, work in Edmonton was exciting and fulfilling. I travelled Alberta and Saskatchewan and the far North in search of stories. Much of my reporting appeared back at the *Sault Star* where Veronica read it with interest and shared it with her friends. Some of the most interesting stories were the stories behind the stories, and I passed these along to Veronica in letters and in tapes we exchanged. I would take a tape recorder with me out onto the Prairies and dictate what I saw, especially at Native sites. Her fascination with Native culture was strong, and grew with every year. I sent her Native crafts from places that I visited and heard later that she sometimes took them to Garden River reserve at the Soo, which she began to visit more frequently just to talk to people she would meet there.

She never came to visit us in Edmonton, not once in almost four years. She pined for her grandchildren, who numbered four after the birth of the twins, Leanna and Melissa, but never made the long journey west.

The North in the late sixties and early seventies was a frontier. Late in 1969, for example, I was writing about how the Northwest Territories' government wanted to get people out of igloos at Bathurst Inlet. Many communities had no roads either leading to them or once you got there. Airstrips were the link to other communities and the outside world. You didn't travel far in the North without climbing onto an airplane, usually a small prop job on skiis or floats.

Veronica's pathological fear of flying included huge amounts of worry about anyone else who flew. She worried about my northern travel, with justification. Once I was in a plane that skidded into a snowbank. In Yukon we nearly crashed in an aborted takeoff during freezing rain. Then there was a landing gear problem in the air over Fort McPherson and an incredible near miss with a Flying Tigers transport plane over Anchorage, Alaska.

News about the North usually was about conflict. Conflicts over development, conflicts with traditional ways of life. There was the Berger Commission into pipeline development and strings of studies and meetings on the never-ending question of settling Native land claims. The best stories were about the people living their lives in an uncompromising land. The Inuk who, stranded with a broken snowmobile, fashioned a new drive shaft from a rifle barrel. The Inuit carver who killed his wife in a drunken rage and spent his days in a Yellowknife jail cell which he turned into a soapstone carving studio and produced some of the finest pieces of northern art.

The most dramatic story of the era was that of Martin Hartwell, the bush pilot who crashed in the Northwest Territories during a medical mercy mission in November 1972. When he was found alive after thirty-two days, I flew to Yellowknife to talk to him in hospital. He broke down and cried while telling his story without admitting what I had learned from a source: he had eaten the flesh of his dead passengers to remain alive. That was the North. You did whatever was necessary to survive.

Most northern stories didn't have happy endings. In fact, most didn't have happy beginnings or middles. Everywhere I travelled as a reporter, I encountered swamps of Native despair. At Prince Albert

Courtesy of the Canadian Press.

Rescued pilot Martin Hartwell in his hospital bed in Yellowknife, Northwest Territories, in November 1972. Hartwell ate human flesh to stay alive. Reporter in the fur-collared parka at right is the author.

Penitentiary Native inmates sat at tables trying to sound out the letters in Dick and Jane beginner readers without teaching assistance. Some were there because they were uneducated. Others were there simply because they were Native.

At Grassy Narrows and Whitedog in northern Ontario, I saw kids glassy-eyed from gasoline sniffing; kids who might not be alive to see another dawn. Mercury poisoning from paper mills and government-forced relocation had killed the traditional way of life and robbed the children of a decent future.

In Fort Chipewyan, Alberta, I saw the despondent faces of the villagers, 90 percent of them on welfare because the damming of the Peace River killed their livelihood. The dam began to dry up the Peace-Athabasca Rivers Delta, an internationally recognized important wetland, making the fish, muskrat, beaver, and other species the Natives lived on less and less abundant.

At Cornwall Island, Ontario, part of the territory the Mohawk call Akwesasne, fluoride poisoning had killed off the island's traditional agriculture industry. Some of the people turned to tobacco smuggling to make money. Automatic gunfire echoed along the St. Lawrence River almost nightly as rival smugglers fought for control.

Environmental issues inevitably were the threads pulling native despair stories together. Whether in Yukon or Labrador, the social nightmares of Native communities often traced back to something man-made, some tinkering with nature that upset a way of life.

Most heartbreaking, however, is the realization that roughly thirty years have passed since I wandered through these scenes of degradation of Native life, and not much has changed.

Today, parts of northwestern Ontario remains a place of Native despair. Catherine Cheechoo, a young Native woman from the region, wrote in the *Toronto Star* on September 21, 2006, that Native suicide in the region is an epidemic. She reported that nineteen people in the Nishnawbe Aski Nation, a region of forty-nine communities of forty-five thousand Natives, committed suicide in the first six months of 2006. Most were young people. She also reported that there were 346 known suicides in the region between 1986 and 2006. The reason: despair linked to unemployment, poverty, overcrowded housing, and substance abuse.

Three decades after my Indian Affairs reporting, a Canadian Press team won a National Newspaper Award for its reporting of the human tragedy occurring at Davis Inlet, Labrador. The Innu of Davis Inlet were labelled the world's most suicide-stricken people by Survival International, a charity that works with indigenous people. Alcoholism among adults and gasoline sniffing among children has destroyed the community's social fabric and fires, family violence, and suicides were commonplace.

Again, almost thirty years after I wrote about the plight of Fort Chipewyan, the Indian Land Claims Commission ruled that the W.A.C. Bennett Dam has destroyed the traditional hunting and trapping economy on the Peace-Athabasca Delta. It found the Government of Canada owes the Native people "an outstanding lawful obligation" for construction of the dam. The government said in March 1999 that it needed more time to study the matter.

In the spring of 2007, residents of Fort Chipewyan continued the fight to get government attention to disproportionate rates of cancer in the community. Some residents and others suspect a link with sickness and the Alberta oil sands development nearby, but they say there has been a clear lack of will by the provincial and federal governments to seriously address the problem.

It is depressing to have written so much over the years about these problems and now to look back on the lack of progress.

The federal government admits that aboriginals are overrepresented in the prison system. Statistics Canada reported in April 1999 that aboriginals, while accounting for only 2 percent of the general population, comprised 17 percent of the prison populations. Poverty is an underlying cause. Census data for 1991 showed that more than sixty percent of aboriginal households in selected cities lived below the Statistics Canada poverty line. A StatsCan report in 1997 confirmed a wage gap between Canadian workers in general and aboriginals.

Little has been done to correct these incredible differences between how Natives live compared with the rest of us. In October 2006 ten to fifteen years after government reports documenting the horrible statistics about Natives in the prison system, the Correctional Investigator of Canada Howard Sapers wrote that the plight of Natives in prisons is "a national disgrace."

Sapers wrote that aboriginal offenders are routinely discriminated against by the correctional system and are far less likely to get parole or be rehabilitated. He said the overall incarceration rate for Native Canadians is nine times higher than for the population at large, even higher for Native women. A government spokesman responded that there is no evidence of "systemic" discrimination. These statistics prove disgraceful discrimination against Natives in the system, whether it is systemic or not. Discrimination against natives is subtle but rampant in this country, especially in the institutions. Governments never will move decisively on longstanding Native issues until they are pushed hard by the electorate. The people of Canada, generous in their support of the Third World, continue to ignore their own dispossessed Native people.

As a reporter I was always just an observer and chronicler of Native problems. On one trip I became a participant. I was dispatched to cover the 1977 meeting of the World Council of Indigenous Peoples in Scandinavia. One night near Karesuvanto, Finland, there was a dinner and some ceremonies that stirred Native pride and the hosts invited the Canadians to drive to a Sami campfire gathering out in the woods. During the ride several miles down a dark country road, I heard some rumblings about a white guy tagging along. When we reached the campfire location and piled out of the car, a couple guys pushed me and hit me on the shoulder. The dinner ceremonies and booze had raised emotions. I was pushed to the ground and stayed there while the group gathered itself then headed for a path led to the campfire. I knew the organizers of the trip, including George Manuel of British Columbia, who was president of the World Council, would have been enraged at my treatment, but I decided to bow out and let things cool.

I decided to walk the several miles back to where we were staying. It just wasn't my night because not long into the dark lonely walk in the Finnish woods, it began to pour. I was so wet I couldn't walk at a decent pace. I spotted an old cabin beside the road and bunked in there until dawn when the rain stopped. The sobriety of morning brought several expressions of regret and apologies. They weren't necessary because I had received a valuable lesson in what discrimination felt like.

The most enthusiastic fan of my Indian Affairs reporting was Veronica. She relished hearing about my travels into northern communities and onto the Indian reserves. However, she reacted oddly when I was back in the Soo on holidays and related the story of my night adventure in Scandinavia. A shadow of fear passed briefly across her face. She seemed to have seen something that no one else had seen and when I asked her what was wrong, she simple said, "Nothing." A few years later I would discover what bothered her that day and understand a fear that she carried throughout her life.

17 — NANABIJOU'S SHADOW

YOU DON'T HAVE TO FLY FROM PLACE TO PLACE IN THE West and North to find North American Natives living in desperate conditions. Most of us have witnessed the denigration of Native culture in or near by our own hometowns.

Veronica, who read my stories and reports with interest, got a first-hand look at native problems during the 1970s when she and Bill Brooks bought a camp at Sunset Point on St. Joseph's Island. The island is a half-hour east of the Soo and the cottage became a place to relax, watch the big ships coming and going from the Sault Locks, view glorious sunsets, and play cards with friends. To get to the island from the Soo, you have to follow Highway 17 passing through two Indian reserves: Rankin Reserve is on the city's eastern edge, and Garden River reserve, on-site home to roughly eight hundred natives, is a touch farther east. Both are Ojibwe territory and both hug the north shore of the St. Mary's River, which is narrow enough to see the United States on the other side.

Garden River is the most interesting of the two because it has existed for more than one hundred and fifty years and has a reputation for clinging to some remnants of Ojibwe culture and spirituality. The Ojibwe purchased Rankin in 1939 and it did not become an official reserve until 1952. It is more of an urban Native setting because it is really an eastern extension of Sault Ste. Marie.

During my *Sault Star* days we generally ignored both reserves, except for when a car struck and killed some reserve resident walking along the busy highway. Or, to report the failed attempts by government to negotiate a wider highway through the Native land. Highway 17 east of the Sault starts out with four lanes, reduces to two on Native land, then resumes to four lanes at Echo Bay. So travelling to and from St. Joseph Island, you had to slow to seventy kilometres an hour along the two-lane stretch through Native territory.

Many people making the drive used to look out on the Native land and comment on the disgraces of Native living. Ramshackle housing, abandoned cars, and broken household appliances lying about. Heads shook to accent the question: Why can't these people live like the rest of us?

Veronica passed through Garden River frequently coming and going from her camp. She saw what others saw but saw it quite differently. She saw a people doing their best to cope with a dominant lifestyle forced upon them. They had lived quite successfully — until European settlement — fishing the river and hunting the forests that surrounded it. Their best fishing areas along the St. Mary's Rapids were taken over by European buildings, including a steel mill and paper mill. Veronica saw a people whose traditions and spirituality were at least equal — and often superior — to those of white people but which had been battered by the effects of settlement.

She made her views clear to anyone who raised the matter. Like the day she drove Mary Jane and some of her young friends to the cottage. As they passed through Garden River, the girls made fun of the rundown look of the place. She stopped the car and gave them a lecture on how the Ojibwe had been forced from their traditional ways into reserve life. It wasn't their fault and no one should make fun of them, in any circumstances.

Another day, Mary Jane returned home from school and reported how one of the Pine children from Garden River was in her class. She said the child had arrived on the first day of classes with new clothing, which quickly deteriorated into dirty rags. Veronica became furious and told her to grow up and understand that Garden River people didn't have the good fortune of others. Veronica knew what many people didn't know because they never bothered to find out. The Pine family had grown from the very best of Ojibwe culture. Shingwauk, the Ojibwe word for pine, was tribal leader at the time the reserve was established.

He was famous for having snowshoed to Toronto to plead for European-style education to help the Ojibwe in their changing lives.

Shingwauk's great-grandson, Dan Pine Sr., became famous in the Sault Ste. Marie area as an elder and healer. He received an honorary MD from Algoma University, despite having only three years of formal education. Some of his twelve children, Donna Pine and Willard Pine in particular, were Native medicine people and counsellors well known and respected beyond the reserve.

Veronica knew all this because on trips to the cottage she got into the habit of stopping at Garden River. She met a few people simply by butting into their lives and asking questions. She didn't talk about her visits, but we knew they were becoming more frequent. We thought little of it.

She would have mingled easily in any Native setting. She was soft-spoken and knew how to blend into a scene when necessary. She knew how to direct questions without being obtrusive. Her looks helped her. She had greyed after all the events in Port Arthur, but traces of the deep black hair of her youth remained, as did the high cheekbones. She had always been slightly plump and was more so at sixty. Dressed in slacks, which she often wore to conceal the one skinny ankle, and a windbreaker, she could have been taken for one of Garden River's late middle-age elders.

She talked easily and knowledgably with anyone interested in animals. She loved all animals, and I believe that she could talk with them. I used to joke that she was a latter-day St. Francis of Assisi who could talk the birds out of the trees. Every morning she would get up between 6:30 and 7:00 and let her collie Shep out onto the grass at the front of her ground floor apartment. Then she would arrange bits of bread or seed along the balcony railing and call to the birds that already had gathered in a nearby tree. First would come the crow, then the smaller birds like the sparrows and nuthatches after he had finished. She talked to each bird individually and some people swore they heard them chirp back at her.

I got to see more of my mother and of Garden River after 1973 when CP moved us to the Ottawa bureau. We did the Ottawa-Sault drive frequently, of course passing through the reserve each time. Previously I had been one of the people who glanced through the car windows and asked why they could not live like the rest of us. Reporting from reserves

Courtesy of the Canadian Press.

Pierre Trudeau and wife, Margaret, stepping off an airplane during 1970s election campaign. Over the prime minister's left shoulder is the author, who was part of the press corps covering the election.

in many parts of the country and observing the workings of government in Ottawa, I changed my views. Ottawa's policy, certainly under Prime Minister Trudeau, was assimilation. Like trying to force carrots to become turnips. Thousands of bureaucrats beavered away on federal policies and programs for Natives with few of them having the vaguest feel for life in the Native communities. It was frustrating to witness the spirit-draining conditions of reserve life, then listen to the politicians in Ottawa while trying to squeeze little pieces of public information from their bureaucrats.

I was given the Indian and Northern Affairs beat in Ottawa, plus the Supreme Court of Canada. Much of the bureau's work involved reporting from the Press Gallery, which I quickly discovered was so focussed on Parliament Hill that it did not see what was happening in the real Canada. One example was the early 1980s hostage taking at an Ottawa bakery. The storeowner went a bit berserk when a sheriff tried to serve him with papers related to financial difficulties. This was a time when mortgage rates were as high as 20 percent and foreclosures were epidemic. It was almost impossible to get reporters to go to the scene because they didn't consider it "a Hill story." Yet, the incident was the direct result of the high-interest rate policies of the politicians on the Hill. It was a beautiful example of how big government affects the lives of the little people, but the Gallery couldn't see it.

Ottawa was a wonderful place to live and raise children. We planned on being there forever, only a days drive from Veronica and Diane's parents. Wire service life was unpredictable, however. I was transferred to Vancouver at Christmas of 1978. We shipped the car to Vancouver, then flew to Sault Ste. Marie for Christmas with Diane's family and Veronica.

There was something different about Veronica that Christmas. She was introspective, the edge of her inherent jolliness not razor sharp. Usually she was the centre of attention at festive occasions, joking and singing. She loved to sing and after a couple of drinks would sing anywhere at the drop of a hat. Her happy disposition always cheered our childhood Christmases, even during the hard years of the early 1960s. It was hard to read what was bothering her. She was lost in thought a lot, and we attributed it to the fact that she was saddened by the transfer that would widely separate us. I learned later that four days after that Christmas, while we were still in town, she sat down at her little kitchen table and wrote her will. She never mentioned it to me. She just wrote it out in longhand, called a friend down from an apartment above her, had her witness it, then tucked it away.

Veronica was strong on gut feelings and premonitions. Obviously she had one during our visit or had noticed something wrong with her health. Two weeks later, while we unpacked boxes in Vancouver, she entered the hospital for a test. The result was immediate and stunning: bladder cancer. She wrote her feelings from that day on a piece of paper:

> It left me devastated; rather like being lifted up into the arms of a storm and being carried with such turbulence into an endless infinity — all this in a matter of seconds — the initial shock of it all. Now, eventually you collect your thoughts, get yourself together and prepare for the routine procedures that lie ahead. Then comes the calming — not serenity, but almost like a grovelling, and I've found that an inner sense of uneasiness has been lifted — but mind you not forgotten. There is no turning back now so "Let us therefore live but one day at a time."

We felt stranded on the West Coast, unable to do much to help her. She went to Princess Margaret Hospital in Toronto. Facing the treatment alone and in a big, unfamiliar city must have been brutal. However, when it was over, she telephoned that she was feeling good and the doctors said the cancer was gone.

Vancouver was like a foreign posting, different lifestyles and impossibly far away from everything. It was claustrophobic. Walls of mountains on the north and the east. The ocean on the west and a foreign country on the south. People seldom spoke of the East. When they did, it was usually with disdain, even though many people I met who were born on the coast had never visited the East. Their interests were in the U.S. Pacific states to the south and Hawaii. To many of them, the country beyond the Rockies was irrelevant.

Veronica called regularly from Sault Ste. Marie and was close to hysterical when she learned I had bought a boat. She was happiest when I lived on the Prairies unable to sail anything larger than a duck punt. Now in her mind, the family madness had struck me again, only this time I was in the big leagues, tempting the Nanabijous of the Pacific Ocean. Then she shocked us with the news that she was coming to visit. She would not fly, of course. She would take the train and come by herself, and she said in advance that under no uncertain terms would she set foot on a boat.

She looked older but healthy when she arrived in the fall of 1979. She was less introspective but occasionally lapsed into brief periods of reflection. We toured the White Rock neighbourhoods and drove into Vancouver to see the sights there. I took her to the marina and proudly showed off my boat. She not only refused to go aboard to have a look, she refused to walk down to the moorage because that was just too close to the water. An invitation to a quick ride out into the channel would have made her swoon.

Although her fears of water and flying still raged inside her, Veronica was less worried about the life horrors that jump up and bite you. The fight against cancer had calmed her and she seemed to approach everything with a sense of finality.

One day she commented on how odd it was that she noticed so many funeral homes during our drives. Another time she pointed out a cemetery noting how much larger it was than the ones back in the Soo.

She wanted to talk, but she couldn't force herself to get started. We were much alike in that respect. Neither of us was able to express our feelings openly. We kept things inside. I know now there were many things she should have told me and many things I should have said to her. I felt anxious when I watched her board the train for the long journey back East. It was like I had let slip by an opportunity for us to talk. We talked by telephone and by letter during the winter and Veronica seemed to have returned to her old self. Her health was good with no signs of a cancer recurrence.

That changed when summer arrived, a summer of big stories for me, most of them tragic. In May, Mount St. Helens in Washington State blew, rattling the dishes in our South Surrey home. Local hero Terry Fox fell ill again with cancer in Thunder Bay, as did Veronica in Sault Ste. Marie.

We buried Veronica just before her sixty-fourth birthday. I emerged from the initial shock of her death obsessed by the death watch on Terry Fox, who was desperately ill in a New Westminster hospital. I established family and hospital contacts, drove through his neighbourhood to familiarize myself with his surroundings, cased the hospital, and laid plans for coverage in case he died. I don't know why I was obsessed with his story. Maybe it was the Thunder Bay connection, maybe it was the strain of dealing with Veronica's suffering and death. I wished that he wouldn't die, but if he was going to die, I was going to ensure the entire world knew of his grit, his determination, and his legacy.

On June 28, 1981, I sat through the night in a small dark office at Royal Columbian Hospital in New Westminster. The office had one window that looked across to the windows of a room that hospital staff would use for the news conference to announce Terry's death. Just as dawn started to lighten the sky, Leslie Shepherd, the reporter assigned to the news conference, flashed a sign at the window. It read "SEND FLASH"

Courtesy of Thunder Bay Tourism & Economic Development.

The Terry Fox Memorial on the eastern outskirts of Thunder Bay. The memorial marks the approximate spot where the one-legged runner stopped his cross-country Marathon of Hope when he suffered a relapse from cancer.

and signalled that Terry Fox was dead. It was 5:19 a.m. I dialled the bureau and a sentence announcing the death of a Canadian hero flashed around the world.

An immense sadness descended upon me after the initial rush of the story. His death was a personal loss to every Canadian. He ran 143 days covering 5,373 kilometres, including a couple loops to raise profile and money. He not only raised an immediate $24 million, he created a legacy in which every year more than a million people in Canada and fifty-eight other countries participate in the Terry Fox Run at 5,500 sites. His impact on cancer research funding has been inestimable. Most of all he is the only modern hero in a country desperate for heroism and leadership. The Terry Fox Story is what Canada should be about.

The great tragedy is what the country missed because he died. What a book he could have written! He could have given us some special insights into why this country is so difficult to govern and why its people are so inward-looking, so self-righteous, and often so negative. Maybe he could have told us more about the things that do hold us together across at least six time zones and three oceans. A country with ten distinct provinces and three territories, dozens of different tongues and two official languages.

Especially sad for me personally was that my memories of him always link me to Veronica and to Port Arthur and our family tragedies twenty years earlier. Years later they built the Terry Fox Monument at the spot on the highway, one kilometre east of Hodder Avenue, where the Marathon of Hope ended. It is a three-metre-high bronze statue that captures the fierce determination of a young man who inspired millions of people, including many cancer sufferers. Another kilometre or two into the bush behind the statue is the spot where I fired that fateful shot in October 1960.

It is also sad that Veronica never met Terry Fox. She was too sick that summer even to be able to go out and cheer him on. She died as his dream ended. It's too bad they didn't meet. They would have liked each other. They were both fighters and dreamers. Terry took his dreams public. Veronica kept hers secret.

18 — CORPORATE CLOWNS

VERONICA WAS A STORYTELLER. SHE LOVED TO LEAN BACK IN a chair and tell fantasies that often had some connection with reality. Like when she took the basics of the LaFrance family history and spun them into the drama of a shipwrecked ancestor marrying the Indian princess. Some mornings, after letting the dog out and feeding the birds, she would set up a portable tape recorder on her kitchen table and sit there staring through the window and tell a story. She loved making up animal stories — adventures of little red squirrels and birds — and she mailed the tapes off to the grandchildren.

In Grade 7, I mentioned to her that there was a public speaking contest and she took immediate interest and encouraged me to enter it. She helped me pick a theme, and when I had written the story down, she helped me practice. The night of the contest, I dressed in a dark little suit that she had bought and stood at the front of a classroom filled with students and their parents and grandparents. Veronica had told me to ignore the people and talk to the back wall, and I did, running through my story about Trixie the dog while she stood at the back of the crowd encouraging me with her eyes. I placed second, beat out by a Grade 8 girl, and the experience gave me confidence to participate in others.

Veronica had dreams of me becoming a globally famous orator, a skinny Winston Churchill. I rather liked public speaking. There was a sense of power in being able to hold people in your spell. There was a large sense of achievement in standing up and telling a story well.

That changed when our troubles began. After the trial for the hunting accident ended, I found I didn't want to stand up and speak anymore. A teacher I disliked began to single me out. Whenever he asked me to stand and answer a question, I saw myself back in the witness stand. He became the Crown attorney, hammering away at me, questioning my answers and trying to put me away. I left high school, not as the flamboyant storyteller and orator my mother had wished, but as someone terrified of standing and speaking in public.

Reporting suited me well in that state. All I had to do was listen to people speak and write about what they said. On occasion, some group asked me to speak to them about a reporting experience but I declined. That changed when I entered CP's management as a bureau chief. I had to go to regional meetings and speak. I developed crutches for getting through those meetings — like putting a colleague on the spot or asking the group a question that got other people talking while I sat back and listened. That couldn't go on forever. I was climbing higher in the company and was expected to speak at meetings and other gatherings.

Just after Terry Fox died, I was transferred back to Ottawa, then was brought into head office in Toronto. I was now in the company's executive ranks and this turned my fear of speaking in public from an awkward affliction into a personal crisis.

Unknown to me, I was brought to Toronto as a child of a covenant made by the CP board of directors. I was to be a key player in a company restructuring that included a plan to eliminate the board of directors of CP's broadcast subsidy, Broadcast News (BN).

In the early 1980s, the broadcasters were feeling their oats and began whinnying about breaking out of CP and starting their own news service. Bob Trimbee, the BN general manager, had been an unsuccessful candidate to replace John Dauphinee as CP general manager, the big boss over both services. The broadcasters had hoped for better times under CP if Trimbee had the job. He did not get it and now they were talking breakaway.

The CP board secretly sketched a plan to eliminate the BN board, knock Trimbee out, and take full control of BN affairs. To do this, they needed a strong editorial manager overseeing the broadcast news service. Enter me. I had to address the BN board at its fall 1983 meeting.

I was sick with fear. I planned to slam my hand in a door the day of the meeting. I thought about throwing myself down the stairs on the way to the meeting, perhaps breaking a leg. I thought about faking a heart attack when called upon to speak. I was willing to suffer anything to avoid making that presentation.

Beside myself with terror, I did something unimaginable. I confided in Bob Trimbee. Telling someone of this terrible weakness was one of the hardest things I ever had to do. His reaction saved my career. He told me to find professional help. The company would pay and he would hide the cost. I took a quick course that involved constant repetition and reinforcement to eliminate the fears. It helped and I made it through the board meeting, but the root problem was still there.

My family doctor suggested the fear was rooted in being put on trial in the hunting accident. Having to tell my story repeatedly and the constant badgering on the stand by the Crown attorney helped to create the phobia. I sought out Toastmasters and discovered there are tens of thousands of people like me. There I learned that studies have shown that for some people fear of public speaking is equal to the fear of death.

There are few afflictions more disturbing, more humiliating than fear of public speaking. I have broken bones, had kidney failure from a virus, lost an eye, had major heart surgery to correct my birth defect, and been in a coma for seven days. None of these has had a more negative affect on me than fear of public speaking. Without Toastmasters, life as I have lived it would not have been possible. It is a superb program of people helping each other and yet another example of building through positive thinking. Ten years in Toastmasters did not eliminate my fear of speaking, but did show me how to control it.

With that problem under control, I faced a new one in my working life. The newspaper business was becoming increasingly corporatized. It had been happening slowly over the years with the family operations such as the Currans, the Davies, and later the Siftons of Saskatchewan being bought out by the Southam and Thomson corporations and Conrad Black's operations. More and more barbarians arrived on the newspaper scene, grabbing more control in the 1980s and consolidating their raping and pillaging in the 1990s. The newspaper business would never be the same after its takeover by consumer goods salesmen, bean counters, and visionless sycophants.

Their arrival coincided with tough business times and new technology. Economic recession demanded more cost effectiveness for all businesses while technology advanced new forms of newspaper production. Cost controls became more critical as advertising revenue fell, newsprint prices rose, and circulation continued a downward trend. At the same time, owners faced huge capital costs needed for modernization and sometimes replacement of their plants. Many smaller papers found themselves like the Curran family in Sault Ste. Marie — strapped for the money needed for a modern makeover.

As corporate power over the news industry increased, publishers offices that had housed genuine news people who had worked through the ranks to the top spot were taken over by people with no news experience but plenty of enthusiasm for the corporate thinking that was the new rage.

Editors found themselves dealing with corporate clones and corporate clowns who took little interest in the traditions of news gathering and the public's right to, and need for, information. All the corporate clowns wanted was to do it more cheaply, and all aspects of newspapering went under the knife. Newsgathering was especially hard hit because it is labour intensive. Editors who resisted the change were labelled old-fashioned and were moved out. Others, unable to think for themselves or afraid for their jobs, adopted the corporate line. A few of the worst egomaniac editors, eager to show their worth and advance themselves, joined the corporatization campaign enthusiastically, becoming banner wavers for vacuous corporate sloganeering. People who were once wordsmiths charged with ensuring truth in language were suddenly "re-engineering to move forward and have their protocols move upward so they could increase market share." It was sad to watch the slashing and dumbing down of news operations.

Newspapers needed to change. Editorial people were too removed from financial, circulation, advertising, and marketing aspects of the business. The industry needed a new Canadian journalism, but corporatization too often brought negative people who lacked the attitude, the skills, and the talent to build a new journalism for a dramatically changing world. Values and attitudes built on decades of family influence began giving way to corporatization, which allowed corporate goals and bottom lines to erode good journalism. Being a powerful executive became more important than being a crusading journalist. The executives whittled, then slashed staff levels. They thinned content, the rich marrow in the bones of good journalism, then thinned it again until the reason for buying the local newspaper was for the ads or simply because of habit.

The changes were dramatically obvious in the smaller cities. Staff numbers were slashed. Newspaper sales fell and continue to fall. Public access to the newspapers was restricted. Where people like Queen Edith once wandered up to the city editor's desk, now the public no longer could enter the newsroom without an appointment. Where any enraged reader or legitimate tipster once could phone and drive a Homer Foster crazy at deadline, callers now faced automated phone systems with call-screening voice mail. Newspapers no longer belonged to their communities. They belonged to big shots sitting in corporate comfort in big cities. This happened at newspapers across Canada until there were no genuine independents left among Canada's one hundred-odd dailies. Most of the small- and medium-sized papers became what you see today — shells sucked so dry by corporate bosses that they no longer have the resources to staff a peanut stand robbery.

The decline of these smaller daily newspapers has been a factor in the transformation of Canada into an overwhelmingly urban society, and we are all the poorer for it. The shrinking of smaller newspapers has created huge black holes that reduce the exchange of news between Canadians. Almost all our news now comes from, and is about, urban areas. As a result, urbanization is smothering many of the beliefs and traits of small-town and country life. The values, lifestyles, and morals of people living in small towns are considered quaint now because they are little understood. This is because there are fewer return news mechanisms linking them. The news is a one-way pipeline now: It is big city news about big city life produced by big city people, and it is news produced mainly for making some corporation in a big city some money. The voices of Canada now are predominantly voices from the big city streets.

The disappearance of Canada's non-urban voices is a tragedy, but any reversal is unlikely. That would involve change, and change is not a word often associated with newspapering. Despite their belief that they are at the forefront of everything, journalists plod along in a craft burdened by antiquities. They hate change, perhaps fearing that change will destroy their Hollywood image as rough-and-tumble iconoclasts, working to rescue society from its ills. Gruff heroes like reporter Hildy Johnson and editor Walter Burns depicted in the stage and screen renditions of *The Front Page*.

American essayist Frank Moore Colby (1865–1925) summed it up nicely when he wrote: "Journalists have always been our most old-fashioned class, being too busy with the news of the day to lay aside mental habits of fifty years before."

Newspapers would do well to heed the words of Murray Davis, the tailor back in Sault Ste. Marie: Be a builder. Get rid of your old mental habits including cynicism, negativism, and egotism. Build instead of tearing down. Build an informed and accurate news file, respect among your readership, and a sense of improving the local community and the state of the world. Build by creating innovative and substantive content, not by constant cost-cutting. You have to spend money to gather news.

CP, because it is a creature of the newspapers, suffered the effects of corporatization. It became more corporate itself; I took on the icy corporate title of vice-president instead of the venerable title of managing editor, which people related to ethics, fairness, and trust.

CP service was a big bill and publishers now reporting to corporate head offices were frantic to cut costs to please their masters. This developed into a campaign to slash CP costs, or even replace its newsgathering function. By 1996, CP was in crisis. I agreed to run the place for no more than a year while the news corporations figured out what they wanted. I was close to early retirement entitlement and knew I couldn't tolerate the new corporate world of news much longer.

The new corporate news people did not stand for the things I learned to stand for while growing up in northern Ontario. They were carpetbaggers, some of them obtuse and sleazy. They practised situational ethics, easily rationalizing any move away from the traditional values of newspapering. Trained corporate seals with all the vision it takes to push nickels and dimes around with their noses. Matchstick men and women who snapped or blew away when a storm blew through.

It became increasingly difficult to tolerate them. Whenever I had to meet with them, my stomach rolled. I applied Veronica's test to them: if you wouldn't bring them home to dinner, you shouldn't be around them.

Thankfully, the year passed quickly. At 10:48 a.m. on June 27, 1997, I looked up at my office TV and saw the familiar Broadcast News television cable report broadcast the following: "BN Cablestream salutes Jim Poling, General Manager of the Canadian Press, who retires today after a remarkable twenty-eight years with the news agency. Congratulations and best of luck, Jim."

I leaned back in my chair and stared at the new jacket hanging on the back of my office door. Summer sunlight falling through the window warmed the tawny buckskin and toyed with tiny blue, orange, white, and green glass beads meticulously stitched into native floral patterns. There was a floral pattern on each breast and a larger one across the back.

The jacket's broad buttons were crosscuts of deer antler and fastened through slits in the jacket front. As a child, I told Veronica that someday I would have a fine buckskin jacket of my own. It would be a magic coat, and when I slipped it over my shoulders, I would become a new person and run free in the woods. She laughed her big laugh, but told me it was good to dream. I knew that when I slipped on this buckskin jacket my life would change forever. Wearing it would mark the end of thirty-five years in daily journalism.

Courtesy of Ron Poling.

Author Jim Poling in the buckskin jacket made for his retirement from the Canadian Press.

I got up and pulled it from its hanger, then paused to assure myself I was doing the right thing. Mine had been a dream career. I was blessed with work that challenged me to wake up excited every morning and to grow as a journalist and a person.

I could feel Veronica's presence as I walked down the hall and into the newsroom for the last time. Finally, I was truly free to run in the forest. Free of the chaos and corruptions of corporatization. Free to do and say what I wanted. Free to wake Nanabijou. Most importantly, I was free to return to reporting. My first assignment would be the one I had put on hold seventeen years earlier when my mother died.

Book Four

Nanabijou Awakened

19 — UNFINISHED BUSINESS

TURBULENCE ROCKED MY MIND THE DAY WE BURIED Veronica in August 1980. Expected perhaps, but this was more than the grief of losing a mother. More than seeing the upsetting bruise left on her mouth by the jostling of the ride from the Soo. More than dealing with her husband Bill Brooks's feelings and my disappointment of not being able to jump into the Terry Fox story. My head swam with questions about an unexpected inheritance: a piece of paper I found hidden in my mother's belongings while making her funeral arrangements. It was a shocking discovery that demanded an explanation from Veronica, but she was no longer alive, and it was inexplicable why she would not have provided it before she died. As the funeral directors lowered her coffin into the hole we had put my dad twenty years before, I felt like screaming: What does this all mean? Why didn't you tell me?

On my way back home to Vancouver after the funeral, I scoured my mind for an answer, rolling the events of that summer back and forth in my mind, freezing frames here and there, summoning details and examining them closely. Veronica suspected she was dying, and perhaps re-examining her final month might reveal some clue to the meaning of the hidden identity card found behind the lining of her jewellery box. However, no clues came immediately to mind and the pressures of work, including the Terry Fox story, forced me to set my investigations aside.

When I retired in 1997, I began a fresh review of that summer of 1980. Terry Fox was shuffle-hopping along the north shore of Lake

Superior and thinking about a halfway celebration. Veronica entered the hospital in Sault Ste. Marie. The cancer treated at Princess Margaret in Toronto had returned and was chewing away her bladder. The doctors wanted to perform surgery to see if there was anything they could do.

I flew to the Soo in mid-August, arriving to find her already in surgery. While I paced, I bumped into her family physician, a silver-haired icon of the city's medical community. He had already delivered me some bad news many years earlier when he noted that my heart defect might make my golden years quite brief, if I even got that far. He had more bad news this day. He murmured that he was sorry, the surgery had revealed nothing more could be done for her. We were talking days, not weeks or months.

A nurse approached and told me I must explain all this to my mother in the recovery room. I threw her a look that I might have given someone who had just escaped from the psycho ward. We argued, she insisting it was my responsibility to tell her, me saying that I could not tell my mother she had only a few days to live.

Another nurse opened double doors at the hallway's end and summoned me into the recovery room. It was cool in there, but Veronica lay in a thin green hospital gown, uncovered by blankets. She always had a problem with feeling too warm. The chrome bar of the side restraint was cold against my sweating palms as I gripped it and leaned over to kiss her. I told her she would soon be on her feet and back home with her beloved Shep, a full-size collie who could have stood in for Lassie on a Hollywood set.

Shep was gone, she said as the tears began to flow. I was taken aback. Gone? Gone where? She explained that the dog could never live without her. He would pine away. She had him put down before she entered hospital.

It was a surreal moment accented by the fluorescent lighting humming with an unnerving persistency, the biting odour of antiseptic snagging at the back of the throat, and the catheter bag pink with blood instead of the yellow of healthy urine. I struggled to find a response. Something had told her that this would be her last trip to the hospital, her last trip anywhere. Shep would have gone crazy waiting for her return. They were inseparable. He was gone and she would be close behind.

I thought back to the mornings I had watched her and Shep share tea and toast, then go out on their walk. They were twin spirits, talking to each other like an elderly lifelong couple. She talked to him as if he was human, and he responded with barks and body language. They had lunch together, then watched television in the afternoons. At evening gatherings in her living room, she would entertain guests by telling Shep to bring out his toys to show the people. The dog would nose open a closet door in the hallway and with his teeth drag out a cardboard box of stuffed bears and rubber duckies. He would take each one out carefully on her command and show it to the folks.

Veronica had an almost supernatural relationship with animals. She talked to birds and could make them come close. Her analogies about life often included animals, and she was forever making up children's stories in which the key players were squirrels and chipmunks, crows, and of course dogs.

Dogs were an important part of her life right from childhood days on Peter Street in Port Arthur. When she had sleepovers with her girlfriends, the little white Pom was always the centre of the party. Then there was Trixie from the days at 402 Dawson Street, hit by a car and blinded, who learned to navigate the house on smell. And Dixie, whom she gave to me at the house on Pine Street when Mary Jane was born. Dixie lived long and went with her to Sault Ste. Marie where she suffered strokes on two occasions when my mother tried to sneak out of the apartment without her. I recall picking her up at her apartment back in the 1960s. We had to sit pretending to watch TV while Dixie fell into a deep afternoon nap. Then we tiptoed to the door and crept out trying not to jingle a key or make the door latch click.

Her love for and understanding of animals was powerful. She even mentioned this in her will, saying she hoped she had left us her love for animals.

As I processed the news about Shep, I shuffled uncomfortably at her bedside, trying to think of what to say next. She broke the silence, saying that I was having a hard time with all this. Indeed I was. I was ashamed at my inability to find the right words that would comfort her. Knowing what to say at times of illness and death comes only with experience. There is little in our early lives to prepare us for such moments. A long pause passed, then we began to talk, saying some of the things that had to be said. She reached out and touched my hand and asked me for a promise.

"Promise to take me home to your dad."

My promise led us into the forbidden land of conversation that both of us had avoided for so many years. We talked about her leaving me behind in Port Arthur and her marriage to Bill Brooks. We talked about many things, some that a son can never repeat. She was so open and what she told me was so personal that it is still impossible for me to comprehend how on her deathbed she held back the most important secret of her life. When she had said everything she wanted to say her face clouded with fear. She balled her fists and closed her eyes and began to pray: "Hail Holy Queen, Mother of Mercy. Our life, our sweetness, and our hope. To thee do we cry, poor banished children of Eve ...."

The words of the Salve Regina, favourite prayer of the nursing order of nuns known as the Misericordia Sisters. Years later I still reflect on how it came to be her favourite prayer as well and where she might have first heard it. I recall the ancient tale that those who hear it recited never forget it. I believe she first heard it as an infant at the place where she was born.

Veronica loved to clown and could never be serious for long. After praying, she lit up her mischievous smile and said: "And, I'm not to be taken home by plane. I'm still afraid to fly."

She was like that for the duration. My sisters and I sat with her and we joked and sang and told stories and reminisced about favourite dogs. One night we ordered in panzerotti and ate and laughed ourselves silly. I can't recall how long the vigil lasted, but it was an oddly pleasant time, once we had had our serious talk. She seemed comforted by having her kids beside her. That is the way people are supposed to die. Although the fear tightened her face from time to time, she displayed a calmness that I guessed came from knowing that she was going home to a long awaited reunion with Ray.

The Vic, the old *Sault Star* watering hole, was a block down the street from the hospital. Veronica was sleeping and I walked over to the venerable tavern for a sandwich and much needed reflection over a couple glasses of beer. I entered through the old Women and Escorts side where Veronica and I had shared a few drafts in years long passed. I sat in a dark corner where the air was thickest with the smell of spilled beer and burned tobacco, and I felt sheltered from what was happening outside those walls. The back door opened, piercing the darkness with unwelcome daylight. My sister Barb walked through the beam of daylight and sat down across from me.

"She's gone," she said.

I was uncomfortable with the knowledge that I had sipped beer in semi-darkness while my mother had died. Yet it was fitting. We spent some of our best moments together talking across little round tabletops marked by the sweat rings of draft glasses. Veronica was at her best when sipping a beer and smoking a cigarette while telling a story. She liked to have people around because no matter what bad news intruded on her life, she always managed to find something to laugh at. Sometimes when she had more than one or two beers, she became an entertainer. She was a good actress, with a voice to match, and was known to break into song in public at times. She was once offered a singing job at the Brown Derby in Duluth, Minnesota, after she took the stage, uninvited, and belted out her version of the old and not well-known song, "Umbrellas."

She was such a kind, gentle, and happy person. I should have stroked her forehead, kissed her cheek, and told her goodbye after the nurse closed her eyes. I should have stood at the edge of the St. Mary's River and cried my eyes out. It was hard-nosed just to have turned on my heel at her hospital room doorway and walked away, but perhaps this reflects the realities of relationships between mothers and sons. Adulthood constantly strains the steel bonds of birth and rearing. In our case, we had suffered more than usual strains. We had lived through outright trauma. Our instincts told us to look after ourselves by doing what we thought was right. She had done what she thought was right by leaving Port Arthur and remarrying. I had done what I thought was right by not assuming the full role of the little man of the family and setting off to create my own life. None of this lessened our love for each other.

In all of this — hours of soul-searching and reviewing in detail the events of that summer of 1980 — I found neither clue nor explanation for why she had not told me about a secret part of her life that was also a secret part of mine.

20 — THE SECRET

WHEN VERONICA DIED, SHE REVERTED TO HER OLD LIFE. That is an absurd statement, but her death seemed to obliterate the years following her move to Sault Ste. Marie from Port Arthur. Death placed her back home in Port Arthur where her central male figures were my dad and I. She had placed me in charge of all her arrangements, leaving her husband Bill Brooks as a bystander.

Bill was shattered. He sat shell-shocked at the kitchen table in their Macdonald Street apartment, which they had shared for fifteen years. Bill's own health was deteriorating with age abetted by hard work in the steel plant, heavy smoking, and drinking.

I had never taken to Bill, although he had treated my mother with love and respect and had provided fatherly guidance to Mary Jane, who was seven when Dad died, and to a lesser extent, Barbara, who was fifteen. I disliked him, probably not so much for who he was, but because it is natural for a boy to reject a man who takes his father's place. We all gathered at the apartment to discuss the arrangements. I told everyone my instructions were to take Veronica home to my dad's grave. This aggravated Bill's grief, and I didn't know how to make it easier for him. I had her handwritten will but didn't want to show it to him because it would only make him feel worse. I sensed that Bill felt I was being arbitrary and rushing things just to be done with him. I couldn't show him the letter with her references to her "beloved husband Ray" or the fact that she had remarried out of necessity, not love. I simply told him her wishes, outlined in the letter and at her deathbed, and tried to lighten the situation by reading an excerpt of the will. It was typical Veronica, following up some decidedly serious comment with some clowning: "I have my insurance with Metropolitan Life. Please don't get an elaborate outfit, as it will take money to get me home. Who knows I just might get up and walk."

Bill stared out the front window while my sisters and I went through her possessions. The dearth of family documents struck me as odd. There were a few papers related to the sale of the house in Port Arthur but not much else. Little evidence of almost twenty years of living with my father and a lifetime with the LaFrances. The only record that the LaFrances had lived was a note from my grandmother saying she grew up in the Ottawa Valley, moved to Chapleau and then to Port Arthur after her marriage, where she stayed for the rest of her life. It seemed to be a statement typed out for legal purposes. There were no scrapbooks, no shoeboxes of household papers or newspaper clippings, or legal papers that most families have piled in drawers or buried in closets.

Barb pulled a wallet-sized card from a slit in the lining of Veronica's jewellery box and asked what it was. She handed me a laminated card, a Canadian citizenship card in the name of Veronica Cecile LaRose. The picture on the card was Veronica's, but how did her birth name get changed from LaFrance to LaRose? I kissed it off as government incompetence. They mixed up LaRose and LaFrance. If the circumstances had been different, and if I had been thinking, I would have realized how stupid my off-the-hip answer really was.

I assumed Veronica needed the citizenship certificate when she and Bill decided to marry in Michigan. To get it, she would have to have produced a birth certificate. How the bureaucrats could get LaRose out of her birth name of LaFrance seemed amazing, but then governments have done a lot queerer things. The certificate gave her correct birth date, September 16, 1917, and city, Edmonton.

My flip answer seemed to satisfy everyone, including myself. Except that later, Barb found a second piece of Veronica's past in the form of a booklet: *Little Baby's Big Days* by Edith Truman Woolf. On the cover was a drawing of a stork bringing a bundled baby to a house in the woods. Inside were drawings and spaces in which to write the big moments

Little Baby's Big Days

by
Edith Truman Woolf

Published by
C.R.Gibson & Company
New York City

Copyright 1   Gibson & Company New York City

It was a close examination of this baby book that led the author to start digging into his mother's past. The baby book was a gift from the Women's Institute of Hanna, Alberta, and contained some discrepancies in birth information.

in baby's life: First Laughs, First Steps, Little Journeys, and so on. The book was inscribed "To Veronica La France from the Hanna Women's Institute May 1918," obviously given to Louise and Joseph during their brief time in the Alberta village. It seemed odd that a women's group would present a gift baby book to a mother eight months after the birth.

My grandmother had filled in the birth details, including Misericordia Hospital in Edmonton and nurse Sister St. Felix, in neat handwriting done with a nib and ink. It was neat, except the last number in the year of birth had been written over. A dark seven had been placed over an eight in the year 1918.

We thought no more of the discoveries, probably because we had to arrange the wake in the Soo, hire an undertaker to drive to the body to Thunder Bay, then arrange a funeral and burial there. The citizenship certificate with the wrong name plucked at my mind, but there was no time to sit back and consider it. It appeared to be a simple mistake.

We all moved through the scenes: the wake at Everest, across the street to St. Andrew's, where a priest who knew nothing about the life of the woman in the coffin — and was too disinterested to ask anyone — performed Catholic Church rituals. He went through the drill, never mentioning her life, a sin, really, because every life is a story worth telling, however briefly, out of respect and for the learning value of the people who hear it. No priest or minister should ever forget that.

Then the graveside ritual. It was a flashback to twenty years earlier at my father's funeral. The pine tree sentinel watching over my father's grave was taller and more gnarled by time. Many of the mourners were the same, much older and conditioned to the ceremonies of death and burial. The grave was a single grave with a small simple black stone. The inscription was unpretentious, reading simply, "Ray Poling 1915–1960." They would place my mother on top of my father and later inscribe the single name "Veronica" beneath his.

Bill was isolated in the crowd, lost in his own world with his own thoughts as the coffin disappeared into the slash of fresh earth taking his wife back to back to the man she loved. After it was done, I went and stood over the grave of my grandparents, Isidore and Louise LaFrance, perhaps waiting for some sign of approval that I had done the best I could for their daughter.

Soon afterwards I was on an airplane to my Vancouver home and a day later the events of previous days seemed but a dream. I waded into work. Terry Fox had returned to Port Coquitlam from Thunder Bay, and his illness and impending death consumed my life. The emotional shocks of losing my mother lessened and the citizenship card and baby book discoveries slid even farther into my subconscious. Not only did I not have the time to consider them, they seemed insignificant.

The wrong name on the citizenship card was easily sloughed off as a mistake. *Little Baby's Big Days* could not be pushed away so easily. It continued to float in and out of my thoughts. I took it out of the folder I kept on my mother, then put it back. Out again, in again. It nagged, like someone hidden calling from a distance in a game of hide-and-seek.

After I retired, I pulled it out and studied it critically. The birth date of September 16, 1918, had been changed to September 16, 1917. No details on the baby's activities until she was eight months old. There was something wrong with all this, so I decided I should get Veronica's birth record. It was something we should have anyway for the family history.

My sister Mary Jane, who lived in Red Deer, Alberta, called Misericordia Hospital in Edmonton and talked to an elderly nursing nun who said all records from the 1918 era burned in a fire. I contacted the Alberta government and learned that the file was privileged, and I could not see it. The person who told me this would not explain why I could not have my mother's birth record, or why there would even be an entire file instead of a simple record. Something was going on and needed to be uncovered.

One rule of reporting is that anything being held back by government must be worth getting. This is especially true in Canada, a country in which people are reluctant to share information. We have a culture of secrecy and our governments operate on the theory that information can be harmful to its citizens. Openness is dangerous and information is protected at all costs, an attitude that has worsened in recent years with new and suffocating changes in various privacy legislation.

Sometimes the only way into government information vaults is through the back door. Reporters know all about this and I was fortunate because I knew someone who had a key. I can't say who the person was, how that person was connected to government, or what that person did. However, one day I received a telephone call and was told to wait by my fax because an interesting document was on the way. I waited, my fingers tapping impatiently. The tapping stopped, and so did my breathing as the first couple of pages rolled smoothly from the mouth of the magic fax.

My eyes tore through the first pages. Then I backed up and fell into my chair. I felt like I had been struck by lightning. I was light-headed and my mind tingled with confusion.

The fax pages contained information obtained from the Alberta Adoption Registry. Veronica Cecile LaRose, the name on my mother's citizenship certificate, was a child of the Misericordia Crèche, the orphanage once operated at Misericordia Hospital in Edmonton. The Misericordia Sisters were famous for their work with unwed mothers. Veronica LaRose was an illegitimate child born to an unwed mother rescued by the Misericordia Sisters. Sometime before her first birthday, she was removed from the orphanage and placed with foster parents.

My mind stopped tingling and exploded with realization. The baby book presented in Hanna almost eight months after the birth. The book not noting any of the baby's weights or characteristics until she was eight months old. Louise and Isidore married thirteen years without a child, suddenly disappearing into the Alberta frontier, reappearing later in Ontario with a baby. My mother was an illegitimate child! The people I knew as my grandparents were not my blood grandparents. Many of Misericordia's unwed mothers were Native, and some other information indicated that Veronica LaRose was a Native child.

I recalled Veronica's story about the LaFrance ancestry. The shipwrecked French baron's son and the Indian princess. It was a fantasy, but now I realized it was based on a real set of facts. The discovery was like falling across a live power line. My head buzzed with confusion about my changed relationship with people who had shaped my early life, especially Louise LaFrance. Despite her gnarled fingers and feet and the pain that sucked away her original beauty, she was a goddess to me.

She was my soulmate and had as much to do with me becoming the person I am as Veronica did. Learning that she was not a blood relative was like discovering your favourite hero is an impostor.

Reason alleviated some of the shock. It wasn't as if I'd just been diagnosed with a terminal illness. The discovery had not changed my life significantly. Then anger knocked aside reason. I felt tricked, deliberately deceived. Veronica had no right to keep the secret of her birth from me. For one thing, doctors had said my heart problem was hereditary and knowing from whom I got it might be important. Why would she keep this secret from me?

I canvassed family members. None had ever heard that Veronica was adopted. I made calls to the Alberta government and soon found myself frustrated again by the secrecy of bureaucracies. Alberta refused to release any information about my mother's birth.

One of the rules of public relations is never make a reporter angry. I was angry and determined to vacuum clean Alberta, the entire country, and the continent if necessary to piece together the story of Veronica's secret and why it was so important that she took it with her to the grave. I would find the answers, even if I had to make a second career of it. Where to start? The best advice seemed to come from the King of Hearts in *Alice's Adventures in Wonderland*: "Begin at the beginning, and go on till you come to the end: then stop."

The beginning was out west in Alberta, and I had no idea that I would find such a fascinating story before I reached the end.

21 — WILD WEST ORPHANS

SHAME WAS THE BEST REASON FOR KEEPING AN ILLEGITIMATE birth secret. Birth out of wedlock in most societies was non-conformist behaviour. Society forced people who couldn't control themselves and behave like everyone else to stand outside the crowd to suffer the humiliation of not fitting in.

This shame didn't result only from a puritanical attitude toward sex. It developed from sound reasoning based on economics. Not so long ago, women without husbands had little economic strength, certainly not enough to support an illegitimate child alone. In Alberta just after the start of the twentieth century, the average industrial wage for women was $344 a year compared with $2,843 a year for men. A woman couldn't afford to raise a child alone, so the burden fell on society, frequently overburdened by the costs of all its other problems. Society is never amused when people who don't behave like the rest of us make us pay more into the pot.

Bastard children were nothing but problems. Someone had to shelter and feed them and pay to look after their health. Then there was education. Without some training, they were continuing problems as adults, living off society's handouts or even turning to crime to support themselves. They helped to swell the poor classes that were breeding grounds for disease, sloth, crime, and other unsavoury societal problems.

Even bastards sired by rich men, who could afford to cover up their mistakes with money, were problems. Society looked the other way when aristocrats played with unwashed trollops but reacted strongly toward any unexpected offspring, branding them lesser class citizens and substandard humans deserving only ridicule. The illegitimates of the rich were potential hazards to parts of society. They weakened bloodlines and threatened the rights of legitimate heirs.

Women felt the full sting of society's slap against illegitimacy because they carried the evidence of their mistake out front. Unwed mothers were considered promiscuous and dirty, vilified because of the problems their bastards created. However, not all men who sired illegitimates escaped the public wrath. In English society, men known to have sired a bastard were charged and jailed if found guilty. Proof of paternity was difficult but the fact that society did jail men for "begetting bastards" shows the extent of society's disgust over the problems caused by illegitimacy.

Killing unwanted babies was an epidemic before the modern era. Then more "enlightened" societies decided that murder was too severe a solution and instead allowed the poor to sell their bastards into slavery. Infanticide was common throughout early history. Europe's Christian churches opposed infanticide and slavery as solutions to the problems created by illegitimate births. They had no means to stop the practices, however, so did the only other thing they could — provided food and shelter to unwed mothers and their children.

That aid only further blackened the stigma of illegitimacy. Society saw bastards as intellectually inferior beings, the reasoning being they inherited the traits of parents dumb enough to create problems for themselves and society. Some orphanages even refused to accept bastards because they feared the children had inherited their parents' moral weaknesses.

Illegitimacy was rampant in North America during the 1800s and early 1900s. Montreal doctors in 1817 complained of "the social plague of infanticide." Bastard babies were left in outhouses, thrown into streams, smothered in garbage heaps by unwed mothers unable or unwilling to care for them. In Western Canada, there were reported cases of infanticide in which magistrates refused to punish the unwed mothers, saying they had suffered enough. If that said something about compassion to these unfortunate women, it said a lot more about the feelings toward illegitimates. The magistrates, while displaying sympathy for the mothers, telegraphed the message that the illegitimates were better off dead.

The illegitimacy plague ran throughout Canada and the United States. The Grey Nuns in Montreal reported in 1867 that they received six hundred and fifty-two abandoned infants that year, three dead on arrival, seven frost-bitten, and thirteen wounded. One arrived in a suitcase, another in a basket, and another in a pail. Most arrived barely clothed and only thirty-three lived the year, a mortality rate of 90 percent. Overcrowding, understaffing, and the need for wet nursing made close individual care an impossibility.

In the 1850s, an estimated thirty thousand kids were homeless on the streets of New York. Not all were illegitimates. Many were the product of marriages but were abandoned when their parents died or simply could not afford to raise them. Either way, they presented enormous problems that were difficult to ignore. Governments, many just trying to establish themselves in what was still frontier North America, were incapable of dealing with so many abandoned children. Laws governing child neglect, children's aid, and adoption would come later, but until then concerned and committed individuals working together became the main source of relief.

One individual, Charles Loring Brace, conceived the idea of shipping street children West to live with farm families. The result was the Orphan Train Movement that between 1853 and the early 1900s placed more than 120,000 homeless kids on farms in the Midwest and parts of Western Canada. The photographs of wan faces staring out from railway car windows are surreal when viewed from today's world.

Individual compassion and the good work of religious orders became the chief sources of mercy for unwed mothers and their children. People often committed themselves after seeing the tragic consequences of illegitimate birth. Marguerite d'Youville founded the Sisters of Charity of Montreal (Grey Nuns) in 1737 after seeing the hand of a baby poking through the ice on a stream where it had been thrown with a knife in its throat.

More than a century later, a young widow named Marie-Rosalie Cadron Jetté began helping unwed pregnant girls in Montreal, finding them places to stay until their *accouchement*, then organizing care for the newborn. Montreal's Bishop Ignace Bourget heard of her work and in 1845 asked her to establish an order to serve the needs of unwed mothers. Three years later, she constituted Soeurs de Miséricorde, or Misericordia Sisters, Catholic nuns bound together by the rules of poverty, chastity, and obedience. They established a hospice with a mission to rescue and reform unwed pregnant women and their illegitimate children. In the beginning, the locations of Madam Jetté's maternity homes were secret because of the hostility of Montreal society. When the sisters brought newborns to church for baptizing, citizens threw garbage at them. People praying at Notre-Dame church would leave when the sisters entered with their big-bellied charges. Young women staying at the Misericordia hospice had to cross a street to get to a chapel for Mass. Citizens lined up to taunt the young women with the big bellies that told of their shame.

Montreal society criticized the sisters for "supporting low degraded creatures." Even Madam Jetté's own children openly criticized her work among the low-lifes. Despite the snubs, the sisters expanded their work. By 1898, the order reported it had helped more than fourteen thousand women. It established orders and unwed mother operations in Winnipeg, Edmonton, and in the United States.

Nowhere in Canada was the problem of illegitimate births more prominent than the frontier town of Edmonton in 1900. Church officials were frustrated trying to deal with the effects of loose morality. Young women routinely fell into sin, burdening society with their bastards and leaving the religious community despairing for their souls. One such case prompted a Monsignor in Edmonton to write the Misericordia Sisters' mission in Winnipeg. A Metis girl was headed straight to Hell, and the Monsignor pleaded with the sisters to rescue her. The sisters responded positively, provided the girl agreed to follow their rules.

Bishop Vital-Justin Grandin wrote back to thank the nuns for agreeing to help and added: "If moral misery were sufficient to draw you to us, I would make initiatives to this direction for we certainly have need of your help, but we are not sufficiently advanced yet for that. If, however, your society could establish a mission without our help, I beg you in grace to come to our assistance."

The bishop's pleas were heard in the convents of the Misericordia Sisters. Months later, twilight descended on the North Saskatchewan River Valley as four robed nuns stepped from a passenger car of the Calgary and Edmonton Railway at Strathcona. They were the answer to Bishop Grandin's prayer, although they certainly didn't look like it. They were nearly penniless and brought little beyond promises of assistance in their mission. They carried their few belongings to a waiting buckboard that took them across the river to Edmonton where they had been promised temporary accommodations with the Grey Nuns.

It wasn't unusual to see clergy travelling throughout the West in those days. Missionary work was a main component of western life. Priests and ministers helped to open the West as they competed for converts among the Natives. In their tracks followed support groups such as sisterhoods providing charity that included health care and education.

The Misericordia nuns were led by Sister St. Francois d'Assise, a forty-two-year-old veteran of charity work. Sisters St. Laurent, Rose de Lima, and St. Frederic had travelled across the country by rail from Montreal to a frontier they had only read about. They had only what they could carry, but their intention was to establish a maternity mission for unwed mothers like ones already created in Montreal, Ottawa, and New York. With them was a young lay nurse, Mary Jane Kennedy, seconded from the Ottawa mission. Three days after their arrival, they moved into a clapboard house at 9937 110 Street in Edmonton, across the street from St. Joachim's Church. It had four rooms on the main floor, plus a loft and was donated by a citizen who also threw in a stove and some kitchen gear. The night before they moved into the little house, the Sisters showed their determination in a letter back to Mother House in Montreal: "Dear Mother, the house we will be living in is a not a castle, rest assured, we would not have wanted it if it would have been. We'd rather start in a manger…"

The next day they began their mission and in three months established a maternity hospital in a donated wooden building at 111 Street and 98 Avenue. The hospital included the Crèche, or nursery, with room for ten babies. The good sisters had their hands full. Their unwed mothers operation was located in the heart of St. Joachim's Roman Catholic parish, which served French-Canadian frontier folk since the

1850s when Fort Edmonton was a trading post. The parish had the scandalous distinction of being the leader in illegitimate births of all parishes in Canada. In the five-year period from 1900 to 1904, between 11 and 18 percent of all babies baptized at St. Joachim's were illegitimate. In France, a rate of 8 percent was considered shockingly high.

One reason for the high illegitimacy rate was the Wild West culture. Where pregnancy out of wedlock was repugnant in the East, it was not such a big deal in the West. Looser standards for living had been in place since the explorers and fur traders went west and took up Native wives in "the custom of the country." It was common for families with French or Scots names to have Native blood.

Misericordia helped many Native and Métis girls, as well as others, and its operations expanded steadily. It became a general hospital in 1906 and added an orphanage wing in 1911. By 1913 the Crèche regularly sheltered an orphan population of thirty.

The Misericordia Sisters filled a huge need in dispensing mercy to unwed mothers and their babies. However, for the young women who sought help, there was a price. When they walked through the door of Misericordia, they entered an asylum-like setting in which temptations would be pushed back by discipline, obedience, and respect for authority. The girls became "penitents" and soon after entering Misericordia had to make a three-day retreat that the nuns described as helping them to "fathom the depth of the abyss to which they were hurrying and with the help of grace conceive a salutary shame." They had to submit to rehabilitation and follow the rules of the Order, which were severe. The nuns considered the girls fallen women, sinners who must repent and find the route of goodness through life. They had to attend services and were encouraged to become nuns. Trips into the chapel were frequent where they fingered rosaries and murmured prayers such as "Hail Holy Queen."

The pregnant women usually entered the maternity home several months before their due date. The idea in most cases was to hide them before their condition began to show. The homes expected those who had the means to pay room and board, but many could not and worked for keep, doing household chores. Their lives during pregnancy were lived in secrecy. They existed behind draped windows and the matrons seldom allowed them outside. Life was regimented drudgery compared to the gaiety — or what the nuns might call looseness — on the outside. Their names were secret to protect the honour and reputations of themselves and their relatives so the nuns assigned them pseudonyms — names of the saints. The births of their children occurred in secret, and in shame. The entire operation was meant to bring the scandal to completion and move the mother back on the road to God, the child into a life with a family that could care for it.

At Misericordia in Edmonton, the sisters took charge of the illegitimate newborn, caring for them in the Crèche. That was only the start of a new phase of their work. They had to get the mothers on track and back into the world, and most importantly they had to find homes for the growing numbers of babies. They worked channels, some of them arcane, to arrange placement. Their best networking was through parish priests across the country. These men knew the lives of their parishioners and were able to spot where a child might be wanted and raised in Catholic traditions.

Adoption laws in the beginning were non-existent. Alberta was part of the Northwest Territories until provincehood arrived in 1905. Even when a legislative assembly was elected and child protection laws were drafted, the placement of orphans and neglected illegitimates was not always done exactly by the book. The goal was placement to keep the orphanage doors from bulging, not satisfying narrow-minded bureaucrats.

When the young women left Misericordia, thinner and lighter physically, and usually relieved of the responsibilities of child rearing, the sisters hoped they were better prepared to deal with a cruel world filled with temptations. A world the nuns saw as "a corrupt world, which after inflicting unhappiness by causing the penitents to lose all honour, reproves their presence by seeing them as objects worthy only of hatred and disgust."

22 — INNISFREE

THE HISTORY OF THE MISERICORDIA SISTERS WAS interesting, but it didn't provide me with any specifics about Veronica, where she came from, and who she was. The information I obtained through the back door was sketchy. It listed the birthplace as Misericordia Hospital in Edmonton, the date of September 16, 1917, and the parents as Elizabeth LaRose of Innisfree, Alberta, and John Coleman, a farmer with no address. There was no other information as to who they were, how Elizabeth ended up at Misericordia Hospital, or what happened to them. The Alberta government continued to refuse to show me the file.

I tracked down LaFrance connections in Chapleau, Sudbury, and Sault Ste. Marie. None had any direct knowledge of Veronica's secret history. Rene Aquin, her first cousin, did recall telling someone in Chapleau about his new posting to Port Arthur as a federal government Indian agent, and that person noting the coincidence because Rene would get to see his "Indian cousin" who lived there.

Most of the people who knew Isidore and Louise had passed away and the few who remained had been young at the time. In Thunder Bay, no one recalled anything. I spent a morning in a basement examining Port Arthur Separate School records from the 1920s and found records of Veronica's attendance at St. Andrew's School. They provided an interesting history but no clues to her secret.

Doris Spooner, Veronica's maid of honour when she married my father, was said to be alive and living in Quebec. I found her in the

Montreal area and she had crystal clear memories of them growing up as children but knew nothing of an adoption.

I connected with a researcher in Edmonton who made a possible connection with a Joseph LaRose and an Eva Piché, a descendant of a well-known Native leader. Something was wrong with the connection, but we couldn't say what it was and were unable to connect Veronica directly with that family.

We found one John Coleman who was a terrific bet to have been Veronica's father. He had lived on a farm near Delville, an area between Innisfree and Edmonton. The LaRose family had passed through his territory on trips to the city. He was an Irish immigrant, single and with no relatives in Canada. He had enlisted in the Canadian Expeditionary Force overseas for the First World War.

I pulled his army records at the National Archives in Ottawa, and at first glance was convinced he was the birth father. He was the right age and had lived in the right area. He had joined in the fall of 1916, was sent to boot camp at a time that would have given him a Christmas leave when he could have hooked up with Elizabeth LaRose. Veronica would have been conceived early in the New Year. But alas, John did not get Christmas leave. He was shipped out to Europe in November, making it impossible for him to be the father. Had he been the father, he would never have seen her anyway. He died in battle a month or two before Veronica's birth.

No other Coleman living in Alberta at the time came close as a possibility for having fathered Veronica. The name was a dead end, so my focus turned to the LaRose family, but some mysterious happening kept derailing a straight connection with Veronica.

I was like a cat with a ball of string. The more I unravelled, the more snagged the story became. The LaRose track looped back on itself and went nowhere. Many a reporter and researcher gets hopelessly lost while following a false track too far. I felt I was miles back in the bush without a compass until a closer look at a 1900 Northwest Territories census turned over a revealing fact. A Joseph and Eva LaRose lived on the same street in Strathcona, now the south part of Edmonton, but in different houses. Why would a husband live in one house with a couple of the kids while the wife lived down the street with two other children?

This clue led to the discovery that Joe had tossed aside his wife, Eva, for a young American woman, also named Eva. There were two Evas and their separate paths had confused the family history trail. More digging revealed that Joe and Eva Number Two later owned property in Innisfree, the place listed as Veronica's birth mother's home.

Innisfree is a tiny homestead community once named Delnorte, but the name changed in 1911 after Sir Byron Walker, president of the Bank of Commerce, agreed to locate a branch in the village. Soft hills there cuddle a beautiful lake marked by an odd-shaped island to create a setting that reminded Sir Byron of Lake Isle of Innisfree in Scotland. The locals called the lake Birch Lake because of the thin Prairie poplar and birch forests that put down thirsty roots beside its shores. Sir Byron said he would build a magnificent bank building if in return the citizens would rename the village Innisfree.

It didn't seem to bother Sir Byron that Birch Lake cannot be seen from the village because a hill, one of the highest in that piece of flatland, blocks the view. Innisfree is built into the north side of the hill while the lake is on the opposite side, roughly two kilometres south of the village centre. It is an energetic stroll up the hill, but from the summit there is a rewarding view of the lake and surrounding hills. First to catch the eye is Crowsnest Island, called so because of the numbers of crows that once nested there. It is a small island measured in square yards rather than square kilometres, and it is peculiar because of the high cliff on its west end that slopes into nothingness at its eastern end. If Birch Lake reminded Sir Byron of Scotland, Crowsnest Island reminded me of a miniature Nanabjiou, the Sleeping Giant at Thunder Bay. Birch Lake became a popular summer recreation spot, its northeast corner the scene of many summer picnics.

The lake was shackled by ice and snow as I stood on the hill and peered over it in March of 2003. It was sunny and springtime warm but there remained a chilliness that made one wonder how people survived the bitter winters out on this prairie many decades ago. I wondered how cold and snowy and windy it was during the winter of 1916–1917 when Elizabeth LaRose walked the village streets as a pregnant teenager.

It was exhilarating being back on the Prairies as a reporter. Sure, it was a personal assignment, with no employer paying the expenses; still, it felt like the old days of being in a strange place and about to discover new and exciting information. The greatest excitement of being a reporter is that you never know when or how you will stumble across something important. If you walk around enough, poke your head through enough doors and ask enough questions, you will find out something new.

A walk through the village's nine or ten streets helped me understand why people had settled there and not beside the lake. The village was built into the side of a treed hill, which provided some protection against the snow-bearing winter winds. I stumbled into the village office where I decided I should buy a map of the area. I chatted with the village clerk and asked her if she knew the name LaRose. She was young and new to the area and the name was unfamiliar. But as I turned to go, she said an elderly woman named Erica might know.

She dialled a number and called Erica Mansell, the old-timer born in Innisfree and who lived up the street. Early in the conversation, she cupped her hand over the mouthpiece and said Erica wanted to know if I was a LaRose. I fumbled that no, I was not a LaRose.

I went to see Erica. She grew up on a homestead not far away and was in her mid to late eighties. The first thing she asked: Was I a LaRose?

Again I stuttered, never providing a complete answer. Instead I explained what I was looking for and that it involved my mother, who had been born Veronica LaRose. She picked up the telephone and called a relative who knew more than she did. "Yes, he's one of the LaRoses," she told the person on the line.

I shifted awkwardly while she continued the telephone talk. I was uncomfortable being called one of the LaRoses. After I left her place, I walked up the hill and sat in the sun while looking out over Birch Lake. My emotions were raw and I tried to sort them out.

Are you a LaRose? Between Birch Lake and me was a shimmering film, like in one of those horror movies. If I said, "Yes, I am a LaRose," I would pass through the watery screen and into another world. I didn't want to enter another world. Until that moment, I had been detached from the LaRose family history, a reporter gathering facts about just another family.

Are you a LaRose? The question kept repeating itself. My mother's mother was LaRose, so what did that make me? This was now too much, too close to reality. I didn't want to be a LaRose. I just wanted to be myself as I had always been, a Poling and a LaFrance.

Erica knew something about the LaRose family. As a child, she had known Eva LaRose and a couple of the younger LaRose kids. She also knew three sisters in Vegreville who had information about the LaRose family.

The next day I sat in the kitchen of one of the sisters listening to what they knew, while they provided me with lunch. It was a flashback to earlier reporting days out West. A stranger knocks at the door, is brought into the kitchen to get warm, and then is fed. There are few regions as trusting and kind as the Canadian West.

The sisters told me that Eva LaRose had lived with one of their relatives. They knew something of the family, although they had not known about Elizabeth's illegitimate child. They knew Margaret, the youngest LaRose child. Eva was pregnant with her in 1917, the same year Elizabeth gave birth to Veronica. Mom and daughter both pregnant at the same time. Margaret had stayed in the area all her life, but regrettably for me, she had died only months before, taking with her much of the knowledge of the LaRose family.

Margaret did have a daughter living in Edmonton. Her name was Marlene. Attempts to find her were fruitless, so I climbed on an airplane for the East. It was a defeat not to find any living descendants of Joe and Eva. I wasn't terribly disappointed, however. Veronica had always said it was best to let sleeping dogs lie. It was better not to make any direct connections.

Reporters never know how to leave well enough alone. Months after promising myself to let the matter sleep, I resumed the search for Margaret LaRose's daughter. I never expected to find her but sent out some letters to people I thought might be connected to her.

On the morning of Mother's Day 2004, more than a year after visiting Innisfree, I opened my e-mail and received a shock. There was a message from a woman in Edmonton. Her name was Marlene and she explained that she was the granddaughter of Eva LaRose, knew the family history, and was willing to help me. We were cousins and her email introduced me into the LaRose family. Soon there were emails from other LaRose cousins. No one in the family knew of Elizabeth's first child, but they provided enough bits and leads that I was able to collect Elizabeth's story and piece together who my mother was and where she came from.

23 — LaROSE

ONE OF THE EARLY CUSTOMERS OF THE EDMONTON Misericordia unwed mothers home was Evangeline May Fuller, a young American woman who had trailed out of the Dakotas with her family in the late 1890s to a homestead in Wabamun, just west of Edmonton. She wasn't typical of the unwed mothers the Sisters had come to assist. For one thing, she had been previously married, had already borne two children, and was now a twenty-year-old widow who had emigrated from the United States with her parents, brothers, and one son.

Eva May, the eldest child of James and Martha Anne Fuller, was born in Spencer, Iowa, a pioneer town in northwest Iowa. James was a chimney builder and Martha was said to have Native ancestry, and after Eva May, they had three sons. James's work took the family from Spencer into the Black Hills of South Dakota where a chance meeting changed the course of a couple of family histories.

James encountered one day in the Black Hills a horse trader named Joe LaRose whose buckboard had broken down. LaRose was a French Canadian with Native features and who had gone west from Quebec for adventure and opportunity. He found it in the Edmonton area where he worked at training horses for the North West Mounted Police and in the livery stable business. James gave LaRose a hand with the repair and no doubt they talked about the opportunities out in the Northwest Territories where the federal government was offering free land to encourage settlement.

Courtesy of Jim Poling Sr.

Joe LaRose and Eva Fuller began living together in 1900, but there is no record of their marriage, even though she carried the LaRose name. She was a young widow, and he had left his Native wife when they met through Eva's father. This photo was taken sometime in the early 1900s.

Some years later, in 1900, James and family pushed even farther west and steered north into the Edmonton area. Joe LaRose was well known in the community and the two renewed their acquaintance, although Joe's attention quickly turned to Eva May, the comely, narrow-waisted widow with brown hair, sparkling eyes, and an ever-present mirthful look. Joe was twice Eva's age, but love sparks flew and she became pregnant.

It was an awkward situation for Joe LaRose, who was already married with a son, two daughters, and a step-daughter. He had married a twenty-two-year-old Native woman named Eva Piché in 1891. She was the daughter of a Cree named Jean Batiste Piché, also known as Erminskin and Charlebois. She also was a widow when she met LaRose, having been married to Xavier Juneau who died young. It was also said that she married or lived with Peter Juneau, possibly her brother-in-law. She had a child named Rosie with one of the Juneaus and brought her to the marriage with LaRose. Together, Joe LaRose and Eva Piché quickly added Octavia in 1894, Alphonse in 1896, and Agnes in 1897. Another child, Peter James, died as an infant.

The affair with Eva May either triggered or completed the breakup of the LaRose family. Eva Piché moved out of the LaRose house in Strathcona, the south side of Fort Edmonton, and took up residence down the street with Rosie and Agnes. Alphonse and Octavia stayed with Joe.

Eva May Fuller arrived at the Misericordia Maternity Hospital in January 1901. The nuns had moved out of their clapboard shack five months earlier and into a renovated shed-warehouse on the southwest corner of 98 Avenue and 111 Street. The two-storey structure had a typical false western façade that disguised the building's homeliness. The only thing that identified it as anything more than just another business was the rough wooden cross that stood atop the highest shoulder of the facade. The shadow of the cross, depending on the time of day, fell across a rough prairie farmyard where chickens, ducks, turkeys, and a cow foraged around a slash of earth where the nuns busted sod for a vegetable garden.

The Sisters had been busy. When they were not tending to expectant mothers and babies, they were out canvassing for donations. They travelled into Fort Saskatchewan and along the streets of Strathcona gathering donated house utensils, furniture, and food. By the time Eva May arrived, they were well established. Eva was there just long enough to deliver the child she called Elizabeth Belle and whom she decided to keep instead of giving her up to the Misericordia Crèche for adoption. She left the maternity home with the baby and moved in with Joe LaRose.

The LaRose household in Strathcona now had four children from three different unions — Alphonse and Octavia from Joe and Eva Piché, Elizabeth from Joe and Eva May, and a two-year-old boy named Stephen

LeRoy Davis from Eva May's first marriage. Eva May had married a soldier named Scott Davis at age sixteen and they had two sons, Frankie and Stephen. The male Davises all would die young and tragically. Scott went off to war, possibly the Spanish-American conflict, and was killed in action. Frankie was two when the family was smoking meat over a fire pit. He toppled into the pit and was so badly burned he died later. Stephen followed his father into soldiering and served in the Canadian army in the First World War. He returned from the war only to drown in Birch Lake during celebrations on July 1, 1919.

No one knows why Eva did not retain the Davis name. She went by her maiden name Fuller and gave that name to her new daughter, Elizabeth. However, when the census takers came along five months later for the 1901 census, the child was listed as Elizabeth LaRose.

The new combined family settled into a domestic routine in Strathcona. There is no record of a marriage between Joe LaRose and Eva Fuller, but an early 1900s photo of the couple appears to have been taken as a wedding photo. Also there is no record of a divorce from Eva Piché, who along with Rosie and Octavia vanished into the mists of history. It is possible that Eva Piché died young, returned to an Indian reserve or Métis settlement, or simply disappeared into a new life in Edmonton. She apparently was not around for one of the many LaRose family tragedies, the death in 1907 of Agnes. The child, who was living with her mother after the marriage breakup, died of pneumonia at age eleven. The *Edmonton Bulletin*, in recording Agnes's death and funeral, noted that her father Joseph LaRose was returning home from his horse business in Montana to be at the funeral. It did not mention her mother Eva Piché LaRose, but perhaps that was an omission that simply reflected the chauvinism of the times. Or, it might mean that Eva herself had died or moved away. She appears not to have had much contact with her son Alphonse. When he signed up for the Army, he listed his mother as Eva May LaRose of Innisfree, who was his stepmother but apparently the only mother he had known since he was six years old.

Records or not, it is likely that Joe and Eva May did marry sometime early in the 1900s. More children followed Elizabeth — six more girls, although one girl named Marjorie died in infancy, and a boy named Joseph after his dad, but called Buster. Life with Eva May and the growing family settled Joe somewhat, and he focussed on building a successful business career, although he seemed to drift sometimes into the shady side of the street. In fact, in the parlance of today's urban society, Joe was a bit of a bad ass and had trouble with the law on at least three occasions.

He was born in Quebec about 1856 but there is no record of where he got his Native features, although French-Canadian–Native unions were common on the Canadian frontier. He drifted west, likely through the States, probably picking up his knowledge of horses in places like Montana. He arrived at Fort Edmonton as a midtwenties gritty wrangler with enough leather in his skin and in his attitude to withstand the brutalities of Prairie weather and frontier living. He was a good fit for the West, gritty and quick to do whatever he needed to survive. He worked with horses wherever he could and dreamed of having his own livery stable.

A history of the Innisfree area east of Edmonton described him as "a regular old-time Westerner who carried a six-gun on his belt and wasn't afraid to use it." He didn't need the six-gun to look the part. He was well put together into a short, sturdy frame and looked well weathered with his olive skin, black hair, and dark eyes. He likely did need the six-gun at times to dampen any violent ambitions in his enemies.

In the spring of 1899, he was before a judge on a charge of horse theft. He had been caught with a pretty bay mare with a star on her forehead and a G burned into her left back thigh. The G was the brand of the horse's owner, one John Grant. "I have nothing to say just yet," Joe told the judge. The rest of the court record is gone and it is not known whether he was found guilty. He likely was because the evidence showed his claim to legal ownership of the beast was thin.

Five years later — in the spring again — he stood before another judge, this time charged with stealing a wallet containing $4 and a promissory note for $400. The wallet belonged to Frank Mariaggi, owner of the Alberta Hotel in Edmonton. Joe said he found the wallet on the floor at the hotel. Again, there is no record of whether he was found guilty or innocent. Three years after that — in October 1907 — he and a business partner were hauled in for operating a feed stable without a licence. They were fined $30 plus $3 in costs or fifteen days in jail.

Joe got a chance for his own operation in 1903 when W.L. Wilkin sold his livery and feed barn operation at the corner of Dennis and Ross in Fort Saskatchewan, fifteen miles northwest of Edmonton. Joe threw in with James Charles Starrett, an Irishman a few years his senior, and they began operations as LaRose and Starrett, Livery and Stable. It didn't last long. Starrett died the following year. Joe carried on for a while on his own then acquired a new partner, William H. Bell, and they operated LaRose and Bell Livery and Feed. They exchanged and sold horses boasting "oldest and most reliable firm in the North West Territories." In 1912, something went wrong with the partnership and the two became competitors, Bell operating the Edmonton Horse Exchange and LaRose the Windsor Sale Stables.

The following year, Joe expanded his business interests. He opened LaRose and Co. Wholesale Tobacconists, plus he was president of something called the Banner Coal Co., which seemed to be a speculative project tied to a land claim he had made southwest of Edmonton. Alphonse, now a wiry nineteen-year-old standing five feet four inches tall, was with him in the tobacco business and the next year they were running the Rex Cigar Store in Edmonton. The Banner Coal Co. was still listed as a business but didn't appear to be producing anything.

The year 1915 brought big changes in the business and the family. A few days into the New Year, Alphonse joined the Canadian Overseas Expeditionary Force and shipped out to Britain en route to France. Joe bought a farm out at Innisfree, seventy-five miles east of Edmonton, and sent Eva and the kids out there while he moved into the Castle Hotel, running the Rex Cigar Store at 10187 104 Street and a new horse business — Capitol Sales and Stable. He commuted between Edmonton and Innisfree then later moved to the farm fulltime.

It is unclear whether buying the farm was spurred by thoughts of retirement or by necessity growing out of failing business ventures. Other folks regarded the LaRoses as well off. They had a big house with a nanny and a cook on 114 Street. Joe had made several land purchases and even owned an interest in the Queen's Hotel in Fort Saskatchewan. However, he seemed to change business partners a lot. Something certainly went amiss in his business life because debts piled up. Between

1915 and 1918 he loaded the Innisfree property with encumbrances totalling $13,000 — significant money in those days. These mortgages against the properties were from banks, individuals, and the Imperial Tobacco Co. indicating his venture into the tobacco business had not gone well. He even owed for lumber purchased to improve the farm and for feed or other farm supplies.

The LaRose farm was known as the Northeast Quarter 10-51-11 west of the fourth meridian, just a kilometre or so beyond Innisfree's northern edge. It had been broken by a homesteader and was a working farm with a barn valued more than the ramshackle clapboard house, granary, shed, well, and Ford tractor. No one ever remembered it as a going concern operation. It could not have produced much more than table food. Joe was close to sixty then, relatively old in those days and certainly too old for dawn-to-dusk farming. He had only Eva and six girls and a young boy to work the place. He did not have the money to hire a hand. His financial affairs were in a serious downward spiral by then.

Eva kept the place running and the kids fed, clothed, and reasonably well directed. By then she was short and plump with dark hair and plenty of energy. She could do anything around the farm, from running down a cow to nailing barn boards. She was a midwife who helped bring many Minburn County babies into the world. She was strong-willed with the type of spirit needed to survive the drastic changes from big house and servants in Edmonton to the harsh realities of surviving on the outskirts of a Prairie village.

Her survival instincts showed earlier when she was ostracized by the women of St. Joachim's Catholic Church in Edmonton, where Joe was a member. Her affair, her trip to the Misericordia Maternity Home, and the breakup of the first LaRose marriage were known in the community. She was snubbed and ridiculed. Despite that, the LaRose children attended St. Joachim's. However, when the family moved to Innisfree, Eva enrolled the family in the United Church because she bitterly resented her treatment by the Catholic Church women. Resentment of Catholicism became a family feature for decades later.

The LaRose kids were tough and handy, as well. Some of the girls later became known as excellent seamstresses while Buster was the village auto mechanic until he moved away. A county history book noted that Joe LaRose's "children had enough Indian blood to be the best built, best looking and most honest kids in the neighbourhood."

Eva had to be tough. She buried three children and a stepchild. In the course of four months in 1919, she would bury son Stephen and husband Joe, whose death was followed by especially hard financial times.

There must have been considerable strain — financial and otherwise — on the LaRose farm even before Joe's death. Inexplicably Joe left the farm and returned to Edmonton late in 1918 or in 1919. He took up residence in the Alberta Hotel on Jasper Ave. and opened LaRose and Son Livery at 9924 102 Avenue. The LaRose and Son name seemed to anticipate Alphonse's return from Europe. However, there was no real evidence to prove whether he left Innisfree to set up business for Alphonse or because the family needed the money.

Alphonse returned and within weeks his dad was dead. Joe LaRose died while living in someone else's home in Edmonton. His financial affairs were a mess. He left Eva May with less than $6,000 in assets and

Courtesy of Jim Poling Sr.

Joe LaRose loved horses and thrived for a while in the livery business in Edmonton. The decline of his business began with the introduction of the automobile. Here he is seen with a pair of his favourite horses.

$16,200 in encumbrances. The net value of his estate was minus $10,800. Much of the debt was owed to Imperial Tobacco, the rest to the Innisfree Co-operative for farm supplies and a doctor. Eva May was now forty and struggling with the hardships of raising a houseful of kids, including the infant Margaret, who was a late-in-life surprise the year before Joe died. All she had was a widow's pension and whatever money she could get by hiring herself out. The situation meant that the kids began moving out as soon as they were old enough to marry or find work.

Elizabeth would be the first to go but her leaving provided added stress instead of relief. Whether she was at home or far away, the eldest LaRose girl was a worry throughout Eva's life. The real worry began in the summer of 1917, two years before Joe's death. Joe was ailing. The bills were mounting and the growing family required more food and clothing. Eva was shocked to find that at thirty-seven and with six kids in the house — the youngest only five — she was pregnant again. This news could not have been greeted with overwhelming joy. That wasn't the half of it. Elizabeth, whose life would mark her as a wild child, announced that she too was pregnant.

Just turned sixteen and unmarried, Elizabeth Belle LaRose found herself on the road to where her life began: Misericordia Home for Unwed Mothers in Edmonton.

24 — ELIZABETH

ELIZABETH LaROSE HAD REASON TO BE FRIGHTENED AS SHE climbed the broad staircase leading up to the balconied portico of Misericordia Hospital in the summer of 1917. First was the building itself, with a design that might have been taken from a Stephen King horror story. It was four storeys of severity dominated by a corner turret and wrought iron widow's walk, where one might expect to see a ghostly figure looking out into a misty night. The stonework of its base gave way to red brick that rose to an iron-railed Mansard roof studded with small, clandestine dormers that watched in silence the street below. The roofline, dormers, turret, and wrought iron all were elements of North American Second Empire architecture, also known as the haunted house look.

If the building wasn't ominous enough to frighten a young girl, the goings-on inside certainly were. Misericordia was no longer just a maternity hospital and unwed mothers' home. The sharp cries and sweet smells of newborns had been overtaken by the sights, sounds, and odours of illness and suffering. In the seventeen years since its founding, its mission became progressively more complicated. Misericordia now was a bustling general hospital dealing with the disease and wounds of a city whose population had exploded to fifty-six thousand. Alberta soldiers with shattered bodies had returned for treatment from the First World War killing fields of France. Crying and moaning from the pain of missing limbs and burned flesh were part of the atmosphere. Added

Courtesy of Glenbow Archives NC-6-33.

Misericordia Hospital in Edmonton in 1912. The hospital grew out of a small wooden refuge for unwed mothers and their babies.

to all that was the shame of being a pregnant unwed sixteen-year-old farm girl about to commit herself to weeks of austere life among the Misericordia Sisters while she prepared for her birthing time.

Despite the increased general hospital work, the Misericordia Sisters had not abandoned their founding role. Their work with unwed mothers continued, although as a small part of the overall hospital. The maternity quarters were more spacious and modern than in the beginning. There was more staff and better facilities. The original hospital-home at 9746 111 Street in the Oliver District where Eva May Fuller gave birth was replaced in 1906 by the four-storey full-service institution on the west side of 111 Street between 98 and 99 Avenues. The Crèche, the home for babies left behind, originally accommodated ten children as part of what was maternity home, convent, hospital, and boarding house. By 1917, the Crèche occupied a narrow clapboard house with a lean-to addition on the west side of the hospital and could accommodate up to fifty orphans.

The West was changing, its itinerant frontier lifestyle giving way to the beginnings of urban industrial life. Edmonton in the fall of 1917 was a relatively recent urban bulge along a bend in the North Saskatchewan River. Although the frenzy of development pushed by the Yukon gold rush of 1898 had fallen back and the war had slowed immigration, the Prairie town still had more than fifty thousand souls relentlessly pushing the last traces of frontier life into the pages of history. Two years previous, they tore down the remnants of Fort Edmonton, first built by the Hudson's Bay Co. as a fur trade post in 1795. The fort had been built and rebuilt on different sites, but this time it would be gone forever as part of daily life in central Alberta.

From the wide steps of Misericordia Hospital, Elizabeth could see the evidence of change all around her. Streets that were once mere horse paths were now broad with boardwalks and lined with tall slim poles bearing as many as seven crossbars that carried lines for electricity and telephone. Automobiles coughing and farting, much like the horses they replaced. There were twenty thousand cars in Alberta in the year 1917 and the livery stables that were once a centre of transportation life in Edmonton were all but gone. Vanishing with them were the horsemen like Elizabeth's father Joseph LaRose, one of Edmonton's old-time livery operators knocked aside by car dealers, mechanics, and filling station operators.

Citizens were becoming more educated, more refined, but although illegitimacy rates were dropping, there was still much rescue and mercy work for the Sisters. What had not changed over the years was the atmosphere of the maternity operation. It remained medieval, thick with shame and guilt. The business of the place was military style, done with religious fervour.

Elizabeth of course could not remember breathing the heavy, dark atmosphere when she entered life as one of its first illegitimates. She probably didn't know that by walking through the doors of Misericordia she was tracing the path of her mother. History repeating itself, although the nuns were not likely amused by the entrance of a second-generation unwed mother because repeat business was not part of their business plan.

Elizabeth likely was at Misericordia at her mother's suggestion and for two other reasons. Joe LaRose's failing financial situation perhaps precluded any birthing beyond the charity of the Misericordia Sisters. The Sisters shook loose cash from relatives who could afford it, but

Elizabeth was just another poor country girl in trouble. Secondly, Misericordia not only would provide shelter, care, and medicine, but also a complete cover-up of Elizabeth's situation. Her stay there would be secret, her name changed for the stay, and her baby could be absorbed into the anonymous world of the Misericordia orphanage operation.

It might seem pointless to protect the reputation of the LaRose family. They lived lives far removed from the rigid standards of Victorian morality. Their bloodlines were so mixed it was hard to tell who was a full brother or sister and whether an individual child's ancestry was French, Anglo, or Native. Still, Innisfree was a rural area where everyone knew each other's business. Many of the folks who homesteaded there or lived in the village were Polish and Ukrainian conservative settlers who carried high standards of morality. Joe might not have cared what they thought, but Eva was in charge of the child rearing and did not want her children viewed as trash.

Not keeping secret the pregnancy would have caused tongues to flap in furious speculation about the father. As it was, Elizabeth was able to hide the father's identity from everyone, including the Misericordia Sisters. When they asked her to present the name of her baby's father, she gave them John Coleman, a farmer. It is possible that she knew John Coleman, had seen his name posted as missing, then killed in action. Or, Alphonse quite possibly knew Coleman and mentioned his death in a letter to home.

In 1916, Alberta passed a law requiring that no father of an illegitimate child be named unless both he and the mother agreed. Maternity homes likely ignored this law, but it certainly provided a good out for Elizabeth if she wanted to keep the name of the father secret. If she said John Coleman, there would be no reason for anyone to go back and match possible conception times with his army movements. Perhaps there were other John Colemans, but searches of records in Alberta have not produced one who was in the Edmonton-Innisfree area at the time of conception. A best guess is that she knew the name and used it to get the nuns off her back. She did not plan to keep the baby, so the father's name didn't matter.

The number of potential fathers around Innisfree was limited. The village was tiny; most people lived on the farms scattered across the

Prairie. Many young men had shipped out like Alphonse LaRose to fight the Kaiser in Europe. The arrival of the Canadian Northern Railway to Innisfree had turned Birch Lake into a summer resort area by 1908–09 and attracted hundreds of vacationing strangers, including young men, who arrived at the Innisfree station to take the hot summer sun and frolic by the water. Elizabeth, however, conceived at Christmas, months after the beach resort closed, and when winter blizzards and cold kept everyone close to hearth at home. There could have been a quick encounter during Christmas festivity visiting between neighbours, although the LaRoses did not mingle socially. Or, a hurried liaison during a trip to the village, but the winter lockdown on the Prairies lessened the chances.

Whatever the circumstances, Elizabeth had committed herself to the Misericordia Sisters for help. On September 16, 1917, they rolled her into the Misericordia labour room where Dr. D. McGibbon and Sister St. Felixe helped her deliver a dark-haired baby girl that the Sisters named Véronique Cécile. Did Elizabeth hold the child and feel the pain that must accompany the thought of giving her up? Perhaps the nuns had her hold it briefly so she could fully understand the consequences that befall a wayward girl.

Did Elizabeth want to keep her baby? Deep down, what mother doesn't? Yet, Elizabeth's later history shows that although she could be kind and loving, she was more capable of looking after herself than her children. After Veronica, she bore three other girls, all of whom lived with relatives or in an orphanage at times. Perhaps she did want to keep Veronica, but the situation at home was difficult. Joe was having business difficulties and spent much time in Edmonton. Eva May was six months pregnant, and there were already five other kids at home.

Joe LaRose was tough and no man's fool and quite capable of leading a potential son-in-law to the altar at gunpoint. Maybe the father, who never will be known, was someone the family did not want associated with Elizabeth and the child, or even possibly someone who impregnated Elizabeth during a rape.

Three days after the birth, the nuns carried Veronica into the Misericordia chapel and placed her on the baptismal font in front of Father Hêtu, who was no stranger to the LaRose family. He had said the funeral Mass for Agnes LaRose ten years earlier.

The baptism is a scene from a black-and-white movie. Father Hêtu is slight and somewhat fragile looking, easily mistaken for a music professor rather than a Prairie missionary. He displays no evidence of the tough resiliency of the Oblates of Mary Immaculate, products of Quebec seminaries commissioned to send strong, committed men to the West to convert the Natives and tend to the needs of the settlers taming the frontier. The Wild West days are about over, but urbanization has not eliminated the godless aspects of Alberta life. St. Joachim's Parish, where at age thirty-eight Father Hêtu became *curé*, is known for its illegitimacy rate. The work of converting Native souls has diminished, but there is still much spiritual work to save souls tainted by the sins of the flesh. His work includes the chaplaincy of Misericordia Hospital and Crèche.

He stood many times over many illegitimate infants, letting the water of baptism slip from his slender fingertips. The water falling in fat and heavy drops, descending slowly through air thickened by the sweet smokiness of burning incense. Dropping almost in slow motion, catching candle reflections like moonbeams on the fall, before spattering onto the softness of the newborn forehead. The drops reconnect into tiny rivulets that seep through black hair impossibly thick for a three-day-old infant. One trickle slips forward, tracking into the corner of an eye, open wide but seeing only the charcoal mist of new life. The child screws up its face and screams. Most babies do when the water wets their heads, but this is not the sharp bird-like protest cry of most babies. It has the melodic huskiness of someone who will love to sing, with gusto. Someone who will laugh at life despite its tragedies.

The priest's tenor voice, sensitive but powerful considering the reedy body from which it issues, joins the crying. Pale white fingers move up, down and across, forming the sign of a cross that casts a shadow over the tiny dimpled chin, flat nose, and high cheekbones, facial features that over the past nine months have emerged from an amorphous scallop of flesh as a one-of-a-kind human face.

"*Je te baptise Véronique Cécile, dans le nom du père, fils et de l'espirit saint …*"

The fingers move with such fluidity that you could imagine creating magic on a piano keyboard as they lift a crystal dish of oil the colour of candlelight. The right thumbs dips into the oil, then spreads it, again in the sign of the cross, on the forehead. The priest murmurs an anointing prayer then dips a wet pointer finger into a silver dish, emerging with granules of white salt. The finger presses it to the baby's lips, which pull inward from the acerbic shock.

Water, the source of all life, although this child will grow to fear and hate it. Oil symbolizing the preciousness of life. This is a life that has emerged from shadows, not sunlight, but nothing makes one life less precious than another. Salt, for the bitterness of living. Veronica Cecile, now calm, will swallow much bitterness on her journey to a final anointing for death. She stops crying. The dark eyes widen, trying to see the shapes in the tiny chapel. Nothing will focus, but she can smell the woody richness of pews and panelling and the ammonia sharpness of starch in the nuns' habits. The pungency of melting candle wax mixes with spent incense and stale breath expelled in the reciting of many prayers.

Lena Kestner, the chief witness of the baptism, rearranges the child's pilch and wipes water and oil from its head. She nods to Father Hêtu as she turns and exits through the dark panelled door that leads into the scrubbed antiseptic brightness of the hallway and into the hospital nursery. Father Hêtu folds his linens, setting them to one side of the baptismal table. The nuns will gather them and take them away for washing, starching, and pressing — all part of God's work in the battle to save lives and rescue souls. The work of the Misericordia Sisters, now in their seventeenth year of delivering mercy to the frontier society of Edmonton, is never done.

The brief ceremony having ended, Veronica is brought up the street to the Misericordia Crèche to begin her new Christian life with the other orphans. There is mayhem there; the screams of infants wailing for feeding and the thumping feet of energetic toddlers wanting to play. Crowds of children and babies in the house are laid out on beds like cordwood ready to be stacked.

Outside, a cool breeze climbs the banks of the North Saskatchewan River, chilling wooden buildings scattered throughout the valley all the way up to and beyond Jasper Avenue. Father Hêtu pulls up the collar of his black overcoat against the chill. It is to be expected. It is past mid-September and the Edmonton winter will begin any time now.

It is possible the snow is already on the road from Edmonton to Vegreville and Innisfree, and Elizabeth must stay in Edmonton where her father is struggling with his businesses in a changing world. Perhaps as she walked away from Misericordia she could hear the hard working nuns during a pause for prayer. Chanting the rosary and singing "Salve Regina," their favourite prayer. In English, it is "Hail, Holy Queen," the prayer that Columbus's men recited the night before they discovered the New World. They say that its lyrical qualities imbed it forever in the minds of those who hear it only a few times. At Misericordia Chapel, it is imbedded in the ceiling and walls. If woodwork could talk, it would surely murmur the words:

> Hail, holy Queen, Mother of mercy,
> Our life, our sweetness and our hope.
> To thee do we cry,
> Poor banished children of Eve ....

Certainly, it must have been heard and never forgotten by the infant Veronica Cecile, now sleeping the sleep of babies in her place in the Crèche.

Sometime soon after giving birth, Elizabeth returned to Innisfree. It is likely she stayed at home to help with the household chores as Eva entered the final stages of her own pregnancy. After a year or so, she married Laurence LaBelle, who, at twenty-seven, was nine years her senior. They lived in Innisfree and had two girls, Phyllis in 1920 and Doris in 1921, and then moved on to Spokane, Washington, where Laurence worked as a millwright for the Great Northern Railroad. A third girl, Betty, was born there in 1923, but the next year Laurence and Elizabeth separated. Elizabeth and the girls returned to Innisfree, where Eva May, widowed for five years, helped to look after them.

Innisfree began to crowd in on Elizabeth again and she and a younger sister, Eva, set out for Vancouver to find jobs. Elizabeth got one with the Hudson's Bay Company and became manager of the toy department. She sent for the girls, and they lived together in Vancouver for several years. In 1929, only twenty-eight years old, she became ill and required surgery. She sent the three girls to Laurence in Spokane, but he had acquired a young wife who wanted nothing to do with three stepchildren, so Laurence packed them off to an orphanage.

The girls and Elizabeth lived apart for more than two years. Elizabeth recovered and moved to Nevada where she found work as a waitress and when she established herself, got the girls out of the orphanage. In 1937 she married Gordon Marin in Nevada, divorced him, and several years later married Jack Redmond.

Elizabeth never spoke of her first child, Veronica. If any of her sisters or her brother Buster knew of the illegitimate birth, they never spoke of it.

In 1951 when Veronica was a thirty-four-year-old housewife tending to her mother Louise LaFrance at 402 Dawson Street in Port Arthur, the mother she never knew died in Nevada. Elizabeth Belle LaRose was fifty when she passed away. She is buried in Mountain View Cemetery, high on a hill outside Reno.

Elizabeth's life was a rough one. Four daughters, all of whom had spent time in orphanages. Moving about, working at jobs that called for long hours and low pay. Three marriages and some illness. She was a party girl, some said an alcoholic, but the drinking never seemed to pull her down into meanness. Nor did it affect her looks. She loved to shop, dressed well and retained her slimness and dark good looks. One of her girls once confided that her mother was kind, caring, and fun-loving, but her downfall was that "she liked men."

Elizabeth certainly didn't make Eva's already difficult life any easier. Eva still had three

Courtesy of Jim Poling Sr.

Elizabeth LaRose at fifty, just before her death in Reno, Nevada. Elizabeth battled alcoholism and beat it before she died. There is no evidence that she ever mentioned the daughter she gave up for adoption.

children at home when Elizabeth returned from Spokane with her brood. Joe's death had left the family struggling economically, and she began to move about, selling the farm, and living in rented accommodations in the Innisfree area.

Margaret, Eva's youngest child born a few months after Veronica, was seriously hurt in a schoolyard accident in Innisfree. She required a lot of medical attention, and Eva worked at the little hospital there to help pay for her treatment. She also travelled with Dr. Adamson as a sort of a nurse and delivered many a baby herself when he wasn't around. She did whatever she had to, including keeping house for David Fowler, a widower who farmed on the east side of Birch Lake. She and Margaret moved into a shack on the Fowler place, but his grandchildren later recalled that Eva May moved into the house and the housekeeping entailed more than just housekeeping. She was living there in 1936 when she keeled over and died at age fifty-six. Dr. Adamson attended and wrote on her death certificate a medical term that simply meant her heart wore out.

What her kids thought of her is visible on her tombstone at Innisfree cemetery. They put the word "MOTHER" on the stone, then added, "A Loving Mother, A Faithful Friend."

25 — THE BROKER

MISERICORDIA SURELY DID NOT GREET THE ARRIVAL OF Veronica Cecile with unrestrained joy. Another of God's little miracles to be sure, but still another unwanted baby to wet nurse, care for, and most importantly, another illegitimate without a bright future. Food, shelter, and care was available through hard work, donations, and faith that God always would provide. Finding an illegitimate child a future that included love, education, and religious direction required a near miracle. Certainly a contact network that could compete with the many other institutions trying to find homes for a flow of orphans that never seemed to subside.

Orphans were as common as stones along a riverbank in 1917–18, not just in Alberta but throughout North America. The Orphan Train Movement continued to dump thousands of children from the U.S. eastern cities onto the North American West. There was a limit to how many children the small although growing populations of the western states and provinces could absorb. Adding to the usual societal problems that created homeless children were the Great War and the Spanish flu. Hundreds of children lost one or both parents to the killer flu while others found themselves without homes because a father died overseas and mother could not support a family, particularly a large one. The flu struck thirty-eight thousand persons in Alberta, killing four thousand. No community, however remote, was immune. Of the 250 people living in Innisfree in 1918, twenty-two, or almost 10 percent, died.

Government reports of the day had much to say about the orphan problem. The Alberta Superintendent of Neglected Children reported handling 905 cases in 1917, including 89 babies born out of wedlock. Not all 905 were children up for adoption, but a large percentage were, and 173 were adopted. Little Veronica regretfully was not one of them. As the Christmas season closed out the year, she had spent the first three and a half months of her life with the other orphans at Misericordia Crèche because there were no takers for her. The following year, 1918, the Superintendent reported 1,037 cases with 182 adopted.

Numerous child-saving agencies tied to government, societies, and religious institutions tried to move along the flow of placements. As fast as the children went out their doors, more flowed in. In 1918, the Edmonton government shelter alone reported dealing with 285 children five years of age and under while matrons at the Calgary shelter reported another 121.

Complicating the problems of child placements were the attitudes of the time. Children, particularly those who created problems and could not be put to good use, were seen as debits, rather than credits. The Victorian age of Dickens and child tragedies such as *Oliver Twist* continued to influence the social fabric. Also, the eugenics movement that discouraged reproduction of people with "bad genes" had arrived from Britain and took a firm grip on North American thinking. It helped to sustain the attitude that the world was better off without illegitimates.

Eugenics, formed from the Greek words "good" and "origin," believed that shiftless people produced children prone to alcoholism, laziness, weak minds, sexual immorality, and other traits that led to criminality. Tied to eugenics was social Darwinism, the belief that wealth distribution is based on the merits of individuals in society. The wealthy have it because they are inherently smart; the poor are poor because they come from inferior stock. Now largely discredited, the eugenics movement caught a lot of attention in the early twentieth century, and by 1917, the year of Veronica's birth, fifteen U.S. states had eugenics laws to sterilize epileptics, the mentally ill, and criminals. Open for debate in North America was the idea of euthanizing children with serious physical and mental defects. Agencies fought this type of thinking, but public attitudes were rigid. The Superintendent of Neglected Children noted the change in his 1917 report: "Experience has shown that Providence and nature hold no grudge against these (illegitimate) children although society has stigmatised them with humiliating names. If normal and healthy, the illegitimate child may, under proper circumstances, develop into a useful citizen."

Added the Children's Aid Society in Calgary: "The appalling sacrifice of life that has taken place on the battle-fields of Europe and throughout the world, during the last four years, greatly enhances the value of every child as a national asset …"

The adoption problem of the times was not so much just getting the kids out of orphanages. There were crowds of people looking for kids as cheap labour. The superintendent wrote in 1917: "Perhaps the tendency to make the most out of child labour has been accentuated owing to war conditions and the scarcity of adult labour."

The challenge was to sort those who wanted a child for greed and those who would provide a real home where a child could grow and disprove the theories tossed about by the eugenics movement. Generally, agencies were cautious with people seeking older children compared with infants. Older and bigger children often were taken to be a little hired man or household maid. Younger and smaller children meant expenses and trouble.

Veronica LaRose lingered for months at Misericordia Crèche. She was heartbreakingly cute, as were all the kids. Photos of the orphanage would open the tightest of hearts. Nurses holding a swaddled infant in each arm while clumps of preschool children stand near their skirts staring into the lens with wide, hurt eyes. The ones like Veronica had much going against them. Infant, illegitimate, and part Native.

One Christmas photo of the orphanage shows two dozen children and babies gathered beside a giant spruce Christmas tree. The tree stands floor to ceiling — the top incredibly only a couple of feet away from a woodstove pipe — but sparsely decorated with a couple of strings of tinsel and a few ball ornaments. The paucity of bright and cheering decorations attests to the poverty of the place and the meagreness of the expectations for the orphans.

Veronica spent her first Christmas there, and the staff had small expectations for her being anywhere else for the second one, or even the third. It would take effort to move her and many of the others out to respectable homes. The best hope for the kids to find a home was in the continent-wide religious networks that reached into parishes where priests watched for potential placement situations to develop. Even remote and small parishes such as Sacred Heart in the northern Ontario backwoods, where Father Romeo Gasçon busied himself for long hours tending to the personal as well as spiritual needs of his Chapleau parishioners. The Sisters laboured in hope, praying for God to find the children homes, while working their networks for potential parents. Each passing month lessened the chances for Veronica's adoption.

Then, as the Prairie winter yielded to the spring of 1918, Veronica Cecile LaRose found herself being carried aboard the Edmonton-to-Hanna train by a big man in a suit and a lady with a large hat. When the passenger coach lurched forward, it sent the big man's left hand into his left vest pocket. Long, strong fingers clutched the metallic warmth of the timepiece as a big thumb gently pushed the clasp release. The gold face cover flipped open to reveal what look like black dock spider legs squashed onto a round white faceplate. The spidery hour and minute hands pointing to black Roman numerals from I to XII and an inner ring of Arabic numerals for the hours thirteen to twenty-four. The man nodded positively then slipped the watch back into its pocket, close to his heart. The spider legs confirmed that the Canadian Northern Railway train southbound from Edmonton was leaving on time. He expected as much. He had spent the last six years in the steam engine cabs of this railway and knew that the only way to run a railway is on time.

The watch is engraved with the letters "JIL" in large Old English script. They stand for Joseph Isidore LaFrance, who at age thirty-five has been a locomotive engineer for almost half of his life. Almost any other day he would be up front, his striped cap head catching the breeze flowing into the engineer's side window. This day he is riding in coach comfort because it is a special day. He and the straight-backed woman with the big hat in the seat next to him and the baby girl Veronica on her lap are on their way to a new life in Hanna, a relatively new town in the Drumheller area northeast of Calgary.

Veronica is bright and alert with dark hair and dark eyes, a handful of energy in fact. At exactly seven months, she is already on the move, crawling and getting ready to walk.

The three are dressed in Sunday best, testimony to the importance of the day. Louise wears a brilliant white blouse closed high at the neck with a silk navy bow that matches the high hat. Isidore is in a well-tailored blue serge suit accenting a stiff rounded white collar and a neatly knotted silk cravate. Beside him somewhere on the seat no doubt is the straw boater, which he wears at a cocked angle that gives him a mischievous air.

Louise LaFrance holds the baby and sings to soothe her to sleep against the whistling, shuffling and click-clack-click of the train pushing south. Unquestionably, it is the happiest day of their lives together. Married thirteen years without children and now a miracle — the answer to years of hoping and constant praying. Now their home would have the sounds of new life and Louise would have her days well filled while her husband was out on road trips. The baby made them a complete family, a railroading family.

Hanna, like Chapleau, is a railroad town. Beyond that, there were no similarities. Chapleau was choked by dark forest while Hanna was in the middle of what the settlers called the Big Sky Country. Open prairie stretched to all four horizons, with herds of cattle grazing a free range once dotted with buffalo. It had been a stage coach stop called Copeville and was destined to remain a couple of lonely buildings struggling on the yawning prairie had it not been for the growth of railways.

Canada needed its West settled and a new railway, Canadian Northern Railway (CNoR), began a feverish program of rail laying track off the main routes of the CPR. One area not served by rail was the east central region of Alberta, a tract along a line drawn from Calgary to Saskatoon, through rolling prairie spotted with pothole lakes black with ducks and geese during spring and fall migrations. CNoR decided to push a line through there and to call it the Goose Lake Line. It would bring settlers and the services and supplies they needed for homesteading. Crews surveyed the line in 1911 and the rails started going down in 1912, reaching Copeville in November. Tents and shacks popped up as settlers from Canada and the U.S. rolled in by stagecoach in search of land to homestead. Within months, there was the beginning of a town, which people called Hanna after D.B. Hanna, a CNoR vice-president, later president of what became Canadian National Railways when CNoR and other lines were merged by the federal government. D.B. Hanna later became the first chairman of the Liquor Control Board of Ontario, established in 1922 when Ontario passed the Temperance Act.

Isidore LaFrance joined the CNoR after leaving Canadian Pacific over the damaged wheel dispute in Chapleau. CNoR was a going concern, frantically building a web of rail lines throughout the West and trying to become a second transcontinental carrier. Its rapid expansion later would create a corporate financial disaster but would provide a lifetime of work.

Hanna hummed with the activities of a real town when the LaFrances returned from Edmonton as proud new parents on April 16, 1918. A ten-stall roundhouse and a sixty-thousand-gallon watering station appeared as Hanna became a key point for rail activity. Passenger rail service had started just over three years before, ending the thrice-weekly stagecoach service from Castor, eighty-five kilometres away. People and goods flowed in on the rails. There were general stores, banks, livery stables, and even a theatre as the town developed not just as a rail centre but a service community for the growing number of surrounding farms, ranches, and homesteads.

Wild West scenes, including horse thievery, faded as law and order was established. The town even had its own constable — Joe Winkler, a tall and lean Texan with a distinctly un-Canadian southern drawl. He had fought in the Spanish-American War with Teddy Roosevelt's Roughriders and moved north when a doctor recommended a cool climate for the malaria he had contracted.

It was a neighbourly place and friends and neighbours were there to meet the new parents and help them settle into family life. The Women's Institute presented Louise with *Little Baby's Big Days,* a booklet to record key events in baby' life. Mrs. E.N. LeBlanc arrived at the house with petticoats and bibs while Mrs. G.B. Wade brought over a dress and petticoat. Gifts began to arrive from the east. Dresses weren't part of Veronica's wardrobe for long. As she began to crawl, then walk, they became impractical because she was a busy child.

"She is such a busy little body that dresses are rather a hindrance," Louise wrote in *Little Baby's Big Days.* "Her chief pastime is throwing gramophone records all over the place." Her parents saw the record tossing as positive because as she grew it was evident that Veronica was blessed with a personality that celebrated living. She had a temper that showed occasionally but she preferred laughter to anger.

"Baby laughs most of her time," Louise wrote. "She is a very happy baby indeed."

Her happy personality was tested soon after arriving in Hanna. Relatives back in Chapleau were shocked but overjoyed by the news of the baby and pleaded with Isidore and Louise to make a trip home. They packed up Veronica and rode the train halfway across the country to Sudbury, then on to Chapleau where a horde of LaFrance and Aquin uncles and aunts and, of course, the two sets of grandparents, doted on this miracle baby. Veronica travelled well, as she would all her life, suffering no ill effects from the long return trip except a case of hives from a change in water. For Louise, the trip accented the huge distance from family and the loneliness of living in the West.

That loneliness was never worse than the Christmas of 1918, when Isidore did not return from an unexpected trip east. He left Hanna urgently in the third week of November when he received word that one of his sisters was ill in Chapleau. She died before he got there, a victim of the Spanish flu pandemic. After the funeral, Isidore fell ill himself and was laid up into January. Louise wrote that it was a sad first family Christmas but made bearable by western hospitality. The Wades invited Louise and Veronica for Christmas dinner, and in the evening they went to Mr. and Mrs. James White's house for entertainment and there Veronica received her first lesson on dancing.

There had been such great plans for a first family Christmas. Louise was stoical and certainly appreciative of the generosity of her friends and neighbours. That Christmas night, she wrote in Veronica's baby book: "The day is over — for all blessings we are truly grateful. Amen."

Grateful, indeed. Louise and Veronica didn't know it then, but they were fortunate to see Isidore again. Many Canadian families lost kin that autumn and Christmas as the outbreak scythed its way through millions of families. So devastating was the epidemic that the average human lifespan in Canada and the United States dropped by as much as ten years. Isidore was fortunate to survive and return to Hanna. When he did, the LaFrances spent as much time as possible doing things together.

The West was new and fresh. There were regular activities at St. George's Catholic Church. There was the theatre and an orchestra and a glee club, plus a drama club. In summer, you could sit outside and hear a free concert put on by the Hanna Citizen's Band. Outside the town, the Prairies waited to be explored.

The automobile revolution was making possible sightseeing trips into the countryside. Isidore found that driving one of the new-fangled motor machines was an extension of the joy he found in locomotive engineering. You could buy a Ford Runabout for $600 and a touring model for $750. Few people had them, but Isidore could afford one on an engineer's salary. What better way to share with Louise and Veronica the Big Sky Country landscape that he saw almost daily from the cab of his locomotive. On his days off, they toured wherever the rough roads led them, marvelling at the sights and the ability to cover so much territory in so little time.

One motor trip was a thirty-five-kilometre adventure across rough prairie road to the Miller Ranch at Hand Hills. It was July 1, 1918, and people had gathered for what would become an Alberta tradition — the annual Hand Hills Stampede. The previous summer, Jack Miller decided there should be some sort of function to raise money for the war effort. He organized a Wild West Stampede that would include horse racing and other rodeo events. The idea was an instant hit. The first rodeo raised $3,200 for the Lone Butte branch of the Red Cross.

Settlers, ranchers, and town folk from all around heard of the Stampede and the next year trekked out to Hand Hills in buggies, on horseback, and some, like the LaFrances, in automobiles. Isidore paid his dollar to enter the rodeo grounds while Louise and Veronica and all other women and children got in free. Spectators sat on the prairie sod and watched events such as the Roman Horse Race, where a rider raced two horses, standing with one foot on the back of each.

Jack Miller didn't realize it, but his rodeo marked the end of an era in the West. Photos of the first rodeos show the usual cowboys, horses, and wagons. Lining a part of the rodeo grounds, however, were some automobiles like the open-touring model the LaFrances drove. These autos ended the horse-and-buggy age and the careers of horsemen like

Joe LaRose. The stampede itself lived on, however, to become the oldest consecutive rodeo in Alberta.

Louise wrote that night that the auto expedition across the Prairies, plus the excitement of the events wore everyone out. Everyone except Veronica, who "came back as fresh as ever."

Louise recorded another trip, emphasizing the incredible distance covered.

"About the end of September we motored to Castor and back. Over ninety-five miles in one day! Miss V sang all the way there and back ... and wasn't the least bit tired."

A passenger in that motor outing was a special visitor from the east, none other than the personable Father Romeo Gascon. He was there to celebrate the Veronica's arrival and to report back to Chapleau the good fortunes of his friends Isidore and Louise.

His lively curiosity and dynamic personality propelled Romeo Gascon into places and situations not usually occupied by priests. He was a miniature whirlwind, interested and active in everything from architecture to printing to golf, baseball, hunting, and fishing. One minute he was conducting choir practice, the next presiding over a meeting of the Kebsquasheshing Golf Club of which he was president. He coached a baseball team called the Young Elephants, ran his own printing press at the rectory, and was an excellent woodworker.

Fire destroyed at least three of his churches and each time he took personal charge of the rebuilding. In 1918 when his beloved Sacred Heart Church in Chapleau burned, he sketched out his own design for a new one and gave it to architects to draw up their plans. The result is the magnificent red-brick winged structure with two bell towers still prominent in Chapleau's downtown area.

Father Gascon arrived in Chapleau in 1911, three years after his ordination and brief service in Cochrane and Cobalt where fires burned both his churches. Water, not fire, is what almost ended his budding career, however. He was fishing on Lake Commanda at Cochrane when he fell into the water. A young United Church minister answered calls for help and pulled Father Gascon to shore, but it appeared to be too late. Two doctors worked on him with artificial respiration but gave up, saying it was hopeless. A third refused to give up and tried more artificial respiration that produced a faint breath, followed by another and another.

Years later, Father Gasçon met the United Church minister at a baseball game in Niagara Falls. The minister recalled how the two doctors had given up on him and Father Gascon replied: "Yes, they are all dead now and I am at a baseball game!"

Father Gasçon, later named a Monsignor, stayed at Sacred Heart Parish for an amazing forty-eight years. He was likely the best-known person in the community and few people had more friends. You couldn't miss him on the street, a small man in a black cassock wearing an impish smile that masked a high intelligence. He made it his business to know his parish families inside out, including the LaFrances and the Aquins. He visited his parishioners regularly and got involved in their lives when he felt it was necessary. He was an arranger — a fixer and dealmaker — in the positive sense.

He met Isidore and Louise the year he arrived, the same year they left. Although their time together in Chapleau was brief, they became good friends. They were all roughly the same age, he having been born in 1883 in L'Orignal along the Ottawa River. When Louise and Isidore LaFrance left Chapleau, they remained in touch. Father Gasçon saw members of their family at church activities regularly, especially Marie Aquin, Louise's mother, who was the lead singer in the Sacred Heart choir. Also, the good father loved to travel. He liked to get out of the Chapleau limelight occasionally and visit friends in far-off places and to golf in Florida.

His connection to Isidore, Louise, and Veronica went beyond the ties of casual friendship. The four were bonded by something special. He travelled to Hanna to help celebrate Veronica's first birthday in September 1918. The LaFrances travelled to Chapleau so Veronica could receive her first communion from him. Later he travelled to Port Arthur to be the officiating priest at Veronica's wedding.

Veronica's past often left me wondering about the powerful bond between Father Gasçon and Veronica. Why was he always showing up on important occasions? I found an important clue to the answer in Thunder Bay when I visited St. Andrew's Church for a moment of reflection during my search for Veronica's past.

I had been an altar boy at St. Andrew's and recalled having to fetch supplies from the rectory basement. In the basement was a small, vaulted room where important items and records were kept. I arranged with the current priest to let me visit the vault. I found the church's official marriage register and looked up the November 30, 1940, wedding of my parents. Nothing I didn't know there. Anything anyone needs to know about a marriage is easily found in official government marriage certificates. I put the register back and went through some other church history records just as a matter of interest.

My news instincts started to tingle. I went back to the register, opened it at November 30, 1940, then closed it. Again, nothing new or exciting.

I left the vault and was on my way upstairs when my news instincts tingled again, quivered, then went off like an alarm. I hauled back downstairs, entered the vault, and pulled down the register. Something told me I had missed something. My eyes had seen something that my brain had not registered.

The marriage register was in Latin with spaces to fill in names, baptism details, parents, and witnesses. It listed Veronica as born in Edmonton and baptized in Misericordia Hospital and the *filliam*, "daughter," of Joseph Isidore LaFrance and Louise Aquin. Beside the word *filliam*, inserted in smudged ink but still legible, was the word *adoptée*. Filliam adoptée. Adopted daughter.

My eyes fell to the signature of the officiating priest. There scribbled with a flourish was the name Romeo Gascon. The signature had the same ink and the same scribble as the word *adoptée*. Father Gascon, I strongly believe, succumbed to emotion during Veronica's wedding ceremony and inked the word *adoptée* on the marriage register. He did it because of his overwhelming pride of his role in this young woman's life. It was his way of releasing the tension of keeping a long held secret. He knew that marriage registers are seldom read once the marriage is registered with government, and few people, aside from teachers and altar boys, would figure out the Latin.

Romeo Gascon and the Misericordia Sisters put together the deal for a baby the LaFrances could never have had on their own. He was the broker in a long-distance deal that saw the LaFrances move to Alberta and return a year later to Ontario with Veronica, her true identity kept secret from the closed and mean-spirited society that could not accept illegitimacy, adoption, and racial differences.

26 — MERCY

ROOKIE REPORTERS WALKING INTO THEIR FIRST NEWSROOM almost always receive the lecture of five Ws: What, Where, When, Who, and Why. What happened, where did it happen, when, to who, and why? Answer the five Ws and you have a reasonably complete story.

My search for who Veronica really was found answers for four of the five Ws. She was born an illegitimate, placed in an orphanage in Alberta, and later found and gave happiness with a childless couple. Why she kept that information secret remained unanswered and never will be known conclusively. Why did she not tell her family? Why was it so important to keep this secret? Why did she concoct the fantastic tale of the Frenchman and the Indian princess? All the whys are unanswered, left to speculation.

The most obvious reason for keeping the secret was the shame attached to adoption. Society of Isidore and Louise's time generally believed that adopted kids, plucked from the shallow gene pools of lower society, were lesser beings with fewer expectations of ever "doing well" in life. Most orphans were products of lower society, the uneducated, the poor, the disadvantaged, the unsavoury. These were people to be shunned, or at least avoided by choice.

The shame of adoption was a cloak worn not only by the adopted child. It covered the adopting parents. Being childless reflected on their virility and their relationship, among other things. Louise and Isidore were healthy and vibrant, both tall and handsome people. They very much wanted children, and their inability to conceive a child would have been the subject of gossip. Their society viewed a couple's inability to have children with less than charitable eyes. There would be suspicions about their marriage and talk of which partner was not healthy enough to create offspring. Whispered gossip heightens the agony of desperately wanting something that you cannot have.

Many people of the day also viewed adoption as a sign of poor judgment. Adopting the orphaned child of a well-known doctor or lawyer might be a great act of mercy and charity. Adopting an illegitimate was something else. Bringing into your family the bastard child of some shiftless low-life could be seen as folly. Bad traits inherited from the parents would be sure to bring the adopting couple grief.

Adopted and having Native background worsened how the child and its new parents were viewed. Bias against a Native child was almost as strong as against a black child. Many saw Natives as genetically inferior, prone to alcoholism, shiftlessness, laziness, and Stone Age spiritualism. That type of thinking regrettably lingers in Canada today.

The LaFrances knew they had to protect Veronica from the consequences of people knowing of her illegitimacy and her Native blood. She would be teased at school, possibly considered lesser and slower than other children, held back from opportunities, and her chances for courtship would be restricted.

Not everyone felt that way, obviously. However, minds were much more closed then and the easiest option was to adopt secretly. Secret adoption was much easier for the LaFrances because of their mobility. The new CNoR lines in the West demanded more and more rail crews, and as a senior engineer, Isidore could arrange his transfer. A year or so out West, then the return to home in Ontario with the results of a much-prayed-for pregnancy.

There was another reason for secrecy. Veronica was not adopted officially. Alberta did not have full adoption laws until 1920. Some adoption controls existed before then, under a Superintendent of Neglected Children. There were rules to protect children and to stop their exploitation, but official adoption rules were not in place. The LaFrances received Veronica under a loose foster care agreement. Presumably this foster care agreement did not give them unassailable legal rights to the child. There was always a chance the birth mother could demand return of the child.

When they left the province within a year or so of receiving Veronica, they possibly did so illegally. They moved to another jurisdiction without officially adopting Veronica. But who cared? The main goal of finding a neglected child a good home was achieved and legalities did not matter. The LaFrances no doubt had all this in the backs of their minds during the early years and keeping the secret helped ensure no problems developed.

As Veronica reached adulthood, there was no need to keep her roots secret. Her marriage to Ray Poling in 1940 created a new identity that lessened the significance of her illegitimacy and adoption. People she knew still looked down on illegitimacy, adoption, and mixed blood, but the discovery of her secret would not have damaged her life significantly. The sting of gossip, yes, and perhaps some shunning, but she was a housewife, not a politician or a socialite, or a career woman who had to watch how people viewed her.

She might have wished to keep her secret to protect her children from the gossip, but even that is doubtful. We grew up in times when adoption still set some kids apart from others. The knowledge of our mother's background would not have made our lives better. However, the distance between Innisfree and us was wide, and few people would have dwelled on the knowledge that our mother had been born in a home for unwed mothers. Besides, sticks and stones might break our bones, but names would never hurt us.

Veronica perhaps feared that knowing the LaFrances were not her "real" parents — the way it was put in those days — might have changed our view of them. Would knowing they were not our "real" grandparents have lessened our respect? Would knowing the truth have set us off some day on a search for the "real" grandparents. These thoughts no doubt went through her head at some time. It is inconceivable, however, that she weighed these as valid reasons to keep the secret in late life, especially with the end of her life in sight. So why? Why take the secret to the grave? The question loomed in front of me every step of the search. Why?

The question angered me. She had no right to hide such information from her children. Did she think she was God, withholding from us who our ancestors really were? Anger turned to understanding the day I stood on the hill overlooking Birch Lake at Innisfree. The elderly lady Erica had asked, "Are you a LaRose?" I had replied no. I was a Poling and how could I be anything else. The newfound knowledge that Elizabeth LaRose was my biological grandmother did not change who I was.

It was the same for Veronica. She had been who she was her entire life, except for eight months. LaRose was only a name on her birth certificate. It didn't mean anything because she was a LaFrance and a Poling, no matter who her biological parents were. Louise and Isidore LaFrance were the only parents she had known. They had shaped her life with love and protection and the rest of the story didn't matter. It was just a story that didn't mean anything because it would not change anyone's life. Veronica never revealed her secret because it would not change who she was.

I should not have been angry with my mother. The fact that she was not who I thought changed nothing. The only important fact was that she had not only given me life, she had shaped my knowledge and attitude so I could make something of it, just like she had.

The best part of being a reporter is the opportunity to learn. For me, an uneducated kid from northwestern Ontario, reporting provided the education I missed by being unable to go to university. Reporting stories, Veronica's included, taught me the importance of learning from individuals' stories. Every life, no matter how simple on the surface, is a story to tell. Not just the stories of the prime ministers, the famous, the elite, and the self-promoters. The stories of average people. Combined, our individual stories are the story of our nation. Our stories tell much about our society and how it changes, often for the better when viewed long term.

The story of Veronica and the LaRoses is filled with tragedies. So are the stories of most families, some more than others. But it is a story that offers hope in a world that increasingly fights to hold its anchorage. Viewed in perspective, the stories of our lives show us progress toward a better world. You can't look back at all the changes that have occurred in our world since Elizabeth LaRose stood at the front doors of Misericordia without realizing that no matter how crazy the world appears today, it has changed for the better.

Technological changes obviously have improved our lives, although don't say that to anyone trying to maintain a perfect Internet connection. Telephones, airplanes, cars, television, miraculous medical equipment, and vastly improved educational opportunities have made life better and have allowed people to understand each other better. Physical life today is unrecognizable to the few still alive who can remember the First World War era. The homesteads of Joe and Eva's time had outhouses and no electricity. Joe's business life was about horses and buggies. Eva kept the family sheltered and fed by working as a housekeeper and a medicine woman, assisting people in times of illness and delivering babies.

Misericordia Hospital has gone through several transformations to become a major corporation. Health care in general has improved so dramatically that quality of living has improved and life spans lengthened. By the time the Spanish flu epidemic of 1918 had finished, the average life span in North America was down to thirty-eight years. It's now nudging eighty years. Surgeons gave me a heart valve and a Dacron aorta that improved and lengthened my life and even allowed me to realize the lifelong dream of becoming a pilot. My Grandmother Poling had no such miracles. When her sticky heart valve made her heart less and less efficient, she died because the knowledge, technology, and skills were not there to help her.

Attitudes have changed as much as the things we can see and touch. We live in a more compassionate and understanding society than Joe and Eva LaRose and Isidore and Louise LaFrance. We remain stricken by greed, violence, and horrid violations of human dignity, but there have been improvements. We are working the ancient taboos and biases out of our lives. Situations once seen as not being normal, therefore not acceptable, are accepted as part of life.

Adoption is an example. Its stigma fades with each passing decade. Those who choose to adopt are congratulated, not whispered about. We view them as intelligent and caring. Those adopted often feel special because they were chosen, not simply accidents. There is even a cautious move toward open adoptions in which unwed mothers have a part in their babies' futures. Illegitimacy is a word seldom used as more single women opt to bear and raise a child alone. The word "bastard" has lost its original mean-spirited smear, reduced to simply another swear word.

Unsettled feelings about adoption, illegitimacy, and certainly Native heritage, continue in our society, however, and much more enlightenment is needed. Outright racism festers in Canadian society. Stories reflecting Canadian attitudes towards its original people are shamefully plentiful. Handful after handful of these stories are easily gathered, and you don't need to be a reporter to do the gathering. Two grabbed randomly illustrate the continuing shameful treatment of aboriginal peoples in Canada.

At a junior hockey game in Quebec a few days before Christmas 2005, fans let loose a torrent of racial slurs against Ted Nolan, coach of the Moncton Wildcats in the game against Chicoutimi Sagueneens. They made war cries, did the tomahawk chop, and shouted derogatory comments about Nolan's heritage. Nolan is famous in hockey circles as the former coach of the Buffalo Sabres of the National Hockey League. He was voted NHL coach of the year. He is Ojibwe from the Garden River Reserve, which Veronica took to visiting in her final years. Nolan is a role model for Native kids who need to see how they can escape the despair of Native life in Canada.

The media reported the incident, the usual outrage was expressed, and apologies were offered. Said Nolan: "It hurt when I was seven years old and seventeen years old, and I just turned forty-seven, and it hurt as much as it did back then."

A couple of months before the Nolan incident, years of government incompetence and neglect exploded at Kashechewan, a Cree community on western James Bay. The town, with a 90 percent unemployment rate, lived under a boil water order for two years as its water facilities deteriorated until collapse. Finally, E. coli was found in the drinking water and much of the community of nineteen hundred was evacuated to the south. Heavy chlorination and other problems left many of the residents with skin infections such as impetigo and scabies.

Whitedog, Grassy Narrows, Fort Chip, Cornwall Island, Davis Inlet — Indian reserves I had written about in the 1960s, '70s, and '80s. Mercury poisoning, fluoride poisoning, drought, alcoholism, despair. Communities where human beings lived and died like dogs. I had written about them as an idealistic young reporter, convinced my reports would shake government and improve lives. Decades later, the same things — and worse — are happening over and over.

We are all to blame for Canadian attitudes toward and treatment of our native people. More blame rests, however, with those who know better and have the power to make change: governments, politicians, and bureaucrats. Citizens can be blamed for not standing up and saying "That's enough, stop it!" Citizens have the power to force the politicians to make change, or to force them from office.

It is scandalous that a country that welcomes millions of immigrants from different cultures and encourages them to be hyphenated Canadians, is incapable of accepting its Native population. We continue to try to assimilate Natives while promoting the value of cultures imported from abroad. Canadian governments have done everything possible to destroy Native culture and in the process have created pockets of Native Canadians desperate and lost in their own land. That is not just my biased opinion. Statistics Canada on its website page titled *2001 Census Consultation Guide* provides facts:

> Aboriginal peoples are among the most disadvantaged groups in Canada. The 1991 Post-censal Aboriginal Peoples Survey indicates that they experience poorer health, lower levels of education, lower average incomes, and higher rates of unemployment, compared with the non-Aboriginal population. High incarceration levels and increasing youth suicide rates indicate the presence of serious social difficulties as well. How Canadian society addresses these inequities and assists in the social and cultural healing processes will be a priority issue for governments.

Even the word "Indian" now is politically incorrect, the correct term now supposedly "aboriginal." Perhaps that is because no one wants confusion with East Indians, who are more politically and economically important than Natives in Canada. Or, perhaps it's because the term *aboriginal* nicely groups Native Canadians with all other First Peoples throughout the world, pushing them into a mass global problem, therefore less visible as a distinct Canadian problem.

Canada cannot realize its true potential until it recognizes and accepts its longstanding problem with Natives and moves positively to fix it. That requires looking within ourselves and facing our prejudices. We cannot tolerate hearing it and deny it when it is raised by other nations, but the heart of the Canadian psyche still holds racist thoughts about its first peoples. Many Canadians continue to view Natives as a low sub-species, people lacking the get-up-and-go spirit to move ahead.

On May 31, 2007, the Ipperwash Inquiry into the September 1995 Ontario Provincial Police killing of Native protester Dudley George near Sarnia found that OPP officers made racist statements about the protesters including the phrase "a big, fat, fuck Indian." It also found that the Ontario premier at that time, Mike Harris, also made racist comments about Natives, but Harris denied it. What more needs to be said about Canadians' real thoughts about its Native people?

The first step to fixing Canada's "Native problem" is to admit its existence and the attitudes that sustain it. Assimilation is no fix. Native people have no future without renewing their culture. There is no culture without language and without re-establishing both, there will be no respect for them as a distinct and worthy part of the Canadian mosaic. Only renewed pride in Native culture, languages, and traditions will remove the despair from Native lives. All Canadians must help in this renewal and help promote Native life as worthy and positive.

It is not a matter of feeling sorry that the European invasion destroyed traditional Native life. It is not a matter of assuaging guilt by throwing tax money at Native communities for infrastructure. It is a matter of changing what is in our minds and hearts when we think of Natives and honestly helping them to help themselves restore traditions and cultures that can fit into twenty-first century life. When that is done, when Native Canadians have the same opportunities and privileges as the rest of us, Canada will become a complete country. Our society must change its attitudes toward Natives just the way it is changing its attitudes toward adoption. Only then will people like Veronica LaRose be able to live without secrets, without fear of waking Nanabijou.

Attitudes about illegitimacy, adoption, and Native blood robbed Veronica of the joy of being able to celebrate her heritage openly. She had a deep interest in Native culture, and whenever it slipped into the open, her friends would laugh and call her "Indian lover." Today when I tell people of my mother's history, I often hear: "I once had an Indian friend" or "I always wondered why you were so wild" or "When are you going to get your card so you can avoid taxes?" Some of it is good-natured, and certainly not mean-spirited, but it reflects a deeply seeded Canadian attitude about Natives.

Politicians say they are doing their best to improve the lives of our Native people. They have dumped tons of money on the problem, but money alone is not the cure. What's needed is for Canadian society to develop a deeper and compassionate understanding of the causes of Native suffering.

An impediment to that is the nature of Canadian governments. Our governments and their bureaucracies have developed a culture that does not promote the sharing of information. Canadian governments are among the most undemocratic of the Western democracies when it comes to sharing information with citizens. They operate from the paternalistic premise that politicians and bureaucracies know what's best for citizens, including what they need to know. Bureaucrats hunker in their closed offices protecting policies premised by the belief that that information can be dangerous and extreme caution must be exercised in distributing it.

Citizens cannot acquire the understanding needed to make intelligent judgments unless they have complete information. They are not getting what they need from the government about how our Native populations live. They certainly don't get it from newspapers, radio, or televisions outlets, most of which couldn't find an Indian reserve unless it was two blocks from an urban intersection. Despite hard and costly lessons like Kashechewan, no change is likely soon. Change comes slowly to governments because they are such big ships, and big ships are hard to turn in small spaces.

Our culture of reluctance to share information openly and without hesitation has other consequences for our society. It explains our tendency not to promote and celebrate Canadian history. Most of us will admit that Canadians do not celebrate history to the extent that other countries do, particularly the United States. Few Canadians have even an elementary knowledge of our history or the stories of our most important historical figures. Examples of neglect of our history are all around us, no matter where we live. Travel to Canoe Lake in Ontario's Algonquin Park and try to find references to Tom Thomson, Canada's most famous landscape artist. He died there in 1917, his death one of Canada's most fascinating mysteries. But you'll find little about him there aside from a cairn hidden on a hilltop in the bush and built by his friends almost one hundred years ago. Instead of celebrating a Canadian hero, we bury his traces in the rocky woodlands that helped develop the character of the painter and Canada itself.

Similarly, Canadians little recognize David Thompson, probably the world's greatest geographer and a giant of North American exploration. The American glorification of Lewis and Clark, who explored the American West, is never-ending, yet they were minor players compared to Thompson, who found the headwaters of the Missouri, the Mississippi, and the Columbia and was first to map a navigable route through the Rocky Mountains to the Pacific. Lewis and Clark relied on some of his work to find their way west.

Why do we like secrecy and why are we reluctant to share information? Some guess that maybe this is rooted in the French-English conflict that formed European Canada. Canadians are afraid to offend and perhaps there is an inherent fear that lifting the dam blocks on information and history might wash open some wounds left by conflicts created by different founding nations. The détente between French and English Canada is so fragile that it came within a handful of votes of flying apart in the Quebec separation referendum of 1995.

Promoting history develops pride in who we are and what we have accomplished. Canadian history shows how we developed a country of three solitudes — English, French, and Native — and maybe we are not comfortable enough with that to want to celebrate it.

Information is the blood of democracy. The governments' job is to encourage its free flow, not restrict it. Reluctance to share information simply continues to foster secrecy. Part of the reason that the Quebec separation vote almost passed was the inability of Prime Minister Jean Chrétien's Liberal government to communicate and openly share information.

Our governments' refusal to give up information easily to its citizens is one of the sad consequences of having built a society that depends too much on government. At the turn of the twentieth century, when

Joe and Eva were raising their child Elizabeth, government was a small factor in their lives. One hundred years later, Canadians are smothered by government, unable or unwilling to do much for themselves. We have become a society addicted to government control. When we don't have everything we want, we cry to the government, a trait that has helped to create an impression abroad that Canadians are whiners.

Government intrusion into our lives has become overwhelming. It not only controls our health care, it manages huge pieces of our lives from what we can watch on television to how many bags of garbage we can dispose in a year and what kind of hooks we are to use when fishing. So much government in our lives robs us of the initiative to think for ourselves. Also, the costs of government now are so high that many Canadians spend more than half their working lives toiling to pay taxes and the proliferation of government fees for services. Complacency about government spending has steadily eroded, allowing scandalous abuses that line the pockets of political friends.

Big government is in our blood and is a major part of the Canadian economy. Obviously a majority of Canadians see it as not a bad thing and maybe it isn't, except one wonders how much more individual commitment would flourish without it.

The most debilitating aspect of big government is that it tries to make everyone alike. Everyone is equal and everyone spouts the same politically correct mantras. Breaking from the pack is discouraged. This explains why the country has few heroes. A country that does not promote individual effort and individual differences produces few individuals who soar to greater heights.

Contrast today's craving for government assistance with the Misericordia story of one hundred years ago. Four nuns carrying their entire worldly possessions by hand arrived in Edmonton as volunteers to help make people's lives better. They built a maternity home, an orphanage and general hospital. Unselfishly they saved lives and changed lives, including mine. Where would my mother have ended up without their help? Would there ever have been a me, and if so, what life would I have had as the child of a Native-breed bastard?

Could such remarkable feats of committed volunteerism occur today? No doubt, yes. There still are dedicated people committed to improving society, but it would be an exception. Government meets most of society's needs today. Canadians want the government to do everything for them and seem unconcerned by the consequences: the financial burden on taxpayers and the loss of personal freedom that accompanies government management of our lives. The power of the collective and its government smothers the power of the individual.

Our American neighbours resist government control of their lives and are willing to make more individual sacrifices to protect individual freedoms from encroaching big government. Canadians are less interested in individual freedoms than the health of society as a whole. Deep down, many Canadians are jealous of U.S. individual freedoms, and this sometimes manifests itself in our growing anti-Americanism and is a sign of an inferiority complex.

Individuals helping each other is what life is about. People are amazingly strong and creative when left to make their own commitments. The Misericordia Sisters certainly were. So was Veronica when for eighteen years she nursed her adopted mother at home, with little help except later from the Victorian Order of Nurses, another charitable organisation. There was no government medical care, no drug plans, and we children didn't always get what we wanted for Christmas because of the burden of care. We did have a grandmother in our home who taught us more about living than a school ever did.

Some changes brought by government obviously are important. Government medical care, which would have helped us immensely during the earlier years of my grandmother's illness, now ensures us comprehensive health services and keeps us from the individual financial hardships seen in the States. We need government direction and controls but not to the point where our attitudes toward individual initiative become distorted. They sometimes are distorted to the point that those who toil for the betterment of the less fortunate are seen as curiosities while our real heroes are multi-millionaire hockey players.

Greed has short-circuited our instinct to distinguish clearly right from wrong and we see examples of this every day in business and government. The federal government sponsorship scandal in which millions of dollars flew away to federal Liberal's friends in Quebec. The implosion of the Conrad Black newspaper empire and the stories of incredible excesses that flowed from it. Isn't it odd that it was the United States, not Canada, which investigated the Black empire?

Canada's history provides direction for building a more complete nation. All we need to do is take it down from the shelf, blow the dust off it, celebrate it, and use its lessons as a guide to Canadian living. Our history holds the stories of Canadian heroes — and there are some despite our tendency to forget them — whose traits provide clues to achieving greatness. To find the real heroes, we must reach beyond the shallowness of twenty-first-century life. Our heroes are not the people celebrated in the daily media — the multi-millionaire hockey, basketball, and golf stars, the powerful CEOs, the star politicians, or the billboard entertainers. We will find the lessons of real heroes by going deep and examining what is important in life. Things like the incredible determination of David Thompson; the vision of Louis Riel, martyred by the Canadian government for his beliefs; the unshakable hope of Terry Fox. And of course the compassion and commitment of the four Misericordia Sisters who opened the Edmonton Mission for Unwed Mothers.

History and its lessons are found not only in libraries and archives. We find them in our own lives. All of us will find examples of incredible grit upon which strong families and great nations are built. Veronica's life of trials, tragedies, and triumphs is not shockingly different from the average Canadian life. Every family has stories of hardship and glory. Their true importance lies in their telling because our family histories are pieces of a larger history. They create a picture of what our country is and what its people have become.

More of our history needs telling from the maternal side. Too often our histories are told from the paternal side because of some unwritten convention in many societies that the macho paternal side matters most. After all, men did the exciting things like carry canoes over dark portages, fight the elements and shoot moose, while women stayed at home and cooked and washed and looked after younger children. In fact, the maternal side often carries the stories of spiritual strength, courage, and determination. The women in my family were real heroes even though they received little recognition. Each lived through periods of soul-destroying adversity yet they had the strength to make life better for those around them.

Eva Fuller LaRose found a reasonably secure and fulfilling life with Joe LaRose. He built modest businesses but became a victim of circumstances that left him scrambling to pay debts in his final years. When Joe died in 1919, she still had at least five children at home ranging from an infant to a fourteen-year-old. Most of them left home young because life was difficult, and Eva moved from house to house working as a midwife, a housekeeper, and doing whatever else she could to put food on the table. She did whatever she had to for her kids and worked until she died at fifty-six while keeping house for someone else. She built a family that has spread out across North America to build good lives for their own families.

Eva Poling was much the same. She wore her heart out worrying about and caring for her husband and eight children. She took in boarders for extra money and paced the hallways late into many nights while her husband or one or more of the boys were out testing the fates on the Big Lake or drinking too much in a downtown beverage room. She taught the children the values needed to live decently and to raise families of their own.

Louise LaFrance turned her pain into love for the people around her. She was a strong and privileged woman before her illness, politically active and a strong force in the Catholic Church in Ontario. Her pain was sometimes unbearable to witness, but she sucked it into a compartment in her mind where she converted it into love and distributed it to her daughter and her grandchildren. You would have thought the pain would have made her mean and uncaring, but it did the opposite. She taught gentleness and the need to be understanding of others.

Veronica, having lived a pleasant childhood and early married life, suffered more than any of them. She had no time to prepare for the tragedies that befell her. She endured the deaths of her mother and her husband, plus a son facing life in prison — all within four months. The supports of her life collapsed, and she ran away to start over and to protect her two girls. In the end, she saved her family and got them on the road to establishing their own.

These were four women who lived different lives doing whatever they had to build strong families. Four women who like the four Misericordia Sisters sacrificed without question or complaint to make life better for others. Totally different individuals who demonstrated a lesson often missing but much needed in our distorted world: Mercy truly is the quality of compassion.

Veronica often said it is better to let sleeping dogs lie. I thought a lot about that and about ending the search into her past. I would have, had it not been for the journalistic training that pushes reporters relentlessly to find the truth. I'm happy I continued.

I'm sure if Veronica was alive and her story was in the open, she would not be ashamed of her LaRose heritage. Her grandparents, Joe and Eva LaRose, were not dream team ancestors. They lived rough and undisciplined lives. Joseph convicted of barroom theft and stealing a horse, Eva and first daughter, Elizabeth, who both gave birth behind the dark curtains of the Misericordia home for unmarried mothers. However, they looked out for their kids, loved and protected them, and produced a wonderful family.

I am not ashamed of Veronica's background. The discovery of her secret has enriched my life. I am proud to think that some of my ancestors were the first people who roamed North America, relying only on their wits and skills for survival. It also explains the powerful connection I feel with the natural world. I am happiest when I am outside among trees, rocks, and water.

People say that blood is thicker than water. Perhaps, but even thicker and stronger than blood are the mental bonds that develop between people. The morning when I awoke inexplicably early in the forestry camp on Lake of the Woods, what woke me before dawn was the end of a remarkable dream in which I saw my Grandmother LaFrance running across a meadow. It was bizarre because I had never seen her walk without crutches, let alone run. Yet in the dream, her legs were straight and strong and her fingers no longer crooked. Her long grey hair flowed out behind her, and her face was free of pain. From the other side of the meadow, Grandpa LaFrance came running. He was just as I remembered him only he was bright and happy, unlike the day eleven years before when I paced beside him in the living room as he alternately held his chest and rubbed his left arm. They called to each other and then I awoke.

I don't believe in supernatural occurrences. I do know my dream was real and that it happened when it did. I believe there are bonds between humans that we don't understand. A bond that allowed my grandmother to connect with me as she lay back to die in her bed. I used to think that the dream came to me because of our blood ties. Now, of course, I know the truth — there were no biological ties between us. We were just two unconnected people brought together by circumstances. Yet the bond between us was as powerful as if she had given birth to me herself. Her blood did not flow in my veins, but her spirit did.

Veronica no doubt had reached that realization long ago, and that's the reason why she never revealed the secret of her birth and adoption. It didn't matter because spiritual bonds are thicker than blood. She never did tell the secret, but she left a subtle hint in the last paragraph of her will: "Always have the courage of your convictions. Always be honest and remember I love you dearly, and always be proud of your name and your heritage. You came from damn good stock!"

I have ignored Veronica's cautions about waking Nanabijou and have no regrets, except one. It's a shame that Veronica and Elizabeth never met each other again after their 1917 parting at Misericordia. Everything I learned about Elizabeth indicated she was a bright, happy, and loving person, much like her daughter. They would have made a great pair, singing over a beer or two and enjoying each other's company. They even looked like each other. The same high cheekbones, dark hair, and dark mischievous eyes. I picture them at a party somewhere, raising glasses in their hands as they belt out a raucous tune. I hope they are doing that somewhere.

INDEX

INDEX